Empowering
Global Citizens

Empowering Global Citizens

A World Course

FERNANDO M. REIMERS,
VIDUR CHOPRA, CONNIE K. CHUNG,
JULIA HIGDON, AND E. B. O'DONNELL

ISBN: 1533594546
ISBN 13: 9781533594549
Library of Congress Control Number: 2016909491
CreateSpace Independent Publishing Platform
North Charleston, South Carolina

Fernando M. Reimers is the Ford Foundation Professor of the Practice of International Education and the director of the Global Education Innovation Initiative and of the International Education Policy Program at Harvard University.

Professor Reimers is an expert in the field of global education policy and innovation. His research and teaching examine how education policy, leadership, instruction and innovation empower children and youth to develop the skills they need to thrive in the twenty-first century. He directs the Global Education Innovation Initiative, he and his colleagues recently finished a comparative study of the goals of education as reflected in the curricula in Chile, China, India, Mexico, Singapore, and the United States. These findings are presented in the book _Teaching and Learning for the Twenty-first Century: Educational Goals, Policies, and Curricula from Six Nations_ published by the Harvard Education Press. This book is also available in Chinese, Portuguese and Spanish language editions. Another recent book, _Fifteen Letters on Education in Singapore_ examines the lessons that can be learned from Singapore's efforts to build a robust teaching profession, and is available in paperback and as an e-Book. He has authored, edited, or coedited fourteen books and ninety research articles and chapters on education.

He teaches graduate courses on education policy and educational innovation at the Harvard Graduate School of Education. These courses are also offered online via the Harvard Extension School. He is also the faculty chair of a number of leadership development programs offered by the Harvard Graduate School of Education, including an annual program for education leaders interested in advancing global education.

He advises governments, international development organizations, universities, public and independent schools, foundations and other educational institutions. He is a member of the Massachusetts Board of Higher Education, where he chairs the strategic planning committee, which works with all public universities in the state to align their strategic plans with the state's Vision Project.

He is a member of the US Commission for UNESCO and advises policy makers in the United States, Asia, Latin America, and the Middle East.

In recognition of his global education leadership, he was appointed as the CJ Koh Visiting Professor to the National Institute of Education in Singapore and received an honorary doctorate in humane letters from Emerson College. He received a BA in psychology from the Universidad Central de Venezuela, and an EdM and EdD from Harvard University.

Vidur Chopra is an advanced doctoral candidate at the Harvard Graduate School of Education, where he focuses on adolescent and youth civic agency in the developing world and particularly in post-conflict countries with large youth bulges. He is interested in the role of formal and non-formal educational opportunities in young people's imaginings of their roles in rebuilding conflict-torn societies and in the potential and promise that education holds for peace building. He has policy-based experience from consulting for United Nations International Children's Emergency Fund and the Office of the United Nations High Commissioner for Refugees and practice-based experience from working for international organizations such as Save the Children and RET International. He has also worked on early childhood development issues in the developing world and has had international work experience in Bhutan, Burundi, Ethiopia, India, Lebanon, Rwanda, Syria, and the United States. Vidur also has an EdM in international education policy from the Harvard Graduate School of Education, an MA in international and development economics from Yale University, and a BA in economics from the University of Delhi in India.

Connie K. Chung is the research director for the Global Education Innovation Initiative at the Harvard Graduate School of Education, a research-practice-policy collaborative that works with education institutions in seven countries. Her field of research is in education for the twenty-first century, civic education, and global citizenship education. She works to build the capacity of organizations and people to work collaboratively toward providing a powerful, relevant, rigorous, and meaningful education for all children that supports not only their individual growth but also the development of their communities. She is the coeditor of the book *Teaching and Learning for the Twenty-first Century: Educational Goals, Policies, and Curricula from Six Nations*.

In pursuing her research interest in ways in which people from diverse backgrounds can learn to work together and to leverage their collective power for positive change in their communities, she was involved in a multiyear, multisite study of education reform and community organizing in the United States, the results of which were published in the book *A Match on Dry Grass: Community Organizing as a Catalyst for School Reform* (Oxford University Press, 2011). She has worked as a staff member, consultant, and speaker with various human-rights and civic-education organizations. She currently serves on the board of two nonprofits, including Aaron's Presents, an organization that offers grants to students in grades eight and below to encourage positive development in those students and in their communities. A former public high school English teacher, she was nominated by her students for various teaching awards. She has taught as an adjunct lecturer on the topics of nonprofit management and multicultural education and also was a curriculum consultant in the development of a kindergarten-through-twelfth grade global citizenship education curriculum. Dr. Chung received her BA in English literature from Harvard College and her master's degrees in teaching and curriculum (1999) and in international education policy (2007) from the Harvard Graduate School of Education. Her doctorate is also from the Harvard Graduate School of Education.

Her greatest sense of satisfaction has come from working with young people, one of whom wrote the following to her at the end of a school year: "I think I learned more about life in this class than in any other part of high school. Thank you for not only teaching us to think critically but also humanitarianly as a citizen of this world. When I talked about my vision of a mentorship program, you really listened. I feel encouraged to make it happen before the end of my senior year and to make things happen for the rest of my *life*."

Julia Higdon received her doctorate from the Harvard Graduate School of Education in May 2015. In her dissertation, Julia used data from the 2009 IEA ICCS (International Civic and Citizenship Education Study) to examine determinants of intercultural attitudes among adolescents (n=16,847) in seven countries across Europe—the United Kingdom (England only), Sweden, Switzerland, Spain, Bulgaria, Poland, and Greece—focusing on cultural contexts and school climates. Julia established the measurement invariance of a variety of measures of intercultural attitudes to support the validity of cross-cultural comparison, using a novel approach in the Bayesian framework. Julia also examined the ways in which intergroup contact, gender, and school climates were associated with intergroup attitudes across these seven countries. She found limited evidence of an association between native-born and immigrant contact and positive intercultural attitudes. However, she found that positive intercultural attitudes were consistently associated with positive and democratic school climates, as well as with gender and attitudes toward gender equality. Julia was working on her dissertation at the time of the writing of this book.

Julia is interested in issues of measurement and promoting the use of cutting-edge statistical methods in applied educational research. Julia is currently a Senior Research Scientist on the Tiger Works Research and Development team at Avenues: The World School.

E. B. O'Donnell is a doctoral student at the Harvard Graduate School of Education and an education consultant. She has over ten years of experience working with nonprofit organizations, international nongovernmental organizations, and schools. Her particular areas of interest and expertise include curriculum development, global education, parental beliefs, early childhood care and education, and emergent literacy and numeracy. She earned a BA in international studies and French from Washington University in Saint Louis, Missouri, and an EdM in international education policy from the Harvard Graduate School of Education in Cambridge, Massachusetts.

Praise for Empowering Global Citizens

In 2015, the international community charted a new course for people, planet and prosperity, set out in the 17 Sustainable Development Goals. Together, they add up to a universal agenda solidly anchored in human rights that calls upon everyone's spirit of solidarity and responsibility to leave no one behind. Education – the fourth goal – is the most transformative force for nurturing the mindsets, values and skills that we need to shape our common future, grounded in awareness of our common humanity, respect for our formidable diversity, and the certitude that, at all ages, we have the capacity to initiate beneficial actions for self and others. It is not by chance that global citizenship education is included in this goal. UNESCO has been leading action to clarify the concept and demonstrate its crucial importance across all societies for learning to live together. Our challenge is to bring this concept to life in 21st century classrooms, in teaching practice, in schools and communities. In this spirit, I congratulate Professor Reimers and his team wholeheartedly for showing how this can be done with this "World Course" that provides a stimulating, interactive and project-based curriculum running the full school cycle, from kindergarten upwards. Its international perspective, humanist approach, historical insight and creative multidisciplinary activities provide an extremely rich and comprehensive resource for educating global citizens who have the values and cross-cultural competences to be artisans of peace and sustainable development. I hope that it will be widely shared and inspire further global collaboration.

Irina Bokova, Director-General, United Nations Educational, Scientific, and Cultural Organization (UNESCO)

Schools increasingly need to prepare the young for an interconnected world where they will live and work with people from different backgrounds and cultures. This book contributes to this noble endeavour, laying out the basis for a comprehensive curriculum to form global citizens to address the challenges and opportunities of the 21st Century. We welcome this initiative to reinforce the attitudes, values and knowledge of future generations on global issues—something the OECD is itself actively promoting in our PISA studies and through our Global Competency for an Inclusive World initiative—so our children can thrive in a rapidly changing world.

Angel Gurría, Secretary-General, Organization for Economic Co-operation and Development

More than ever, our world needs citizens and leaders who are capable of informed empathy. This means that a modern education must go beyond providing students with the knowledge and technological skills they need to operate in an increasingly connected world. We must also help students develop social and emotional capacities to listen to the perspectives of others and approach problems in collaborative, conscientious ways. *Empowering Global Citizens: A World Course* is a wonderful tool that educators can use to create this kind of learning environment for their students. It is heartening and exciting to imagine what a generation of students equipped with this kind of education will be able to accomplish in the future.

Yo-Yo Ma, Cellist

The future of industry and business depends increasingly on talented individuals who can understand and create opportunities amidst the complexity created by a deeply interdependent and rapidly changing world. This provocative book explains how such talent can be systematically cultivated, from an early age, with innovative global education programs. Anyone interested in the future competitiveness of industries and nations should read this book.

Jorge Paulo Lemann, Swiss-Brazilian Businessman

Empowering Global Citizens. A World Course is the kind of curriculum that the world needs to realize the Sustainable Development Goals for all and achieve peace. The curriculum promotes so many characteristics that students, who are our future world citizens, need today--critical thinking, cooperation, ethics, intercultural competency and awareness and so much more. It should be a required curriculum for every student in every school.

Sakena Yacobi, Founder and Director, Afghan Institute of Learning

As the world continues to become more crowded, connected, and complex, the need to teach and understand the principles of Global Citizenship will become the intellectual currency and common language for a greater global good. Mother nature has no compassion, but human beings do and we must grow that capacity! As a Global Teacher Prize Top Ten Finalist and 2016 Project Based Learning Champion, I believe empathy, compassion, ownership, voice and choice will drive the next generation of teachers and students, makers and doers, innovators and iterators, disruptors and change agents towards a more just, robust and equitable world. Professor Reimers and his team have compiled a comprehensive blue-print and action plan to educate and empower a legion of legacy Change Makers for this and future generations; *Empowering Global Citizens: A World Course* is a must read for teachers, students and equity warriors around the world so that together, we can all prosper and grow something greater!

Stephen Ritz, Green Bronx Machine, Teacher, Public School 55, The Bronx, New York

As an Internet entrepreneur who has built one of the world's most popular social media, I see everyday how important it is to have the 21st century skills of digital literacy, global citizenship, and social responsibility. I applaud Harvard Graduate School of Education's Professor Fernando Reimers and his team for designing a complete and integrated curriculum on how to develop the cognitive, intrapersonal, and interpersonal skills necessary to work in the global and technological 21st century workplace, and sharing his curriculum free for all to read and enjoy. This isn't just a useful guide for educators who want to educate students to be agents of change. This has been essential reading for me, and has taught me how to better design corporate training programs for my employees, as well as to how to broaden my own cultural horizons.

Pony Ma, Founder and CEO, Tencent Inc.

For our society to meet the challenges and realize the opportunities of the next century, we will need a new definition of citizenship—one that encourages and equips citizens to think and act beyond their own borders. This volume puts forth an innovative and comprehensive K-12 curriculum designed to prepare truly global citizens. It is a timely and essential handbook for educators who seek to have an impact the world over.

James E. Ryan, Dean of the Faculty and Charles William Eliot Professor, Harvard Graduate School of Education

Empowering Global Citizens is an invaluable resource for educators who understand that the only path to an inclusive, peaceful, sustainable world is to develop today's students into leaders who are equipped to work together for positive change across lines of difference. Professor Reimers and his colleagues provide the rationale for developing global citizens, as well as practical tools for developing intercultural competency, ethical orientation, and the knowledge, skills and mindsets necessary for leading us forward in our interconnected and challenging world.

Wendy Kopp, Founder, Teach for America and CEO and co-Founder, Teach for All

Fundamental education reform will determine whether and how we adapt to an increasingly technology-driven and interconnected global society. Global citizenship education will be a key component of this reform and *The World Course* provides an important and practical path forward for future curricula.

Klaus Schwab, Founder and Executive Chairman, World Economic Forum

The immense challenges that we face today require a collective effort that goes beyond the borders of any one community or country. Global citizenship education is recognized in Goal 4 of the Agenda for Sustainable Development, the "education goal", as a crucial tool in putting learners on the path to meeting modern transnational challenges and contributing to a more peaceful and sustainable world. As we embark on a new education agenda, GCE is of paramount importance. With *Empowering Global Citizens: A World Course*, Fernando Reimers and colleagues offer a timely and pertinent contribution in this regard. Their work not only details the rationale for GCE and the pressing need for its wide adoption, it also serves as an invaluable guide for those who seek to translate the principles of GCE into practice at every level of a child's education, sowing the seeds for the sustainable, peaceful future we all desire.

Gwang-Jo Kim, Director, UNESCO Asia and Pacific Regional Bureau for Education

How wonderful to see this thoughtful argument for rigorous education and detailed curriculum geared to cultivate understanding and much needed abilities to solve global issues and advance human rights. Making their ideas and resources available through Creative Commons, the authors inspire engaged discussion and collaboration.

Martha Minow, Morgan and Helen Chu Dean and Professor, Harvard Law School

I wish we had this book when I was growing up. Empowering Global Citizens is a visionary and practical approach to help students understand the complexities, inter-dependencies and opportunities that exist in our rapidly-globalizing world.

John Wood, Founder, Room to Read

Table of Contents

Global Education for the Twenty-First Century: Designing a Global Citizenship Course

Fernando M. Reimers, Vidur Chopra, Connie K. Chung,
Julia Higdon, and E. B. O'Donnell

Global citizenship education is essential for creating a world with sustainable peace—a world without poverty or hunger and where all have health and education. A world where women and men have the same opportunities, where all have clean water and sanitation, where we use renewable energies, where there are good jobs for all, and where there is economic growth and prosperity created by industry and innovation. A world where we reduce inequalities and create sustainable cities and communities and where we consume responsibly and no longer behave in ways that change the climate or harm life on this planet. A world where we honor and protect life underwater and on land. A world of peace and justice for all. These are the Sustainable Development Goals (SDGs), the compact adopted by the United Nations in 2015 to advance sustainable global well-being (United Nations, 2015). Quality education for all is not only one of those goals but also central to the achievement of all of the other SDGs (Reimers & Villegas-Reimers, 2015).

If the purpose of education is to empower all students to become global citizens, we must elevate our aspirations of what it means to educate children well. The urgency to educate all students to become global citizens calls for innovative curricula that can support new ways of teaching and learning. These curricula must also provide all students with effective opportunities to develop the dispositions, knowledge, and capabilities necessary to understand the world in which they live, to make sense of the way in which globalization shapes their lives, and to be good stewards of and contributors to the Sustainable Development Goals. However, curricula are, of course, not self-executing. To support powerful learning from students through curricula, we need teachers who are well qualified and prepared to teach them—teachers who have adequate instructional materials and resources that can personalize learning, who work in schools and systems that establish adequate partnerships with parents and communities, and who are supported by effective leadership that supports cultures of continuous improvement and learning (Reimers, 2009 Powell & Kusuma-Powell, 2011 Kay & Greenhill, 2013). All of those elements are important because together, they form a system that supports deep learning and teaching. But a curriculum, while not the only element of such a system, is a singularly important element of that system. Given that the Sustainable Development Goals call for a new and urgent conversation on global citizenship education, such a conversation must begin with a discussion of curricula.

This book presents a global citizenship education curriculum. We present a comprehensive, rigorous, and coherent curriculum to be implemented from kindergarten to high school that has intentionally been designed to educate global citizens. We also provide a rationale for global citizenship education; a review of its historical roots; and an examination of different approaches to global education, discussing the role of experiential learning, student-centered learning, and the relationship between global education and twenty-first-century education. Finally, we present the conceptual foundations of the curriculum we developed. It is our hope that this book will serve as a provocation and stimulate further curricular and pedagogical innovation and adaptations of the ideas we provide here, which are aligned with the goals and conceptual underpinnings of our work.

We originally designed this curriculum in the hope that it would be adopted by Avenues: The World School, an innovative elite school currently operating in New York City that plans to eventually establish campuses in major global cities around the world. Following this chapter, we present the curriculum itself as we designed it before Avenues: The World School began operating. We note that this curriculum is the foundation for the World Course, which is a prominent component of an Avenues education. The World Course has been further developed at Avenues since its opening; however, that development is not the focus of this book. As we developed this curriculum for a well-resourced school which would be established in New York City, some of the activities and resources presented here may need to be adapted for use of this curriculum in different circumstances. For instance, some activities involve exploring the city of New York, or visiting the Metropolitan Museum of Art, or they involve interviewing parents involved in occupations likely to reflect those of parents of students in the Avenues School. While the same activities may not be feasible in other geographies, the principles which underlie the choice of these activities can be generalized, such as drawing on local resources and institutions such as museums, engaging parents and community members as sources of knowledge and experience, or exploring the particular cities where the school is located, whatever those may be. Similarly, the resources listed in this curriculum are all in the English language, uses of this curriculum in schools where other languages are used for instruction will necessitate identifying appropriate resources in those languages.

The goal of this book is to make this curriculum widely available to educators around the world in the hope that they will use it in whatever way they find appropriate as they seek to support their students in becoming global citizens. We believe that we are at the dawn of a new era, one in which global education will be a part of the significant transformation that will take place in education in the twenty-first century. Such a transformation will require not linear extensions of what has been taught in the past or of the ways in which it has been taught but a fundamental rethinking of the teaching and learning enterprise. Innovation of such a reach and depth will require the efforts of many different individuals and organizations. We hope that many of those educational innovators will work to create more effective and relevant modalities of global citizenship education. To facilitate such creative elaboration upon our work, we have used the least restrictive Creative Commons license and published this book in paperback and as an e-book. We expect that those using this curriculum will make adaptations and modifications to what we propose here to best serve their local contexts, as the educators who first received this curriculum have done. We fully expect that wide global use of the World Course will require adaptation to particular contexts, as well as updating of the instructional resources included in this book as new resources become available. Our goal in presenting a fully developed curriculum which reflects the principles articulated in this chapter is to illustrate a rigorous and coherent curriculum, designed on the basis of clear curriculum mapping aligned with the goal of developing global citizens. We see these principles as generative to allow others to develop a curriculum appropriate to their particular settings and circumstances, drawing on what we have offered, but adapting and reinventing as necessary.

1. The Long Roots of Education for Cosmopolitanism

The idea that schools should help students learn about different people and cultures is as old as the field of education itself and can be traced through history and modern education. Historically, education aimed to help people transcend their own immediate circumstances in order to adopt a more cosmopolitan outlook. Cosmopolitanism is the notion that humans are bound by a shared set of values—that is, by commonalities that transcend other socially constructed aspects of our identity. This idea is at least two thousand years old and is expressed in the statement "*Homo sum: humani nil a me alienum puto*" (Nothing human is alien to me) by Terentius, a playwright in the Roman Republic.[1]

---

1   Terentius, or "Terence," whose full name was Publius Terentius Afer, was a theater writer of the Roman Republic (195–159 BC). Born in North Africa, he was brought to Rome as a slave to a Roman senator, who eventually freed him.

The resistance of various religious leaders to the violent colonization of Latin America by the Spanish conquistadores further developed this interest in cosmopolitanism. For instance, Dominican friars Anton de Montesinos and Bartolome de las Casas challenged the violence against the indigenous populations on the grounds that indigenous people had the same rights and dignity as the conquistadores. Montesinos's sermon, "I Am a Voice Crying in the Wilderness," given in the Dominican Republic in 1511, nineteen years after Columbus had landed on the island, influenced changes in the New Laws of the Indies so much that the crown censored and punished the abuse, enslavement, and murder of indigenous people (Fajardo, 2014; Jay, 2002). De las Casas, who witnessed Montesinos's sermon and was influenced by him, challenged the institution of slavery and the violence against indigenous people and argued that all mankind was one (Hanke, 1994; Huerga, 1998). The notion of "natural rights" of different people and the idea that all humanity is one, which was advanced in the early sixteenth century, are cornerstones of the idea of human rights.

Both the cosmopolitan aspiration to construct humanity as one and the entire idea of human rights benefitted from a new impetus during the Enlightenment, the philosophical movement that advanced the notion that individuals could improve their circumstances individually and collectively as a result of the cultivation of human reason and the development of science (Reimers, 2013a). These ideas were foundational to the creation of democratic societies, which recognize the rights and responsibilities of individuals, and were central to the creation of public education. During this era, Hobbes argued that the state had to justify the exercise of power to each member of the polity, and Locke saw human rights as protections that individuals needed against abuses by the state (Reynolds & Saxonhouse, 1995; Goldie, 1997). Rousseau, the first Enlightenment philosopher to write explicitly about human rights, argued that since humans are naturally free and equal, the social contract should preserve that equality among all people (Rousseau, 1974). Kant proposed the need for cosmopolitan law to prevent war, an idea that is ethically based on the shared right of humans from different jurisdictions to natural resources (Kant, 1795).

In the twentieth century, the genocide perpetrated by the Nazis caused, at the end of World War II, two important developments in the quest for cosmopolitanism. The Nuremberg trials of the perpetrators of the Holocaust brought forth the notion that there are ethical obligations to humanity that transcend national law; this notion was the foundation of the idea of crimes against humanity. These views on shared obligations and the human rights that people have above their rights and duties to nation-states and national legal canons formed the foundation of the creation of the United Nations and of the Universal Declaration of Human Rights.

The United Nations, the global architecture built after World War II to advance peace and security, is a clear cosmopolitan expression that recognizes that the advancement of human rights and peace is an undertaking that calls for cooperation across the boundaries of nation-states. The Sustainable Development Goals, which were adopted at the seventieth general assembly of the United Nations, in September 2015, are the most recent expression of that cosmopolitan aspiration.

As an institution of the Enlightenment, public education is, at its core, an institution created to advance the cosmopolitan idea of humanity as one and human rights as a shared responsibility (Reimers, 2015a, 2015b).

The long-standing cosmopolitan character of education is reflected in the way that ideas about the purposes of education and about the curriculum and pedagogies used to achieve those purposes have generally traveled across national boundaries. The expansion of public education in particular depended on multiple forms of exchanges between educators across national boundaries and on extensive borrowing and transfers of educational approaches and practices from one cultural context to another. In the early years of the French Republic, for instance, Marc Antoine Jullien proposed that the systematic comparative study and diffusion of educational innovation was a way to advance public education. In the early years of the American experience, John Quincy Adams extensively documented the educational practices of Silesia, where he served as ambassador, for the benefit of his contemporaries. Horace Mann, the founder of public education in the United States, benefited from the systematic study of the educational systems of Prussia and France, and the founder of public education in South America, Domingo Faustino Sarmiento, benefited from exchanges with Horace Mann and his wife, Mary Tyler Peabody Mann, as well as from the study of the early American experience with public education (Reimers, 2016).

Such an extensive cross-national exchange and the roots of the public school system in the Enlightenment imprinted a cosmopolitan character on the resulting global movement to expand education to all. Greek and Latin were subjects in the curriculum at many colleges and schools in Europe as well as in the Americas in order to enable students' access to common content.

With the creation of public education systems two hundred years ago, in part to advance the consolidation of nation-states, school-based education adds to the cosmopolitan aspiration of education the purpose of consolidating national identity through the teaching of a common language, a set of common cultural views and knowledge, and the knowledge of a shared national history. But this new set of nationalistic goals notwithstanding, the common school curriculum also included geography, and the structure and content of the curriculum were influenced by examples taken from other countries. In that sense, traditional education was cosmopolitan insofar as the "classics" defined what should be learned much more than regional or local experience did. In the United States, for instance, it was only at the beginning of the twentieth century that local literature was included in the college curriculum, which had been largely composed of classical texts.

Global education was also advanced by movements to advance peace, which emerged in the late 1800s and the early 1900s. Peace-education movements often resorted to education as a way to share knowledge about the dangers of war and to help avert it. Many of these education efforts were aimed at adults and did not involve formal education in schools; but at the beginning of the twentieth century, the peace movement included support for school-based peace education.

In 1912 a school peace league had chapters in nearly every state in the United States that were "promoting through the schools…the interests of international justice and fraternity" (Scanlon, 1959, p. 214). They had ambitious plans to acquaint over five hundred thousand teachers with the conditions for peace (Stomfay-Stitz, 1993). In the interbella period between the First and Second World Wars, social studies teachers started teaching international relations so that their students wouldn't want to wage war against foreigners. Convinced that schools had encouraged and enabled war by indoctrinating youth into nationalism, peace educators contributed to a progressive education reform in which schools were seen as a means to promote social progress by providing students with an awareness of common humanity that helped break down the national barriers that lead to war (Harris, 2008).

A number of progressive educators at Teachers College at Columbia University advocated for education for global understanding, emphasizing cooperation rather than competition as the goal. James Earl Russell, the third president of Teachers College, offered a course on "foreign education systems" in 1898 with the purpose of helping teacher candidates develop global awareness. Russell supported the creation of the first university-based center of comparative education at Teachers College, where faculty such as John Dewey devoted significant time to learning about education systems in other countries and to contributing ideas to the advancement of public education abroad.

A leading figure at Teachers College's Comparative Education Center was Professor Isaac Kandel. At a lecture given to the National Association of Secondary School Principals in 1925, Kandel advocated for infusing high school curricula with information that would prepare students for international understanding (Kandel, 1930). Kandel defined international understanding as "that attitude which recognizes the possibilities of service of our own nation and of other nations in a common cause, the cause of humanity, the readiness to realize that other nations along with our own have by virtue of their common humanity the ability to contribute something of worth to the progress of civilization" (Kandel, 1930: 228). He distinguished international understanding from communism, or as antithetical to nationalism. To foster international understanding at the high school level, Kandel proposed not a new subject but a special emphasis on the international dimensions of the existing subjects, including the arts, science, geography, literature, and history. Kandel saw the existing curriculum as holding the potential to foster international understanding as a result of a specific emphasis on highlighting cosmopolitan linkages among people. In effect, he was advocating for the infusion of global education into the existent curriculum of other disciplines.

One alternative to the idea that global education could be infused into the curricula of other disciplines was the notion that global education required a specific study of international subject matter. Another view on global education emphasized the importance of experiences and interactions with people from diverse cultural backgrounds and national origins that exchanges and study abroad provide.

A contemporary of Kandel who also advocated for using global education to foster international understanding was Stephen Duggan, the first president of the Institute for International Education, which he founded with Nobel Laureates Elihu Root, a former US secretary of war, and Nicholas Murray Butler, the president of Columbia University. Duggan, who was known as the apostle of internationalism, was also the first president of the Council on Foreign Relations. The Institute of International Education was established to support international understanding as a way to achieve lasting peace. The institute's founders believed that student-teacher exchanges were a valuable way to foster such international understanding.

The institute also sponsored the creation of international relations clubs on college campuses. In addition, in the 1920s a few colleges in the United States, including Harvard University, offered their students the opportunity to participate in simulations of the League of Nations with the purpose of educating them on global issues, interdependence, and the factors that threatened peace and security.

Following World War II, the creation of the United Nations and the adoption of the Universal Declaration of Human Rights, which included education as one of the basic rights whose pursuit would help achieve peace, accentuated the cosmopolitan aspiration for education—that is, that education would help students discover their common humanity with others. The preamble to the constitution of UNESCO, the specialized agency established to advance the achievement of the right to education, makes explicit reference to the need to educate students on the focus of the United Nations and on advancing human rights. This idea gave impetus to the view of global education as a specific subject matter that would require direct study and interaction with diverse peers, not indirect infusion into other disciplines. In collaboration with governments around the world, UNESCO advanced a number of programmatic initiatives to promote global education, peace education, and human-rights education. These included a series of affiliated schools, starting with thirty-three schools in fifteen countries in 1953, whose goal was to "encourage the development of education in the aims and activities of the United Nations and the Specialized Agencies and in the principles of the Universal Declaration of Human Rights." UNESCO also contributed to the development of curricula for peace and human-rights education.

In the 1960s two important education programs emerged to promote global understanding. One of them, the International Baccalaureate (IB) Organization, was established in 1968 in Geneva to develop and support a university preparatory curriculum—a diploma program—for students who had to move between countries as a result of their parents' occupations. In developing this curriculum, the organization initially built upon a UNESCO handbook published in 1948 that presented a framework for peace education (Maurette, 1948). Over time, the International Baccalaureate Organization grew to offer a primary-years program, a mid-years program, and a high school diploma. Core components of the high school diploma program include the following: an independent research project that students conduct, resulting in a substantive paper that reflects an in-depth understanding of a topic, and a subject called "theory of knowledge," which was designed to help students understand the relationship among the various subjects and to reflect on alternative ways of knowing, with a focus on the areas of natural sciences, human sciences, arts, mathematics, ethics, and history.

The midyears program emphasizes holistic learning, intercultural awareness, and communication. The focus is on approaches to learning, community and service, human ingenuity, health and social education, and environments (Hayden & Thompson, 2011).

The primary program emphasizes interdisciplinarity in the studies of identity, one's location in space and time, communication, understanding the world, understanding human organization, and understanding the planet. These themes are explored through the study of six subjects: languages, social studies, mathematics, arts, science, and personal and physical education.

In 1962 Kurt Hahn, a German educator, established the United World College (UWC) of the Atlantic in South Wales. His goal was to foster international understanding among students between the ages of sixteen and twenty from diverse countries through a shared residential pre-collegiate educational. The explicit goal of the United World College is to foster peace and sustainability. The organization has expanded to fourteen colleges located in different parts of the world. The curriculum goes beyond imparting knowledge to its students and actively promotes a series of values aligned with international understanding, including valuing differences, personal responsibility and integrity, mutual responsibility and respect, compassion and service, respect for the environment, idealism, and personal action. The early development of the International Baccalaureate was intertwined with the early development of the United World College, as the experiences of students in the UWC in Wales were studied by those developing the IB diploma, and the UWC was one of the first adopters of the IB.

2. Alternative Approaches to Global Education

The approaches to global education that were developed during the twentieth century vary along at least two related dimensions: the purposes of global education and the definition of "global competency."

The purposes of global education have included the advancement of personal and national goals through a better understanding of others as well as international cooperation toward the mutual advancement of shared interests. Different curricula emerged from these diverse purposes, including education in world history or geography, education for international business, education for the advancement of human rights, peace education, education for conflict resolution, international and area studies, security studies, and peace studies, for example.

More recently, researchers have noted that most global citizenship education curricula encourage students to understand globalization, to adopt a self-critical approach to how they and their nation are implicated in local and global problems, to engage in intercultural perspectives and diversity (Pashby, 2008), and to recognize and use their political agency toward effecting change and promoting social and environmental justice (Eidoo et al., 2011). Schurgurensky (2005, in Eidoo et al., 2011) observes that "transformative citizenship learning involves the nurturing of caring and critical citizens who raise important questions and problems in overt ways" and "probe the status quo" (Eidoo et al., 2011). Andreotti (2006) further draws the distinction between "soft" and "critical" global citizenship education and looks to critical literacy for a pedagogical approach that "prioritizes critical reflection and asks learners to recognize their own context and their own and others' epistemological and ontological assumptions." Furthermore, she argues that in order "to think otherwise" and to transform views and relationships, learners must engage with their own and others' perspectives. Andreotti's "critical" global citizenship model promotes citizenship action as "a choice of the individual after a careful analysis of the context of intervention, of different views, of power relations (especially the position of who is intervening) and of short- and long-term (positive and negative) implications of goals and strategies" (p. 7). Key concepts of critical GCE include "transformation, criticality, self-reflexivity, diversity, complicity, and agency" (Eidoo et al., 2011).

Also undergirding these various approaches to global education are diverse ideas about what global competency entails. One approach views global competency as knowledge and, to some extent, as the ability to use knowledge or skills to solve problems. This idea translates largely into *curricular approaches* that focus on giving students access to specific content and subject matter—such as geography or world history or the study of international organizations. Additionally, these approaches focus on efforts to infuse existing curricula of more established disciplines—such as science or history or literature—with topics that are global in nature, as Kandel suggested in 1928. Examples of global-in-nature topics include specific curricula on global education, such as development studies or international affairs, and Oxfam's Global Citizenship Curriculum, an initiative of Oxfam in the United Kingdom consisting of a series of lesson plans—plus support for teachers—that foster the development of global citizenship (Oxfam, 2015). In the United States, infusing global education into the more established subjects of a curriculum, such as social studies, history, language, or sciences, is the prevalent approach to global education. A few states, such as Wisconsin, have developed curricular maps that explicitly identify opportunities for infusion of global topics into the entire curricular framework for the state. More recently Wisconsin's Department of Public Instruction created a Global Education Achievement Certificate to encourage and recognize students' rigorous work in global education (Wisconsin Department of Public Instruction, 2005, 2008, 2011). More recently, the Asia Society published a framework to infuse global education into existing curricula in schools and districts (Boix Mansilla & Jackson, 2011).

An alternative approach to global education views global competency as a disposition—that is, as a way of thinking and doing and as a value. This idea translates into *pedagogical approaches* to global education. The following educators reflect this perspective: Maria Montessori's emphasis on pedagogy as essential to the development of peaceful and democratic dispositions, in contrast to the authoritarian pedagogies that she believed reflected and reinforced a mind-set accepting of authoritarian regimes; John Dewey's emphasis on pedagogy as the way to cultivate autonomy of the mind; and the International Baccalaureate's emphasis on interdisciplinarity and research. A study of the effects of a cosmopolitan pedagogical framework used in three educational programs in Chicago's public schools demonstrates that it can teach global competencies that encompass hope, memory, dialogue, and other cosmopolitan values to underserved students (Sobré-Denton, Carlsen & Gruel, 2014). The emphasis on experience and, therefore, on pedagogy was a key tenet of the progressive education movement, of which Dewey and Kandel were proponents. The following key tenets of the movement were adopted at the founding of the Progressive Education Association, in 1919:

- freedom to develop naturally
- interest as the motive of all work
- the teacher as a guide, not a taskmaster
- the scientific study of the pupil's development
- greater attention to all that affects the child's physical development
- cooperation between the school and the home to meet the needs of the children
- the progressive school as a leader in educational movements (Little, 2013)

Some approaches emphasize the role of *experience in learning* over intellectual engagement with cosmopolitan knowledge exclusively. Study abroad and exchanges, for instance, reflect this emphasis on embedding students in a cultural setting different from the one they are most familiar with in order to expose them to interactions with people of different cultural backgrounds, which can be a path to developing cross-cultural understanding. Rooted in this view on the importance of social experience with cultural differences are a range of programs that focus on the *structure of the social context* that students will experience in their schools and classrooms or in particular activities designed to expose them to culturally diverse contexts. These programs and activities are based on the assumption that exchanges among culturally diverse learners and teachers will enable them to discover the common humanity they share with others across lines of difference. This view is central to the approach reflected in the student- and teacher-exchange programs of, for instance, the Institute for International Education, the United World Colleges, the Fulbright Exchange Programs, the Peace Corps, the myriad programs of study abroad supported by higher education institutions, and other programs that deliberately bring together students or teachers from diverse backgrounds. One of the areas of current experimentation involves using technology to facilitate remote collaboration among students in different countries, an area pioneered by iEarn, an organization operating in over 140 countries and connecting over thirty thousand schools in projects in which students and teachers can collaborate. Such collaborations have been found to be beneficial to the development of global competency. For example, an intervention that used virtual collaboration among students from China and the United States on international business papers resulted in gains in global competence by both groups of students (Li, 2013). Virtual learning exchanges have been used to promote collaboration among primary through secondary school students with peers around the world, allowing them to share information on their local cultures, histories, religions, and geographies; discuss US civil rights issues, climate change, poetry, chemistry, and mathematics; play chess matches; and debate contemporary global issues (Roemer, 2015).

Why Is Global Citizenship Important in the Twenty-First Century?

In addition to the long roots underlying the desire to help students develop cosmopolitanism discussed earlier, there are new and emerging motivations. This section expands upon the familiar reasons for global education introduced in the preceding section, the promotion of peace and sustainability, the sustenance of global compacts, and the generation of opportunities for individuals and nations, which range from the opportunity to access humankind's cultural heritage to the opportunity to prepare to obtain jobs in a highly globalized economy. A subsequent section will examine new rationales.

GLOBAL CITIZENS MITIGATE GLOBAL RISK

In the aftermath of World War II, after more than fifty million lives had been lost, after the first and only instances of nuclear warfare, and after the victors, rather than forging even closer bonds, began carving up the world on either side of the Iron Curtain, a group of individuals—representatives from over fifty countries—came together to imagine a series of institutions that would help ensure that another war of this devastating scope never took place again (UN, 2012). The United Nations (UN) was born out of a hope to sow seeds of peace and cooperation among the countries of the world and to unite humanity in a common cause. Those who led its creation expressed a desire for a new kind of citizen—a global citizen—who would balance his personal and state's interests with the needs and practicalities of a global world order. The United Nations Educational, Scientific, and Cultural Organization (UNESCO) crystalized, in the preamble to its constitution, the idea that peace and stability are ensured not only by treaties and military clout but also—and primarily—by the attitudes and beliefs of individuals: "since wars begin in the minds of men, it is in the minds of men that the defences of peace must be constructed" (UNESCO, 2012).

The need for global citizens who are the defenders of peace has not diminished in the intervening decades. Today's wars are neither easily defined nor constrained by national borders. Newer organizations have joined the United Nations in recognizing both the lasting need for co-operation in order to achieve peace and the new challenges for global stability facing humanity today. Global education remains one of the antidotes to conflict and one of the remedies during and after conflict (Reimers & Chung, 2010).

Each year, the World Economic Forum (WEF) publishes a Global Risks Report that identifies the fifty most important risks and trends that threaten global stability. The risks, which are identified by a group of over 750 experts, must be global in scope, must affect at least three distinct industries, must have substantial potential economic impact, must include some element of uncertainty (that is, the likelihood of their occurring in the next ten years and the scope of the impact of the risk must be uncertain), and must require a variety of stakeholders to work together to mitigate the risk (WEF, 2016). The risks are divided into five categories: environmental, technological, societal, economic, and geopolitical. Besides identifying the risks, the report also quantifies and describes the interconnectedness of the risks themselves (WEF, 2016).

Today's world needs leaders who are versatile and interdisciplinary thinkers able to work toward finding solutions to these pernicious and entangled threats as well as informed citizens who are aware of these risks and of the way in which their own actions can minimize their impact. The aspiration to build the defenses of peace in the minds of people, as reflected in UNESCO's charter, has therefore grown more complex. The UN secretary general's special initiative Education First, which was launched in 2012, has a specific focus on fostering global citizenship: "Education is much more than an entry to the job market. It has the power to shape a sustainable future and better world. Education policies should promote peace, mutual respect and environmental care" (Ban Ki-moon, 2012). The recently approved Sustainable Development Goals represent a positive, aspirational way to address and overcome these risks, and the notion of global citizenship emanating from that compact is one that reflects the skills and dispositions that could effectively address those risks.

Global Citizens Protect Global Compacts

In addition to helping people understand and mitigate global risks, global citizenship can support the institutions that allow for global governance in addressing those risks. Shortly after the founding of the UN, the international body adopted and ratified an unprecedented legal document that defines and affirms the rights of all men and women through the Universal Declaration of Human Rights. In the words of Hernán Santa Cruz of Chile, a member of the committee that drafted it, this extraordinary document guaranteed "the supreme value of the human person, a value that did not originate in the decision of a worldly power, but rather in the fact of existing" (UN, 2012b). The declaration asserts the right to dignity, employment, education, religion, freedom, and more for all men and women of the world. This momentous document requires global citizens to act on its behalf to ensure that the universal rights of every man, woman, and child are protected.

In a similar way, as the turn of the millennium approached, the United Nations members' states reaffirmed their dedication to the promotion of peace and cooperation by establishing another global compact that identified a series of global targets for human development, poverty alleviation, and social justice. The following goals compose the Millennium Development Goals, which were to be achieved by 2015:

Goal 1. Eradicate extreme poverty and hunger.
Goal 2. Achieve universal primary education.
Goal 3. Promote gender equality and empower women.
Goal 4. Reduce child mortality.
Goal 5. Improve maternal health.
Goal 6. Combat HIV/AIDS, malaria and other diseases.
Goal 7. Ensure environmental sustainability.
Goal 8. Develop a global partnership for development (UN, 2012c).

In September 2015, a new global development compact—the Sustainable Development Goals (UN, 2015)—was approved by the United Nations at the Seventieth Session of the General Assembly:

Goal 1. End poverty in all its forms everywhere.

Goal 2. End hunger, achieve food security and improved nutrition, and promote sustainable agriculture.

Goal 3. Ensure healthy lives and promote well-being for all at all ages.

Goal 4. Ensure inclusive and equitable quality education and promote lifelong learning opportunities for all.

Goal 5. Achieve gender equality and empower all women and girls.

Goal 6. Ensure availability and sustainable management of water and sanitation for all.

Goal 7. Ensure access to affordable, reliable, sustainable, and modern energy for all.

Goal 8. Promote sustained, inclusive, and sustainable economic growth; full and productive employment; and decent work for all.

Goal 9. Build resilient infrastructures, promote inclusive and sustainable industrialization, and foster innovation.

Goal 10. Reduce inequality within and among countries.

Goal 11. Make cities and human settlements inclusive, safe, resilient, and sustainable.

Goal 12. Ensure sustainable consumption and production patterns.

Goal 13. Take urgent action to combat climate change and its impacts.

Goal 14. Conserve and sustainably use the oceans, seas, and marine resources for sustainable development.

Goal 15. Protect, restore, and promote sustainable use of terrestrial ecosystems; sustainably manage forests; combat desertification; halt and reverse land degradation; and halt biodiversity loss.

Goal 16. Promote peaceful and inclusive societies for sustainable development; provide access to justice for all; and build effective, accountable, and inclusive institutions at all levels

Goal 17. Strengthen the means of implementation and revitalize the Global Partnership for Sustainable Development.

Achieving these ambitious goals requires the hard work, expert knowledge, and collaboration of groups of supranational institutions, public and private, and of individuals from all nations. They require the cooperation of governments, international and local nongovernmental organizations (NGOs), and other global and national institutions. Global citizenship is a condition of support for the work of those institutions, whether it's expressed in the form of elected officials devoting taxpayers' funds to international-development assistance or public diplomacy efforts, in the form of individuals who fund international nongovernment organizations, or in the myriad ways in which ordinary people can now take responsibility to address some of the global challenges and goals mentioned above.

GLOBAL CITIZENSHIP BENEFITS INDIVIDUALS

The individual advantages of cosmopolitanism have been evident for centuries. Globalization, which will be discussed later, has enhanced those advantages. Businesses are increasingly enmeshed in both the global and the local through supply chains, broad customer bases, and the proliferation of large multinational conglomerates. It could be argued that the heir to the age of empires, when a few countries controlled much of the world, is the age of the multinational corporation, when companies have operating budgets larger than the GDP of some countries. In some real ways, Yahoo is bigger than Mongolia, Nike is bigger than Paraguay, and Amazon is bigger than Kenya (Trivett, 2011).

McDonalds, for example, operates in more than sixty countries—more countries than initially ratified the UN charter (McDonalds, 2012). Not only its leadership team but also a significant proportion of its rank-and-file corporate employees need strong inter- and intrapersonal skills, intercultural competencies, knowledge of different countries and their business and food cultures, and positive attitudes and dispositions toward others. These skills, attitudes, and understandings are becoming more and more important for gainful employment whether one is working for a corporation or pursuing entrepreneurial endeavors.

Even for people whose ambition is to live life and to work in their own hometown, the local is becoming increasingly global. An article in the *New York Times* describes "glocal students," or students who pursue a global career by taking advantage of local opportunities, such as increasingly diverse local institutions of higher education (Saalfield & Appel, 2012).

Tony Wagner, a proponent of twenty-first-century education, makes the case for global competency as follows: "the skillfulness of individuals working with networks of people across boundaries and from different cultures has become an essential prerequisite for a growing number of multinational corporations" (Wagner, 2008).

Recognizing the importance of global competencies in the twenty-first century, the Organization of Economic Cooperation and Development is planning to add to the regular assessments of student knowledge and skills—which cover literacy, mathematics, and science—the assessment of global competency (OECD, 2016; Reimers, 2013b).

In the United States, more international students than ever are enrolled in American colleges and universities. Approximately 3.7 percent of all college students in the United States are international students. While this percentage seems small, it represents more than seven hundred thousand people, and if the current trends continue, this number will double within the next five years (IIE, 2012). However, despite the fact that the local is becoming more global, there is still a strong need for students to have opportunities to learn and to practice how to be citizens in the new global climate. A study of 454 international students enrolled at ten public universities found that 38 percent of the foreign students had "no strong friendships with US students" (Marklein, 2012). That statistic points toward a deficiency in the theory of action of these programs, which assumes that bringing people together alone contributes to international understanding.

3. New Calls for Global Education in the United States Today

The mediocre performance of American students in international comparative assessments of students' knowledge and skills, such as the Trends in International Mathematics and Science Study (TIMSS) and the Programme for International Student Assessment (PISA), and the acceleration of globalization have resulted in the evolution of a global education discourse that seeks to make American children and classrooms more globally oriented, aware, and prepared for the challenges of twenty-first-century citizenship and workplaces (Council of Foreign Relations, 2012; Di Giacomo, Fishbein, Monthey, & Pack, 2013). Much of this discourse has translated into internationalizing state standards and the Common Core and ensuring that American graduates are as well, if not more, prepared than their peers in other countries in the core subjects of language, mathematics, and science (Reimers & Villegas-Reimers, 2014). This has also resulted in growing interests in supporting students with greater knowledge about the world and about globalization and teaching them relevant skills, as reflected in an unprecedented move by the US Department of Education, which adopted an international education strategy. This strategy defines a "globally competent student" as one who can investigate the world, weigh perspectives, communicate effectively with diverse audiences, and take action (US Department of Education, 2012).

Echoing similar themes, a recent report of the College Board calls attention to

> what may be the biggest challenge facing the United States in the coming decades. As other countries become increasingly competitive through rising levels of interaction in the globalized economy, the U.S. is faced with the challenge of retaining the competitive advantage it has built through decades of economic growth. If the

US does not enact measures to counter this growing competition, it faces the risk of being outmaneuvered, outperformed, and outpaced by countries that have the ability to adapt to ever-increasing rates of constant change, something that will characterize global markets for the foreseeable future. In order to achieve this goal, the U.S. must possess a citizenry who demonstrate sufficient levels of global competency—that is, they have the right skills, aptitudes, and dispositions necessary to navigate and excel in a highly fluid, globalized, and increasingly competitive environment. (Balistreri et al., 2012)

The Council of Foreign Relations issued an education report that highlights the deficits in the global competency of American students:

American teachers, administrators, policymakers, and parents all need to think about how to better prepare students for life in a world that will affect them, directly and indirectly, in countless ways. Young people will need not only the skills outlined here but also a deep and diverse knowledge base about the world around them. The histories and foreign policies of other countries, the nature and function of the international system, and an understanding of the challenges and opportunities globalization offers—these could all be elements of a curriculum dedicated to shaping the globally literate citizens our civil service, military forces, economy, and society writ large will need. (Klein & Rice, 2012, pp: x–xi)

In recent years, the Asia Society and the Longview Foundation have worked with more than twenty-five states through the States Network on International Education in the Schools. This network seeks to support states in developing their capacities to make students more globally competent and to make schools more prepared to implement a global education curriculum well (Asia Society, 2008). This network builds on the previous efforts of the Asia Society to identify and disseminate good practice in international education through a competition, the Goldman Sachs Foundation Prizes for

Excellence in International Education. This competition, which was conducted for several years, allowed the Asia Society to identify and analyze good practices at each level of education, including at the district and state levels. More recently, the Asia Society produced a series of publications outlining approaches to globalize education as well as a framework to infuse global education in the curriculum (Asia Society, 2016).

Similar efforts have taken place at the tertiary level. These include an annual competition organized by the National Association of Foreign Student Advisors, the Senator Paul Simon Award for Campus Internationalization, which every year recognizes several colleges and universities for their demonstrated success in fostering the internationalization of their programs (NAFSA, 2016). A recent publication of the National Research Council presents the results of an evaluation conducted by the National Academy of Sciences at the request of Congress. The National Academy of Sciences evaluated Title VI and Foreign Languages and Area Studies Programs and other federally funded programs that support international studies and foreign-language instruction in colleges and universities (O'Connell & Norwood, 2007).

TEACHER PREPARATION AND PROFESSIONAL DEVELOPMENT

A number of programs focus on supporting the global competency of teachers, as that is a critical aspect of global education (O'Connor & Zeichner, 2011; Zhao, 2010). Universities and teacher-preparation departments have intentionally been integrating international modules into general education courses. For example, at The William Paterson University in New Jersey, preservice teachers must take at least twelve credits worth of courses in global or international education. Similarly, at the University of North Carolina at Charlotte, undergraduates must take at least one non-Western course to graduate, with the aim that students who may decide to become teachers in the future will have had some basic, minimum exposure to a non-Western knowledge base that supports the development of global competency (Longview Foundation, 2008). It may be argued that the broadening of general education courses can pique an interest in international understanding among teacher candidates. However, given the low threshold of the minimum required credits in such courses, a more stringent and defined set of requirements is needed to develop the knowledge of teachers.

Other strategies to support teachers in global education have included hiring teacher educators who have traveled internationally, who have some global or area-specific expertise, and who are committed to drawing on that expertise in their teaching. For instance, regional universities in Oklahoma specifically require "global expertise" in postings for new hires. Similarly, at the University of San Diego School of Leadership and Education Sciences, candidates are asked about their foreign-language proficiency and the contributions they could make toward internationalizing the school's curriculum (Longview Foundation, 2008). In examining strategies to bolster international competence among undergraduate teachers, Schneider (2007) recommended interfaculty collaboration between the departments of education and the arts and sciences. She found that much regional expertise lay in the area-studies centers that are often housed within arts and science departments. Bringing this expertise to schools of education would allow for greater diversity in the course selection offered and would also enrich existing courses, thereby making schools of education less parochial in their approach to global competency. Universities such as Indiana University and the University of Maryland, College Park, have established funds and incentives to support curriculum development that focuses on global awareness, in some cases specifically for educators (Longview Foundation, 2008).

A fairly common strategy to broaden teachers' global understanding has been, at least since the establishment of the Institute for International Education, supporting teachers in study-abroad programs. These can range from anything to a week spent abroad observing classes and seeking out the best practices that are transferable (Stewart, 2012) to spending an entire semester abroad, in the case of preservice teachers. For example, the University of Minnesota, Morris mandates that teacher candidates complete their practicum experiences in settings that are culturally different from ones they know closely. Similarly,

Michigan State University and the University of North Carolina at Chapel Hill have partnerships in South Africa and Germany, respectively, where pre-service teachers can fulfill some course requirements abroad. Other universities, such as the Ohio State University, the University of Oklahoma, the University of San Diego, the University of Wisconsin–Madison, and Miami University, offer opportunities for students to practice teaching in a classroom outside of the United States (Longview Foundation, 2008).

Given the thin evidence base around the effectiveness of study-abroad programs, it is unknown whether the initial euphoria of a study-abroad program lasts long enough to translate into demonstrable gains in the knowledge and skills of teachers when teachers implement a global education curriculum. In addition, some of these programs don't seem to be targeted enough and may be offered more broadly to the student population at large in the hope that those students who become teachers will graduate with some global experience or expertise.

Moving beyond teacher preparation and certification, some states have undertaken professional-development activities to prepare teachers to teach about the world. California's International Study Project supports teachers in low-performing schools to develop their competency and to upgrade their skills in teaching subjects that have international content—specifically international studies, world history, and geography. Similarly, the University of Vermont's Asian Studies Outreach Program runs a statewide program that introduces the study of Asia to Vermont schools (Asia Society, 2008). Organizations such as Primary Source, World Savvy, iEARN, and several other area-study centers within universities typically offer curricula and professional-development opportunities for teachers who are keen to integrate international content into their existing curricula.

FOREIGN LANGUAGE STUDY

In their nationwide survey of foreign-language education in elementary and secondary schools in the United States, the Center for Applied

Linguistics (CAL) (Rhodes & Pufahl, 2009) found a 6 percent decline in elementary schools and a 17 percent decline in middle schools offering foreign languages between 1997 and 2008. While Spanish was the most commonly taught language (in 88 percent of elementary schools and in 93 percent of secondary schools), the teaching of French, German, Japanese, and Russian decreased during this period at both the elementary and secondary levels. About 4 percent of all elementary and secondary schools offered the study of Chinese. There was a stark increase (14 percent) between 1997 and 2008 in the percentage of uncertified foreign-language teachers at the elementary school level. This statistic is not alarming, given the recommendation to master languages such as Mandarin, Arabic, Russian, and Korean, which are difficult for native English speakers to learn (Longview Foundation, 2008).

Between 2005 and 2008, there was a 200 percent increase in the number of schools teaching Chinese, and forty-four states now offer Chinese language programs (Asia Society, 2008). The Longview Foundation (2008) points out that there is virtually no pipeline of recent high school graduates who have studied the less commonly taught languages such as Mandarin, Arabic, Russian, Korean, and Hindi/Urdu, which are increasingly important to the strategic security and economic interests of the United States. While there is a recognition that schools are expanding their foreign-language offerings, the unilateral thrust to offer Chinese in classrooms is also driven by the Chinese government's initiative of sending Chinese teachers across the world to teach about the country's culture and language and paying part of their salaries, thereby minimizing the expenditure incurred by schools in the United States. (Dillon, 2010).

The Wyoming legislature passed a law requiring that k–8 students be given the opportunity to study a foreign language and in 2004 channeled $5 million into funding the development of a k–6 language program to be piloted in fifty Wyoming elementary schools for five years (Asia Society, 2008). New Jersey executed a four-year pilot program (2009–2013) to improve language proficiency and piloted high school world-language reform along with the development of stronger proficiency assessments and measures (Global Washington, 2011). STARTALK!, a component of the National Security Language Initiative, seeks to improve the teaching and learning of strategically important world languages that are not widely taught in the United States. It offers k–16 students and teachers across the country the opportunity to learn Arabic, Chinese, Dari, Hindi, Persian, Portuguese, Russian, Swahili, Turkish, and Urdu over the summer (https://startalk.umd.edu/). However, since some of these programs are residential, there is inequality in students' and teachers' access to these programs, as they haven't been systematically scaled within school districts. Other states, such as West Virginia, Ohio, and New York, have drawn out extensive and strategic language plans and road maps that articulate their visions for second-language learning and acquisition (Asia Society, 2008). Wilkinson (1998) identifies the need for more research into exploring the pathways of classrooms' foreign-language instruction and study-abroad programs that overcome the limitations of "teacher talk" and classroom-sanctioned behaviors while teaching foreign languages.

INTERNATIONAL EXCHANGE, PARTNERSHIPS, AND STUDY ABROAD

It is widely believed that students who participate in study-abroad programs develop a deeper respect and understanding of global issues, stronger intercultural communication skills, better foreign-language skills, and improved self-image (Norris & Gillespie, 2009; Kitsantas, 2004). While there has been an exponential surge in opportunities for undergraduate international experiences (Salisbury, Umbach, Paulsen & Pascarella, 2008), evaluations of the effects of study abroad on school students are hard to come by.

One of the purposes of study-abroad programs is to provide an immersive experience that will support foreign-language acquisition. However, Wilkinson (1998) found that increased nonclassroom interactions don't always result in significant linguistic gains or in deeper cultural understandings. Other factors that influence the benefits of study-abroad experiences include increased interactions with host families (Schmidt-Rinehart, 2004), the duration of the study-abroad program itself (Wikinson, 1998; Rivers, 1998), and students' goals while studying abroad (Kitsantas, 2004). There are also several methodological limitations to these studies, such as their reliance on retrospective surveys (Norris & Gillespie, 2009), the lack of a fair comparison group, and small sample sizes (Wilkinson, 1998; Williams, 2005). Given the weak evidence base concerning the impacts of study abroad, specifically on school students, we must be cautious with regard to the anticipated outcomes of such programs.

Connecticut has recently adopted eighty-five sister-school relationships with schools in the Shandong province in China. This arrangement offers teacher-, principal-, and student-exchange trips (Asia Society, 2008; Global Washington, 2011). States such as North Carolina, Virginia, and Wisconsin have also sent delegations of policy makers, business leaders, and educators on trips to India, China, Mexico, Japan, Germany, Thailand, and France to establish district education and school-to-school partnerships (Asia Society, 2008).

LEVERAGING TECHNOLOGY IN THE CLASSROOM

The development of information technology has increased both the amount of opportunities available for bringing the world into the classroom and the "intensity of interconnectedness" (Fujikane, 2003, p. 144). For example, the Global Scholars Program is an online global-awareness education initiative that engages students between the ages of ten and thirteen in global cities around the world in the study of a rigorous yearlong curriculum on topics of global relevance.

To examine the efficacy of integrating technology into a social studies curriculum, Johnson, Boyer, and Brown (2011) undertook an evaluation of GlobalEd, a problem-based learning simulation based on real-world scenarios and problems that leverages technology to facilitate communications between groups of middle and high school students in geographically diverse school locations. In their study of 260 participants in middle schools in Connecticut, Maryland, New Hampshire, and Massachusetts, the authors found that such simulations provided students with the necessary scaffolding to work collaboratively in building new knowledge and skills relevant to global problem solving, communication, and decision making. However, this gain in skills was specific to the female students, and there was instead a decline in the level of skills of the male students.

Given the promise of technology in bridging geographies and in working collaboratively with diverse student populations, the Asia Society (2008) has documented the integration of technology into global education curriculum in classrooms. Several states have expanded the availability of online international courses and have created virtual school-to-school partnerships with schools in other parts of the world. For instance, Delaware, New Jersey, Ohio, and Washington departments of education have partnered with iEARN to offer professional-development support for teachers around online project work with schools in other geographies. Similarly, the Florida and Michigan Virtual High Schools offer online courses to students in world cultures, history, global studies, and Mandarin. Indiana and Kentucky have also recently developed distance-learning courses in Mandarin for their students. However, it remains to be seen whether these interventions are being scaled across the state or whether they are just smaller pockets of innovations whose success is yet to be determined. In addition, as identified by Patterson, Carrillo, and Salinas (2011), there exist several logistical, technical, and intercultural challenges to successfully implementing global-learning virtual classrooms, and one must account for them before scaling such programs.

In this section, we have summarized various programs, strategies, and innovations being implemented around global education by states with the purpose of illustrating the wide variation in approaches in use, rather than of being comprehensive in examining every available program. We find that while these varied approaches represent positive steps toward developing global competency, for the most part, they are self-contained approaches that target particular dimensions of global competency and span a short period in the educational trajectories of students. While these various approaches could be integrated into a comprehensive strategy of global education that supports the continuous development of global citizenship over the schooling trajectories of students, examples of such extended and comprehensive programs of global education are more rare. It is likely that each of the discussed strategies could provide synergies by upholding the development of global competency in America's classrooms; for example, online student exchanges could motivate the study of foreign languages, and study-abroad programs could significantly deepen the value of online study and foreign-language study. For example, a study found a positive relationship between global competence and second-language motivation in critical languages among university students (Semaan & Yamazaki, 2015).

In addition, while there are pockets of excellence and innovation in each of the states, there is much that is still unknown about the effectiveness of these approaches and about how these strategies would scale up and generalize to different settings. An ethnographic study of the efforts of a suburban high school in Pennsylvania to integrate global education into the curriculum through a global-studies initiative and credential shows that only a small group of students benefited and that the pressures of system-wide accountability on schools limit the potential for this program to reach a significant number of students (Cozzolino, 2014).

4. Rethinking Global Education

Whereas education has long had cosmopolitan aspirations, the acceleration of globalization and new developments in our understanding of human development require new and more intentional approaches to global education that reflect more ambitious and transformative opportunities.

GLOBALIZATION

In addition to the enduring historical reasons for fostering cosmopolitanism discussed earlier, the acceleration of globalization has increased the importance of educating students on global citizenship.

During the last decades of the twentieth century, a number of scholars argued that an acceleration of a series of processes of social change was resulting from the growth and intensification of relationships between people transcending national boundaries. The combination of these processes was called "globalization." Globalization includes the creation of a global society, the development of global consciousness, and increased global interdependence, meaning that local events are significantly affected by remote and global events. While there is some agreement that there were other eras of globalization in the past, there is an emerging consensus that globalization is intensifying (Albrow, 1990: 9; Giddens, 1990: 64; Held et al., 1999: 16; Robertson, 1992:8; Scholte, 2000: 46; Waters, 2001: 5).

Globalization, the acceleration of global integration, creates a renewed reason for global education, with the aim of preparing students to understand the process itself and to live and function in increasingly globalized contexts. Globalization is making all of us increasingly global citizens, in that much of our lives and circumstances are shaped by events that are global in nature. Just as most individuals do not have much of a choice with regard to being subject to rights and responsibilities in nation-states—although some individuals may choose which nation-state they wish to be a part of—they do not have much of a choice regarding the fact that we are all affected by international regulations and processes, which also give us opportunities, challenges, rights, and responsibilities. Widespread forced displacement caused by conflicts and natural disasters, health epidemics that span continents, and questions around the ethics of whistleblowing and the boundaries of technological development have forced educators and society at large to confront new challenges within and outside of nation-states that were earlier unimagined. These challenges have crept their way into schools and classrooms and affect the very processes of teaching and learning. As with national citizenship, which, as Kandel noted a century ago, is not antithetical to global citizenship, individuals can be equipped with the disposition to be more efficacious in exercising such rights and responsibilities, in seizing the opportunities, and in understanding and addressing the challenges. As global citizens, we can contribute to the mitigation of global risks, the creation and sustenance of global compacts to steward shared interests, and the advancement of personal and national interests. In this sense the new global education differs from the traditional education for cosmopolitanism in that there is now a greater need not only for an international understanding in order to sustain peaceful relations among nations but also for an understanding of the process of globalization itself and for the ability to live and to be efficacious in more globally integrated societies and institutions.

NEW WAYS TO THINK ABOUT HUMAN DEVELOPMENT AND LEARNING

Over the last several decades, the study of human development has contributed to an expanded conception of humanity, one that goes beyond knowledge and dispositions and consequently to a new way of thinking about learning and teaching. In the education field, these developments have found expression in a movement to advance what are called "twenty-first-century skills" (Reimers & Chung, 2016). There are clear parallels between the emphases on the twenty-first-century skills movement and those on the progressive education movement, of which Dewey and Kandel were proponents (Little, 2013). Tom Little (2013) has drawn parallels between the principles of progressive education articulated by the Progressive Educators Network in 1987 and the emphasis of twenty-first-century education on a number of subjects. The principles of progressive education as defined by the Network of Progressive Educators include the following:

- a curriculum tailored to individual learning styles, developmental needs, and intellectual interests
- the student as an active partner in learning
- arts, sciences, and humanities equally valued in an interdisciplinary curriculum
- learning through direct experience and primary material
- a focus on multicultural and global perspectives
- the school as a model of democracy
- the school as a humane environment
- commitment to the community beyond school
- commitment to a healthy body through sports and outdoor play

Twenty-first-century education emphasizes the following:

- project-based learning
- critical thinking
- cooperative learning
- individualized instruction
- self-direction and independence
- global competency and awareness
- using technology as a learning tool

A recent review of the research evidence on twenty-first-century competencies categorizes them as cognitive, interpersonal, and intrapersonal (Pellegrino & Hilton, 2012). Cognitive competencies encompass cognitive processes and strategies and knowledge and creativity; intrapersonal competencies include intellectual openness, work ethic/conscientiousness, and positive core self-evaluation; and interpersonal competencies include teamwork and collaboration as well as leadership (Pellegrino & Hilton, 2012). Notice that this review does not include global competency as a distinct competency, which is consistent with the view of some that global affairs and globalization represent merely a domain in which twenty-first-century skills can be developed or applied (Boix Mansilla & Jackson, 2011). Our view is that while the study of globalization indeed offers a uniquely valuable context in which to develop twenty-first-century skills, there are particular competencies necessary for understanding and functioning efficaciously in global contexts. So global competency encompasses, for example, a particular capacity for empathy with people from different cultural backgrounds as well as the intercultural competency needed to collaborate with colleagues from different national, religious, ethnic, and cultural backgrounds. It similarly includes a deep understanding of and an interest in topics that are global in nature, including, for instance, shared natural-resource challenges, concern for global conflicts and peace, an understanding of the historical sources of such conflicts, and knowledge of international institutions. Global competency equally requires an understanding of the global risks outlined earlier, the skills needed to educate oneself on those risks, and the capacity to live in ways that contribute to the mitigation of those risks.

GLOBAL EDUCATION: CURRICULUM AND PEDAGOGY

Following our definition of global competency as distinct from knowledge or dispositions that can be developed only from education infused in an existing curriculum and also building on Dewey's notion that how we teach is what we teach, we conceive of global education as encompassing both distinct curricula and distinctive pedagogies. These curricula and pedagogies are intertwined and mutually reinforcing, and neither can achieve the goal of global competency without the other. For these reasons, the curriculum we present in this book provides suggested activities that in effect provide examples of a pedagogy of global education.

5. Designing the World Course

In the years 2011 and 2012, we designed a global citizenship education curriculum to be taught in a distinct course that would require six to eight hours a week from kindergarten to high school. Our proposal was to create a new subject that would serve as an organizing core framework around which all other subjects in the curriculum would be integrated. We called this subject the "World Course" and developed it to be taught initially at Avenues: The World School, an innovative global network of elite independent schools, none of which were in operation when we developed the course. The first Avenues campus was then being established in New York City. We agreed with the leadership of Avenues that we would develop this course with their financial support because they intended to use the course. We also agreed that we would subsequently publish the curriculum such that it could be used by other schools and teachers outside of the Avenues network in the United States and abroad.

As we developed the curriculum, we benefited from periodic presentations of our work in progress to the coheads of the Avenues campus in New York; the division heads of the early learning center, lower school, middle school, and upper school; and the director of educational design. We also benefited from conversations with the coheads at the start of this collaboration and upon conclusion of the curriculum. The feedback we received in these exchanges from these seasoned educators helped us to ground our curriculum design in the practicalities and challenges of implementing the curriculum and to balance it with other demands in a new school, such as the demands to teach other subjects and to prepare students for college admission. These conversations helped us appreciate the challenges of negotiating the innovative dimensions of the new subject we were proposing with the demands, expectations, and capacities of students, teachers, and parents. They further helped us to anticipate the ways in which Avenues would integrate our curriculum into theirs, which would have to be responsive to the unique context that emerged as the school evolved in ways that would require modifications to our initial designs. The same is likely to happen in any school that attempts to implement the curriculum presented in this book.

These adaptations or deviations from initial designs are known in the specialized literature as the distinction between fidelity of implementation and integrity of implementation. Proponents of *integrity of implementation* recognize that local actors will give priority to what matters most in their specific school, integrating what works best for the local circumstances and specific needs, which challenges the expectation of *fidelity of implementation*, or the carrying out of a program's designs as intended: "The real challenge of implementation, then, is to figure out how to thoughtfully accommodate local contexts while remaining true to the core ideas to ensure improvements in practice that carry the warrant of effectiveness" (Le Mahieu 2011 & Bryk et al., 2015). Because we are more interested in integrity of implementation than in fidelity of implementation, we explicate the goals and principles that guided the design of our curriculum in the rest of this chapter so that those who need to make adaptations can do so in ways that preserve the integrity of our design.

As explained earlier, the overarching goal of our curriculum is to support the development of global citizenship, which is understood to be the result of competencies in understanding, caring about, and having the capacity to influence global affairs and to advance human rights. We built on a conceptualization of global competency that included knowledge, affect, and skills (Reimers, 2009, 2010.) Central to our conception of global competency is the notion of human agency—of empowerment—and we therefore sought to cultivate the mind-set that individuals can make a difference, the desire to take initiative, the ability to act in leadership roles, and an understanding of responsibility.

The principles that guided our curriculum design were defining clear outcomes for knowledge, affect, and action and focusing on interdisciplinary units that would be aligned with coherent themes in each grade as well as with an overall scope and sequence. Finally we audited the entire curriculum to ascertain whether there were adequate opportunities for developing the intended capabilities throughout. We balanced such curriculum mapping with various features designed to support personalization, i.e. providing students opportunities to develop their own interests, to discover their passions, and to learn deeply about issues that were of interest to them. In particular, we depended on project based learning, student collaboration, engagement of parents and community members, and student agency in shaping the high school curriculum as ways to personalize learning.

One of the pedagogical principles on which this design was grounded was to rely extensively on project-based learning and on active learning methodologies, such as Design Thinking, that place students at the center of their learning. We also sought to give students abundant opportunities to demonstrate understanding in the form of products that could be shared with peers, teachers, and other audiences, including students in other grades in the school and parents.

We also sought to create multiple opportunities for students to directly collaborate with peers in other countries with the use of technology for project-based work and remote communication. We viewed this collaboration as a way to help them find their common humanity with diverse students.

The curriculum also provides multiple opportunities to directly engage students and teachers with parents and community members who can directly contribute knowledge and experience to support global education and thereby help students identify authentic connections between the local and global.

Throughout the entire K-12 curriculum, but particularly in grades nine through twelve, are opportunities for students to pursue their personal interests with greater depth, and to co-construct with their teachers a significant portion of the curriculum.

As we undertook to design the World Course, we sought both to use a twenty-first-century-skills framework to guide the development of the curriculum and to include in it opportunities to develop specific global competencies. The first implication of this aim is that it is necessary to dedicate time to the curriculum and to recognize that attempting to achieve global competency through curriculum infusion would at best produce only partial and inadequate results. The second implication of this approach is that the design of the curriculum has to start with the explicit identification of the competencies that define a globally competent graduate. Those competencies can then be used to map out the sequence of the curriculum and the pedagogies that support the development of those competencies.

We defined those competencies as encompassing intercultural competency, ethical orientation, knowledge and skills, and work and mind habits:

1. Intercultural competency

This includes the ability to interact successfully with people from different cultural identities and origins. It encompasses interpersonal skills as well as intrapersonal skills and ways to govern oneself in the face of cultural differences.

    A. Interpersonal Skills

        i. Work productively in and effectively lead intercultural teams, including teams distributed in various geographies through the use of telecommunication technologies

        ii. Demonstrate empathy toward other people from different cultural origins

        iii. Demonstrate courtesy and norms of interaction appropriate to various cultural settings

        iv. Resolve culturally based disagreements through negotiation, mediation, and conflict resolution

    B. Intrapersonal Skills

        i. Curiosity about global affairs and world cultures

        ii. The ability to recognize and weigh diverse cultural perspectives

        iii. An understanding of one's own identity, of others' identities, of how other cultures shape their own and others' identities, and of where one is in space and time

        iv. The ability to recognize and examine assumptions when engaging with cultural differences

      v. The recognition of cultural (civilizational, religious, or ethnic) prejudice and the ability to minimize its effects in intergroup dynamics

     vi. An understanding and appreciation of cultural variation in basic norms of interaction, the ability to be courteous, and the ability to find and learn about norms appropriate in specific settings and types of interaction

2. **Ethical orientation**
   A. Appreciation of ethical frameworks in diverse religious systems
   B. Commitment to basic equality of all people
   C. Recognition of common values and common humanity across civilizational streams
   D. Appreciation of the potential of every person regardless of socioeconomic circumstances or cultural origin
   E. Appreciation of the role of global compacts such as the Universal Declaration of Human Rights in guiding global governance
   F. Commitment to supporting universal human rights, to reducing global poverty, to promoting peace, and to promoting sustainable forms of human-environmental interaction
   G. Ability to interact with people from diverse cultural backgrounds while demonstrating humility, respect, reciprocity, and integrity
   H. An understanding of the role of trust in sustaining human interaction as well as global institutions and recognition of forms of breakdowns in trust and institutional corruption and its causes

3. **Knowledge and skills**
In addition to highlighting the cosmopolitan links infused in the curriculum, as Kandel recommended a century ago, a global education curriculum should provide students with the knowledge and skills necessary to understand the various vectors of globalization. These include culture, religion, history and geography, politics and government, economics, science, technology and innovation, public health, and demography.

A. Culture, religion, and history and geography
   i. World history and geography, with attention to the role of globalization in cultural change
   ii. The study of religions as powerful institutions organizing human activity
   iii. Historical knowledge, which includes various perspectives and an understanding of the role of ordinary citizens in history
   iv. World geography, including the different areas of the world, what unites them, what differences exist, and how humans have changed the geography of the planet
   v. World religions, history, and points of contact between civilizations over time
   vi. Major philosophical traditions and points of connection
   vii. Performing and visual arts (e.g., theater, dance, music, visual arts, etc.) as a means to find common humanity
   viii. Different arts and ability to see connections
   ix. Ability to view art as expression, to use art for expression, and to understand globalization and art
B. Politics and government
   i. Comparative government
   ii. How governments work in different societies
   iii. Major international institutions and their role in shaping global affairs
   iv. Contemporary global challenges in human-environmental interaction
   v. Sources of these challenges, options to address them, and the role of global institutions in addressing these challenges
   vi. History of contemporary global conflicts and the role of global institutions in addressing these challenges
C. Economics, business, and entrepreneurship
   i. Theories of economic development and how they explain the various stages in economic development of nations, poverty, and inequality

ii. Institutions that regulate global trade and work to promote international development

iii. Contemporary literature on the effectiveness and limitations of those institutions

iv. The impact of global trade

v. The consequences of global poverty and the agency of the poor

vi. The demography and factors influencing demographic trends and their implications for global change

D. Science, technology and innovation, and globalization

E. Public Health, population, and demography

4. **Work and mind habits**

A. Demonstrate innovation and creativity in contributing to formulating solutions to global challenges and to seizing global opportunities; seek and identify the best global practices; and transfer them across geographic, disciplinary, and professional contexts

B. Identify different cultural perspectives through which to think about problems

C. Understand the process of cultural change and that there is individual variation within cultural groups

D. Carry out research projects independently

E. Present results of independent research in writing, orally, and using media

HOW ARE THESE CHARACTERISTICS OF A GLOBALLY COMPETENT GRADUATE RELATED TO TWENTY-FIRST-CENTURY SKILLS?

The characteristics mentioned above include cognitive, intrapersonal, and interpersonal skills. They are, however, more specific than and distinct from twenty-first-century skills. For example, we define "global capability" in the following way: "Innovation and creativity in contributing to formulating solutions to global challenges and seizing global opportunities. Ability to seek and identify the best global practices and to transfer those across geographic, disciplinary, and professional contexts." Whereas innovation and creativity are "general" twenty-first-century skills, the ability to identify solutions in a global context and to adequately transfer solutions across geographic contexts involves the analytic ability to recognize similarities and differences across cross-cultural contexts.

In creating the World Course curriculum, we sought to create something different from the prevailing approaches to global education reviewed in preceding sections of this chapter. We endeavored to create a curriculum that would embody specific principles and frameworks. In our view, global education is not only about informing students of global issues but also about supporting them in embracing and taking responsibility for the principles of common humanity and shared global risks. As such, our curriculum focuses not only on knowledge and ideas but also on developing the skills needed to put that knowledge to use and the attitudes necessary to inspire meaningful action in the pursuit of global stability and peace. This combination of knowledge, skills, and attitudes is summarized by our use of the term "global competency" throughout this discussion. Furthermore, in consideration of the history of global education as well as of the state of global education today, we made the decision to attach global education to the ethical framework reflected in the Universal Declaration of Human Rights and to the specific goal of being able to contribute to solving pressing current world risks, such as those defined by the SDGs. When we developed the World Course, the development compact of the time was reflected in the Millennium Development Goals, and the Sustainable Development Goals had not yet been approved by the UN. In this book we have updated the references to MDGs with references to SDGs.

Anchoring our curriculum design in these frameworks was crucial for three reasons. First, a shared humanity, which is exemplified by a shared commitment to universal human rights, binds people together across borders and boundaries. The ability to recognize oneself as human and deserving of inalienable rights—and others as human and also deserving of inalienable rights—undergirds the willingness to take action when human rights are violated. Furthermore, universal human rights are the philosophical basis of democratic societies and a philosophy that is shared across many cultures. Second, global education must be salient in the way that disciplinary education has been salient, and these frameworks provide salience by defining Global education's theory and purpose. Third, the problems themselves, both those that are current and those that will arise in the future, are complex, serious, and unanticipated. Solving these problems is therefore critical, and adopting problem solving as the goal of global education infuses global education with urgency, purpose, and meaning. Global education is optimal as a method to solve these problems because it requires innovation and collaboration across cultures, societies, and disciplines. Because global education is optimal as a method to solve pressing world problems, it should be a priority in education systems, an idea that is reflected in the adoption of global education curricula that are clear in philosophy and in goals, such as the World Course.

The difficulties in the area of global education center around a lack of conceptual and operational clarity. A significant difficulty in creating a global education curriculum, as opposed to a disciplinary curriculum, is that global education as an idea lacks clarity sufficient to engender the kind of common understanding and consensus needed to operationalize the idea into any curricular content. An additional difficulty lies in the lack of clarity around the idea of global citizenship as well as in the lack of clarity around the underlying philosophy and goals of global education. In this chapter, we attempt to resolve this lack of clarity.

One way in which global education lacks clarity concerns the fact that global citizenship shares similarities with national citizenship, yet it is distinct in that being a global citizen crosses national boundaries by definition. National citizenship, since the Treaty of Westphalia over 350 years ago, is a status bound to the nation-state that is both inclusive and exclusive. It is inclusive in that it defines who qualifies as a member, or a citizen, and exclusive in that it also defines who does not. Global citizenship, by contrast, crosses multiple borders—political, cultural, social, and historical—and is entirely inclusive. Boundaries, some of which are clearly established in the context of national citizenship, fade in the context of global citizenship such that global citizenship runs the risk of becoming a meaningless concept. There is a legal foundation for national citizenship that does not at present exist for global citizenship, although international human rights law does provide some legal foundation for rights and duties that transcend those stipulated by national legal covenants. However, national and global citizenship are similar when the emphasis is shifted away from *definition* and toward *purpose*. National citizenship and global citizenship are pragmatic, as they are safeguards of rights and access to resources. However, global citizenship rights emphasize human rights, which are shared by all. Because the relevant rights are shared across national, ethnic, and linguistic lines, they carry with them a responsibility that also crosses these lines. This responsibility is the heart of the pragmatism of global citizenship.

Westheimer and Kahne's (2004) work in developing a typology of citizenship is also useful as a groundwork for the conceptualization of global citizenship. They identify three kinds of citizen: a personally responsible citizen (a responsible member of a community who, for example, obeys the rule of law and volunteers to assist others); a participatory citizen (an active participant in efforts to remedy injustice and to make improvements in the community); and a justice-oriented citizen (a critical member of a community who seeks to understand the causes of problems and injustice). Global citizenship must encompass these expressions of citizenship. In order to effect change on a global scale, one must be personally responsible, must participate in efforts to remedy injustice, and must seek to understand the causes of problems and injustice worldwide. In order to meet global challenges, participation must be innovative and include collaboration across political, cultural, and other boundaries. Therefore, to this typology we add innovation and collaboration as components of our framework for global citizenship. The collaborative citizen reaches out across borders to work with peers—and, specifically, to purposely work with peers who have differing perspectives—to solve global challenges. The innovative global citizen synthesizes knowledge from across multiple disciplines to develop new approaches, new ways of viewing problems, and new solutions.

Further difficulty exists at the level of education, in that global education must include complex competence that is both interdisciplinary and disciplinary. This idea represents a departure from the disciplinary focus of current education systems and presents a real challenge in the field of global education. Part of what makes education within disciplines comparatively more salient is that the overarching ideas behind the disciplines are clear, and creating curricular content is therefore straightforward insofar as the curriculum should reflect those ideas. Furthermore, the history of the discipline is traceable, as is the future of the discipline, by specific goals. Take, for example, the discipline of history. This discipline has a discrete set of knowledge and skills, such as knowledge of the historical causes of conflicts and the ability to review primary and secondary documents to build that knowledge, respectively. It also has goals, such as avoiding future conflicts through helping students understand and be able to articulate a history that a nation or people share, and the existence of diverse historical narratives. Global education must achieve the same clarity in overarching knowledge and goals, which the World Course achieves through its attachment to the framework of universal human rights, articulated knowledge and skills, and the goal of solving pressing world problems.

CREATING THE WORLD COURSE

To create the World Course, we first spent some time defining the characteristics of a globally competent graduate, as described earlier. To do that we drew from a range of literature, including from frameworks such as the Human Rights Declaration and studies and analyses of future global risks such as those outlined in the World Economic Forum's global risk assessment framework and in the development goals advanced by the United Nations. We also drew from our knowledge of the history of the prevailing approaches in the field that are reviewed in this chapter. We then engaged in a survey of existing global education curricula, as discussed in the literature above.

We found that the existing global education curricula were approached in one of two ways: they were either infused into other curricula—that is, current curricular content was examined for opportunities to include global content and revised accordingly—or viewed as separate curricula. Current approaches in national civic education have fallen into these same categories, and there are cross-national differences regarding whether civic education is infused into the curriculum or taught separately as a subject (see Schulz, Ainley, Fraillon, Kerr, & Losito, 2009, p. 43–46). It is our position that both infusion and a separate curriculum are necessary to achieve complex and deep global competence. Infusion is necessary because the competence developed within disciplines should include global content. Without global content, disciplines are simply incomplete and cannot prepare students to be successful in globalizing societies. We are not arguing against infusion, and we consider it necessary for this reason. However, we argue here that developing a separate curriculum is also necessary. This is because there are certain competencies that are not included in traditional school curricula, such as demography, and topics that are not organized or sustained, such as the study of global poverty. The complex nature of these competencies requires that time be devoted to them in a sustained way. The World Course is therefore presented here as a complete curriculum for kindergarteners through twelfth graders that should be taught separately but *alongside* the revision of disciplinary curricula to include global issues. These two approaches are mutually reinforcing.

We developed our curriculum from this review of existing curricula and from the definition of a globally competent graduate. Once we had agreed on the graduate profile presented earlier, we set out to identify curriculum content that would support the development of those competencies.

Within the framework of universal human rights, and to make real and meaningful progress in solving pressing world problems, we created a complete curriculum that (1) is *deep and rigorous*, meaning that it is *coherent and sustained* from kindergarten through graduation, develops *depth* of competence *as well as breadth*, and *increases in complexity* as students progress; (2) *unifies disciplinary and interdisciplinary competence* as well as *cross-cultural competence*; and (3) supports *lifelong transformative action* by graduates who will pursue many different occupations and paths in life.

We designed the World Course to be deep and rigorous and to those ends. It is coherent vertically and horizontally. It is vertically coherent in that the content of each grade level is unified along a particular theme and horizontally coherent in that particular content and topics are sustained throughout the entire sequence. For example, the theme of the fifth grade is freedom and the rights of individuals, and students engage in the study of social change around the rights of individuals. This theme builds from the creation of a classroom community and then moves to historical explorations through research in various independence movements (e.g., those of the United States, France, and Haiti and the South African resistance to oppression). As a one-year course, it is underpinned by the idea of universal human rights, yet it addresses the students' local contexts and lived experience as well as their shared national and international history. The World Course is also horizontally coherent along strands that are traced from year to year. For example, we determined that understanding identity is fundamental to intercultural competence, and thus we threaded the theme of identity throughout the curriculum in every grade and at increasingly complex levels. For example, in kindergarten, the students examine their own cultures and customs as well as those around them in their class and their neighborhoods. Later, in sixth grade, students begin looking at the way that values and identity shape people and institutions, including governments. In high school, in the Global Conflict and Solutions course, students examine ethnic identities that separate groups as one way (out of several) to approach the Palestinian–Israeli conflict.

In addition to coherence, we developed a curriculum that is sustained from kindergarten to graduation for two reasons. First, a sustained curriculum reflects the depth and complexity of global issues as well as the depth of the competence needed to solve them. It is hard to imagine developing mathematical competence in a year or in a unit, yet that is the expectation that is implied when global education lessons or courses are presented in such a short time frame. A study that is sustained enables the complexity and depth to increase over time. That is preferable to the overwhelming nature of studying complex topics too quickly. Second, we must be successful in developing a lifelong commitment to universal human rights and to the competency required to solve pressing world problems *across individuals with different backgrounds, experiences, and future plans,* not simply among students who already possess this inclination and are within an environment that promotes such goals. Developing competency in global affairs across entire student populations, which should be the goal of education, requires the systematic development of competency in students who possess very different inclinations and who are situated in very different environments. Consider the example of global poverty as a pressing world problem. To solve global poverty, graduates competence must reflect the deep complexity of the problem, and it must be embraced by those entering not only into international development but also into business, medicine, education, service, and other fields. The ability to understand how choices made at the local and individual levels have implications for poverty at the group and global levels requires a sustained examination of this topic that increases in complexity as students gain competence over time.

The World Course unifies disciplinary and interdisciplinary competence as well as cross-cultural competence. As we argue above, interdisciplinary competence is vital to solving global problems, yet it should be mutually reinforced by disciplinary competence that is also global in nature. This unification is most evident when one examines its vertical and horizontal coherence as well. Disciplinary knowledge is a vertical focus; for example, both the fourth and fifth grade courses feature a focus on history and on developing the skills of a historian or an archaeologist. The discipline of history is also threaded horizontally throughout the curriculum with a focus, for example, on historical agents of change within each topic. Each year draws upon content that crosses and combines disciplines, which is most clearly evident in the projects discussed in detail in the section in this paper on pedagogy. Students are required to draw upon knowledge across disciplines in the creation of a product such as a media presentation or a mock summit. It would not be possible to create these projects solely within a science class or a history class, for example, as both of those disciplines, and others, must be brought to bear on the topic of the project. Transformative action, which is addressed through pedagogy and curriculum, is a main focus of the World Course. The pedagogical practices that support transformative action, such as student choice, are discussed in detail in the section on pedagogy. However, transformative action is also addressed within the curriculum through an examination of others, both historical and contemporary, as agents of change as well as through introspection and self-reflection on how each student is also an agent of change.

In order to innovate and collaborate on a global level, young people need to develop the skills to understand perspectives and practices other than their own and to operate between local and global levels. Supporting students in stepping outside of themselves and developing the ability to understand multiple perspectives on multiple contextual levels is complex and challenging. Part of the challenge is that it requires exploration both of the self and of others as well exploration of local and global communities. In addition to these explorations, another part of the challenge lies in navigating the linkages between the self and others and between the local and the global. A third part of the challenge lies in exploring linkages over time through historical, present, and future perspectives.

In order to be clear and accessible, global education must be tied to definable and defensible frameworks and goals. Here, we have argued that the humanity we share undergirds the project of global education as a commitment to the framework of universal human rights. Furthermore, the goal of global education is to make meaningful progress in solving pressing world problems, which infuses global education with urgency and purpose. As such, the World Course is deep and rigorous, unifies disciplinary and interdisciplinary competence as well as cross-cultural competence, makes connections between the self and others as well as between the local and the global, and supports lifelong transformative action by graduates who will pursue many different occupations. To this end, we envision the graduate of the World Course as an individual who is an expert in working in teams that cross borders and that marshal deep disciplinary and interdisciplinary competence to solve problems, who has the intercultural competence to bring diverse people together for such purposes, and who has made a lifelong commitment to human rights.

2. How Is the World Course an Adaptive Approach to Global Citizenship Education in the Twenty-First Century?

As discussed in the preceding section, we see the demands created by globalization as requiring specific instruction that will enable students to understand and to be prepared for globalization. Infusion approaches are insufficient because in practice, they dilute responsibility for such instruction and minimize the opportunities for completeness, clarity, rigor, and adequate and sufficient progression in supporting the development of global citizenship. In this respect, we disagree with the view espoused by Isaac Kandel a century ago that intercultural understanding can be fostered solely as a result of the emphasis of existing subjects on it.

Consequently, if a specific curriculum is necessary to develop global knowledge, what curriculum should be taught? Existing options include relatively short and fragmentary curricular sequences, such as UNICEF's and its partners' lessons on the Sustainable Development Goals; the World's Largest Lesson; Oxfam's Global Citizenship curriculum; and some advanced-placement subjects—that is, college-level courses taught in high school—such as world history, geography, or economics.

While the AP curriculum emphasizes breadth of knowledge and the US standards movement lists discrete skills, knowledge, and attitudes that people wish to impart to students, the World Course curriculum seeks to develop a depth of knowledge and the kind of "expert" thinking required to solve problems. In our desire to integrate into the curriculum knowledge, skills, and attitudes—that is, not only to impart knowledge but also to focus on teaching skills and attitudes—that would prepare learners for the twenty-first century, we found that a focus on developing an interdisciplinary approach to curricular development was necessary. For example, when we looked at the AP curriculum as a possible framework for our curriculum's design, we were impressed by the breadth of knowledge required by the program; however, we ultimately felt that we wanted to emphasize depth of knowledge, given the kind of "expert" thinking required to solve problems. We concluded also that the available AP courses were insufficient to teach the foundational knowledge that global citizenship requires; for example, there are no AP courses on public health, demography, technology, or innovation, all of which, in our view, are indispensable components of an adequate understanding of globalization.

In addition, rather than imposing on the students a list of the discrete skills, knowledge, and attitudes that we wished to impart to them, we wanted the students to find and make meaning in their learning. Thus, the World Course curriculum focuses on learning that is integrated and grounded in current social, political, economic, and other concerns and specifically on issues that are complex and without easy answers or solutions. We believed that students would find value in—and would desire to engage with—issues that are "real" and authentic; similarly, we believed that in being asked to engage with these real-life issues, the learners would be more motivated to learn the skills and knowledge necessary to understand and solve these issues. For example, the curriculum centers on issues like immigration and the impact of human migration on the environment and on the kinds of knowledge, skills, and attitudes that are necessary to address these issues. That approach led us to fields such as demography, which is not a subject taught in many schools but is a topic that we thought was essential for learning how to address issues about population growth and its impact on sustainability. Another difference between more traditional global citizenship education curricula and the World Course is our curriculum's focus on social entrepreneurship; while a few business classes may be taught in high schools, we deliberately brought the subject to the lower grades and coupled it with the development of students' understanding of international development and notions of justice and equity.

In our examination of the IB programs, we appreciated the emphasis on interdisciplinarity and on the development of research and analytic skills, but we missed an explicit curricular sequence and the kind of content that would provide all students with foundational knowledge about globalization and global affairs.

Like other global education curricula, we focused on intercultural competencies to develop the values, attitudes, and perceptions of students. For example, we wanted students to understand how cultures can shape identities, including their own. With our curriculum, we sought to develop empathy in the students through perspective-taking exercises. We also draw upon literature and the arts to encourage creative expression in the global-studies course. As students learn about other cultures through their artistic traditions - music, dance, theater, and other forms of storytelling and emotional communication, they can experience emotional connections which transcend linguistic barriers. Many art forms, particularly performing arts, require collaboration, creativity, and the embrace of uncertain situations, which makes them a potentially effective medium for cultivating in students the ability to appreciate and engage with the unknown, therefore teaching them to be more empathetic and open minded. Participating in an artistic performance is more likely to leave an impression on students learning about other cultures than a history textbook describing the culture because the arts engage emotions, the body, and the senses, in addition to the mind.

In addition to individual development, we focused on the students' development as team members who would be able to work productively in and effectively lead intercultural teams. We built in curricular opportunities for student to develop skills in negotiation, mediation, and conflict resolution.

AGENTS OF CHANGE

We focused on introducing choice, developing capacity to solve problems and make a difference, and motivating students to contribute to the world around them in small and large ways. We sought to cultivate in the students a focus on being innovative and creative in formulating solutions to real global challenges and seizing global opportunities. To that end, the curriculum is largely project based, with a cumulative sequencing of units within and across grades. We include discussions of how geographic, disciplinary, and professional contexts matter in devising effective solutions to global challenges. In particular, we sought to ground students in the reality of the world but also infused into the curriculum the notions of agency and possibility, along with concrete skills and projects that would teach them to be agents of change.

In addition to placing curricular emphases on fairness and global citizenship, we also wanted to make sure that the students felt that they had the freedom to choose how to engage with these issues, and not that the emphases were heavy-handed. For example, at the high school level, the final projects are broadly conceived and open to the students' own conceptions of how they want to apply these skills and knowledge, whether they want to be a scientist, an artist, or a politician. We wanted to develop a strong core body of knowledge and skills that could be ably used by learners who have developed an attitude of compassion, responsibility, and efficacy about changing the world around them. While the students will be thoughtfully guided by their teachers in developing these projects, they will ultimately be encouraged and able to carry out their projects independently.

PROJECT-BASED AND GROUP LEARNING

Emphasizing the development of knowledge, skills, and attitudes thrhough project-based, cumulative sequences of units within and across grades, our various units about different cultures and regions of the world were intended to cultivate the students' ability not only to seek and identify the best global practices and to transfer them across geographic, disciplinary, and professional contexts but also to recognize how these different geographic, cultural, and other perspectives matter in devising effective solutions to global challenges. Instead of being asked to merely engage in individualized learning, students are asked to interact with others, learn with others, and influence others. For example, in grade five they are asked to create an awareness project about the SDGs; then in grade six, they are asked to implement an advocacy project about the SDGs.

ASSESSMENT: MORE THAN A NUMBER

From kindergarten, students not only learn but also are engaged in *demonstrating* their understanding of what they've learned throughout the year. We integrated formative and summative assessments into the course because we believe that global competency and twenty-first-century learning require authentic forms of assessment (Greenstein, 2012). More than merely displaying knowledge, students are asked to engage in creating a product, whether that product is a puppet show (kindergarten), a book (first grade), a business plan (third grade), a game (fourth grade), or a social enterprise (eighth grade). Learning is constructed as *cumulative,* with knowledge building on prior experience and understanding. For example, in third grade, students learn to understand global interdependence through participating in creating a social-enterprise project in chocolate manufacturing. The learning objective is to build an entrepreneurial spirit in young children through an understanding of global food chains and the ethics of free trade and child labor using the case of chocolate. The primary geographic focus is on West Africa's chocolate-manufacturing countries.

The year ends with a capstone activity that gives the students the opportunity to engage in complex, activity-based tasks that incorporate the skills, knowledge, and attitudes they have learned during the year. The capstone activity for the third grade is to create a marketing campaign for the chocolate they have made and to differentiate their product based on the culture of their target market. They build toward this capstone activity through the following units: 1. Setting the Stage for the Life of a Chocolate; 2. The Life of a Chocolate and Its History; 3. Let's Make Our Own Chocolate; 4. Understanding the Culture of My Market; 5. Marketing My Chocolate in School; 6. Child Labor; 7. Taking My Chocolate to the Market; 8. Beyond Chocolate

Other capstone activities include the following: kindergarteners take part in a puppet show performance on understanding difference, first graders create a "Book of Me," second graders educate others, third graders create a business (chocolate), fourth graders create a game about civilizations, fifth graders create an awareness project on SDGs, sixth graders implement an advocacy project about an SDG, seventh graders participate in extended service learning, and eighth graders create a social enterprise around an SDG. In many cases, the capstone activities build on one another; in fifth grade, for example, students are asked to create an awareness project to inform others about the SDGs, and in sixth grade, they are then asked to implement an advocacy project about the SDGs.

Our aim is to enable students to demonstrate innovation and creativity in formulating solutions to real global challenges and seizing global opportunities. Our various units about different cultures and regions of the world are intended to foster the students' ability not only to seek and identify the best global practices and to transfer them across geographic, disciplinary, and professional contexts but also to recognize how these different geographic, cultural, and other perspectives matter in devising effective solutions to global challenges.

References

Martin Albrow, *The Global Age*. (CA: Stanford University Press, 1996).

Vanessa Andreotti, "Soft versus critical global citizenship education," *Policy & Practice: A Development Education Review*, Vol. 3, Autumn (2006): 40–51.

Asia Society, Center for Global Education, How-to Guides. (2016) Retrieved from http://asiasociety.org/education/how-to-guides.

Sarah Balistreri, Sarah, F. Tony Di Giacomo, Ivanley Noisette, and Thomas Ptak, *Global Education, Connections, Concepts and Careers*. (NY: The College Board, 2012).

Ban Ki-Moon, *Statement from the Secretary General on the Global Education First Initiative*. (2012) Retried from http://www.unesco.org/new/en/gefi/about/an-initiative-of-the-sg/.

Veronica Boix Mansilla and Anthony Jackson, *Educating for Global Competence: Preparing Our Youth to Engage the World*. (New York: Council of Chief State School Officers (CCSSO) & Asia Society—Partnership for Global Learning, 2011). http://cal.dpi.wi.gov/sites/default/files/imce/cal/pdf/book-globalcompetence.pdf.

Anthony S. Bryk, Louis M. Gomez, Alicia Grunow, and Paul G. LeMahieu, *Learning to Improve: How America's Schools Can Get Better at Getting Better.* (Cambridge: Harvard Education Press, 2015).

Maria Cozzolino, *Global Education, Accountability, and 21ˢᵗ Century Skills: A Case of Curriculum Innovation.* (Doctoral dissertation, University of Pittsburgh, 2014).

Joel Klein and Condoleezza Rice, *US Education Reform and National Security.* Council of Foreign Relations Independent Task Force Report No 68. (Washington DC: Council of Foreign Relations, 2012).

F. Tony Di Giacomo, Bethany Fishbein, Wanda Monthey, and Catherine Pack, *Global Competency Education: Research Brief.* (New York: The College Board, 2013-1).

Sam Dillon, *Foreign Languages Fade in Cass, Except Chinese. The New York Times.* Jan 20, 2010. http://www.nytimes.com/2010/01/21/education/21chinese.html?_r=1

Sameena Eidoo, Leigh-Anne Ingram, Angela MacDonald, Maryam Nabavi, Karen Pashby, and Saskia Stille, "Through the Kaleidoscope: Intersections between Theoretical Perspectives and Classroom Implications in Critical Global Citizenship Education," *Canadian Journal of Education*, Vol. 34(4), 2011.

Luis Fajardo, "Fray Antón de Montesinos: su narrativa y los derechos de los pueblos indígenas en las constituciones de Nuestra América," *Hallazgos*, 01 January, 2013(20) *Directory of Open Access Journals* (DOAJ, 2013).

Anthony Giddens, *The Consequences of Modernity.* (Cambridge, UK: Polity, 1990).

Mark Goldie, (Ed.), *Locke: Political Essays.* (Cambridge and New York: Cambridge University Press, 1997).

Laura Greenstein, *Assessing 21st Century Skills: A Guide to Evaluating Mastery and Authentic Learning.* (Thousand Oaks, CA: Corwin, 2012).

Lewis Hanke, *All Mankind Is One: A Study of the Disputation between Bartolomé de Las Casas and Juan Ginés de Sepúlveda in 1550 on the Intellectual and Religious Capacity of the American Indians.* (DeKalb, IL: Northern Illinois University Press 1994, circa 1974).

Ian Harris, "History of Peace Education" in *Encyclopedia of Peace Education.* (Teachers College, 2008.) http://www.tc.columbia.edu/centers/epe/entries.html.

Mary Hayden and Jeff Thompson, *Taking the MYP Forward.* (Melton, UK: John Catt Educational Ltd, 2011).

David Held, Anthony McGrew, David Goldblatt, and Jonathan Perraton, *Global Transformation.* (Stanford, CA: Stanford University Press, 1999).

Alvaro Huerga, *Fray Bartolomé de las Casas, vida y obras.* (Madrid: Alianza, 1998).

Institute of International Education, "International Student Enrollment Trends, 1949/50-2011/12." *Open Doors Report on International Educational Exchange.* (2012) Retrieved from http://www.iie.org/opendoors

Feliz Jay, *Three Dominican Pioneers in the New World: Antonio de Montesinos, Domingo de Betanzos, Gonzalo Lucero.* (Lewiston, NY: E. Mellen Press, 2002).

Isaac Kandel, "International understanding and the schools. Address delivered before the National Association of Secondary School Principals" In Isaac Kandel, *Essays in Comparative Education* (pp. 228–235). (New York: Teachers College, 1930).

Ken Kay and Valerie Greenhill, *The Leader's guide to 21st Century Education: 7 Steps for Schools and Districts.* (Boston: Pearson, 2013).

Joel Klein and Condoleezza Rice, *US Education Reform and National Security* Council of Foreign Relations. Independent Task Force Report No 68. (Washington DC: Council of Foreign Relations, 2012).

Paul LeMahieu, *What We Need in Education Is More Integrity (and Less Fidelity) of Implementation*. Carnegie Foundation for the Advancement of Teaching. 2011. http://www.carnegiefoundation.org/blog/what-we-need-in-education-is-more-integrity-and-less-fidelity-of-implementation/.

Yulong Li, "Cultivating Student Global Competence: A Pilot Experimental Study," *Decision Sciences Journal of Innovative Education*, 11 (2013): 125–143.

Tom Little, "21st Century Learning and Progressive Education: An Intersection." *International Journal of Progressive Education*, Vol. 9(1), 2013.

Mary Beth Marklein, "Record number of foreign students in U.S," *USA Today*. November 12, 2012. Retrieved from www.usatoday.com/story/news/nation/2012/11/12/record-number-of-international-students-enrolled-in-colleges/1698531/.

Marie Therese Maurette, *Is There a Way of Teaching for Peace?* (Paris: UNESCO, 1948).

McDonalds, "Where We Operate." (2012) Retrieved from http://aboutmcdonalds.com/country/map.html

National Association of Foreign Student Advisors (2016) Paul Simon Awards. http://www.nafsa.org/Explore_International_Education/For_The_Media/Press_Releases_And_Statements/NAFSA_Presents_2016_Simon_Award_Winners/.

Karen Pashby, "Demands on and of Citizenship and Schooling: 'Belonging' and 'Diversity' in the Global Imperative" In Michael O'Sullivan and Karen

Pashby (Eds.), *Citizenship Education in the Era of Globalization: Canadian Perspectives.* (Rotterdam: Sense Publishing, 2008).

Mary Ellen O'Connell and Janet L. Norwood, (Eds.), *International Education and Foreign Languages: Keys to Securing America's Future.* (Washington, DC: National Research Council, 2007).

Oxfam Education for Global Citizenship, "A Guide for Schools." (2015) Retrieved from http://www.oxfam.org.uk/education/global-citizenship/global-citizenship-guides.

OECD, "Global Competency for an Inclusive World." (2016) Retrieved from http://www.unesco.org/new/en/gefi/about/an-initiative-of-the-sg/.

James W. Pellegrino and Margaret L. Hilton (Eds.), *Education for Life and Work: Developing Transferable Knowledge and Skills in the 21st Century.* (Washington, DC: National Research Council, 2012.) Pages 1–67. http://www.nap.edu/catalog.php?record_id=13398.

William Powell and Ochan Kusuma-Powell, *How to Teach Now: Five Keys to Personalized Learning in the Global Classroom.* (Alexandria, VA: ASCD, 2011).

Fernando Reimers, "Introduction: How Learning from Singapore Can Support Improvement at Home" In Fernando Reimers and Eleanor B. O'Donnell (Eds.), *Fifteen Letters on Education in Singapore.* (Raleigh, NC: Lulu Publishing, 2016).

Fernando Reimers, 2015a., "Educating the Children of the Poor: A Paradoxical Global Movement" In William Tierney (Ed.), *Rethinking Education and Poverty.* (Baltimore: Johns Hopkins University Press, 2015).

Fernando Reimers, 2015b., "Making Democracy Work: A Civic Lesson for the Twenty-First Century" In Dan Eshet and Michael Feldberg (Eds.),

Washington's Rebuke to Bigotry: Reflections on Our First President Famous 1790 Letter to the Hebrew Congregation in Newport, Rhode Island. (Brookline: Facing History and Ourselves National Foundation, Inc., 2015).

Fernando Reimers, 2013a., "Education for Improvement: Citizenship in the Global Public Sphere," *Harvard International Review*, Summer (2013): 56–61.

Fernando Reimers, 2013b., *Assessing Global Education: An Opportunity for the OECD.* Prepared for the governing board of PISA. October 2013. Mimeog.

Fernando Reimers, *The Three A's of Global Education.* (London: Oxfam, 2010).

Fernando Reimers, "Educating for Global Competency" In Joel E. Cohen. and Martin B. Malin (Eds.), *International Perspectives on the Goals of Universal Basic and Secondary Education.* (New York: Routledge Press, 2010).

Fernando Reimers, "Leading for Global Competency," *Education Leadership* September 2009. Vol 67 (1).

Fernando Reimers, and Connie K. Chung, "Teaching Human Rights in Times of Peace and Conflict," *Development*, Vol. 53(4), 2010.

Fernando Reimers, and Connie Chung (Eds.), *Teaching and Learning for the Twenty-First Century.* (Cambridge, MA: Harvard Education Press, 2016).

Fernando Reimers, and Eleonora Villegas-Reimers, "Getting to the Core and Evolving the Education Movement to a System of Continuous Improvement," *New England Journal of Public Policy*, Vol. 26, Fall/Winter (2014).(1): 186–205.

Fernando Reimers and Eleonora Villegas-Reimers, "Taking Action on Global Education," (UNESCO Bangkok Office News, 2015.) http://www.unescobkk.org/education/news/article/taking-action-on-global-education/.

Noel Reynolds and Arlene W. Saxonhouse (Eds), *Thomas Hobbes: Three Discourses. A Critical Modern Edition of Newly Identified Work of the Young Hobbes.* (Chicago: University of Chicago Press, 1995).

Roland Robertson, *Globalization.* (London: Sage, 1992).

Michael Roemer, "The Internet & Internationalization in Primary through Secondary Schools," *Journal of the European Teacher Education Network,* Vol. 10, 2015. Pp. 47-56.

Jean Jacques Rousseau, *The Essential Rousseau: The social Contract, Discourse on the Origin of Inequality, Discourse on the Arts and Sciences, The Creed of a Savoyard priest.* Translated by Lowell Bair. (New York: New American Library, 1974).

Saalfield, P. and Appel, R., "Business Schools: Looking Local for a Global Reach," *The New York Times.* May 17, 2012. Retrieved from www.nytimes.com/2012/05/18/world/asia/18iht-sreducbric18.html.

Jan Aart Scholte, *Globalization: A Critical Introduction.* (New York: Palgrave MacMillan. 2000).

Wolfram Schulz, John Ainley, Julian Fraillon, David Kerr, and Bruno Losito, *ICCS 2009 International Report: Civic knowledge, attitudes and engagement among lower secondary school students in thirty-eight countries. (Amsterdam:* The Netherlands: International Association for the Evaluation of Educational Achievement (IEA), 2009).

Gaby Semaan and Kasumi Yamazaki, "The Relationship Between Global Competence and Language Learning Motivation: An Empirical Study in Critical Language Classrooms," *Foreign Language Annals,* Vol. 48, (2015): 511–520.

Miriam Sobré-Denton and Nilanjana Bardhan, *Cultivating Cosmopolitanism for Intercultural Communication.* (Florence, KY: Routledge. 2013).

Miriam Sobré-Denton, Rob Carlsen, and Veronica Gruel, "Opening doors, opening minds: A cosmopolitan pedagogical framework to assess learning for global competency in Chicago's underserved communities," *International Journal of Intercultural Relations*, Vol. 40 (May 2014): 141–153.

Vivien Stewart, *A World-Class Education.* (Alexandria, VA: ASCD, 2012).

Vincent Trivett, "25 US mega corporations: Where They Rank if They Were Countries," *Business Insider*. June 27, 2011. Retrieved from www.businessinsider.com/25-corporations-bigger-tan-countries-2011-6?op=1.

United Nations. "UN at a glance." Retrieved from http://www.un.org/en/aboutun/index.shtml.

United Nations, "The Universal Declaration of Human Rights: History." Retrieved from http://www.un.org/en/documents/udhr/history.shtml.

United Nations, "Millennium Development Goals." Retrieved from www.un.org/millenniumgoals/global.shtml.

United Nations (2015). General Assembly. Seventieth Session. Resolution adopted by the General Assembly on 25 September 2015.

http://www.un.org/sustainabledevelopment/sustainable-development-goals/

http://www.un.org/ga/search/view_doc.asp?symbol=A/RES/70/1&Lang=E

United Nations Educational, Scientific, and Cultural Organization (UNESCO). http://portal.unesco.org/en/ev.php-URL_ID=15244&URL_DO=DO_TOPIC&URL_SECTION=201.html

United States Department of Education, "Succeeding Globally Through International Education and Engagement." (2012) Retrieved from http://www2.ed.gov/about/inits/ed/internationaled/international-strategy-2012-16.html.

Tony Wagner, *The Global Achievement Gap.* (New York: Basic, 2008).

Malcolm Waters, *Globalization* (2nd ed.). (London: Routledge, 2001).

Joel Westheimer and Joseph Kahne, "What kind of citizen? The politics of educating for democracy," *American Educational Research Journal,* Vol. 41 (2004): 237–269.

Wisconsin Department of Public Instruction.
http://dpi.wi.gov/international-education
International Education Recommendations:
Global Literacy for Wisconsin (2005),
Pathways to Global Literacy|| (2008).
The Wisconsin Global Education Achievement Certificate (2011).

World Economic Forum (WEF) *The Global Risks Report.* (2016) Retrieved from https://www.weforum.org/reports/the-global-risks-report-2016/

Yong Zhao, "Preparing Globally Competent Teachers: A New Imperative for Teacher Education," *Journal of Teacher Education,* November/December 2010 Vol. 61 (5): 422–431.

The World Course

The World Course
Kindergarten: Our World Is Diverse and Beautiful

Theme
Our world is diverse and beautiful, and we can learn about it different ways, like counting, interviewing, describing, storytelling, and viewing pictures.

Description
In this grade, children explore themselves, their families, and the world around them. The focus is on exploration, experimentation, experience, and the different methods of knowing and learning.

Each unit focuses on a central question or questions and is interdisciplinary (covering literature, science, arts, geography, etc.) in nature. The units connect with one another, moving from exploration of the self to surroundings.

Throughout the units, children learn about the beauty of difference and that it exists all around us. The last unit is on folktales that emphasize the concept of fairness in the midst of this difference.

The culminating activity is a puppet show featuring the different products they have created during the year.

The children's parents will be invited to speak with the class about their experiences of different countries and contexts as they relate to the various topics addressed during the year. We hope that starting explicit parental involvement in kindergarten will cultivate a school culture that encourages and embraces partnerships with parents.

Looking Forward
We Are One People with Universal Human Needs

Overview of the Units

1) Getting to Know You: Colors, Clothing, and Choices
2) Where Do We Live? What Is around Us?
3) Where Do We live? How Do We Move Around?
4) What Do Different People Do in My School and in My Neighborhood? How Do We Help One Another?
5) What, When, Whom, How, and Why Do We Celebrate?
6) If Things Look Different, How Can We Be Fair?

Capstone
Produce a puppet show that reflects understanding of diversity.

Unit	**K.1**
Topic	**Getting to Know You: Colors, Clothing, and Choices.** **This unit is a review of colors and clothing with discussion on the factors that influence the choices behind what they wear.**
Theme	**ICC: interpersonal; culture: arts, music, and literature; and global risk: environment**
Region	**Various**
Length	**Five weeks**

Goals and Objectives

1. **Learn** to describe the different types and colors of clothing worn by themselves and their classmates.
2. **Inspire** students to be curious about other people.
3. **Act by** asking questions and learning about their classmates' favorite things.

Skills and Knowledge

1. Students will learn to ask different kinds of questions.
2. Students will understand that choices of clothing are influenced by a variety of factors.
3. Students will recognize that a single piece of clothing may look different in different parts of the world.

Overview

Students begin the year by getting to know one another and talking about the meaning behind their names. They then learn about one another by asking one another about their favorite things and begin to recognize that different people have different favorite things, that colors can mean different things in different parts of the world, and that even the same piece of clothing (e.g., pants) can look different depending on the weather, season, culture, and region.

Activity K.1.1
The Story behind Our Names

The students take home a question sheet and get help from parents in filling out the answers to the following questions:

1. What is your name?
2. What does your name mean?
3. Why do you have this name?
4. Who gave you this name?
5. Who was the first person in your family to have the same name?
6. Which famous people have your name?
7. If you have a nickname, what is it?

Students can create different visualizations of their name (e.g., posters, handicrafts, drawings, etc.). They then do a short show-and-tell for the class about their names.

Students can also make blogs and share information about their names on iEARN.

Resources K.1.1

- https://iearn.org/cc/space-2/group-115
- http://www.oxfam.org.uk/education/resources/your_world_my_world/files/lesson2_looking_at_our_names.pdf

Activity K.1.2
My Favorite Things: What Is My Favorite Color? What Are My Favorite Things?

— The students review colors by singing songs about them and looking for items in the room with specific colors.

— Students then cut out pictures from magazines (from different countries) with items that have that color. They can also learn how to say the names of colors in different languages (e.g., Chinese or Spanish).

— At the end, the students ask one another, "What is your favorite color?" They then tell one another their favorite color, make fingerprints in their favorite color, look at one another's prints, and talk about how those prints are similar and different.

— They review counting by counting how many of their classmates like a certain color. (This simple survey of the class can be repeated throughout the year with other questions as a way for the children to begin thinking about patterns and data gathering.)

— An optional activity would be to begin to teach them about how different colors mean different things in different cultures (e.g., red can mean "danger," be a warning, or signify luck, and white and black are colors of mourning in different cultures).

— This activity can be extended such that children can list and ask one another about other "favorite things" like foods, animals, and activities (as a way to extend their vocabulary). To add a global connection, the teacher can give examples from different parts of the world for each of these categories (e.g., foods from different cultures or animals on different continents). At the end, the classroom walls can be covered with each child's picture and name and a web of his or her favorite things.

— The class can partner with another kindergarten classroom from another part of the world, and children can share their similar and

different "favorite things" with one another via simple lists, pictures, or videos.
  – They can also learn the song "My Favorite Things" from *The Sound of Music.*

Resources K.1.2

- http://www.songsforteaching.com/colorssongs.htm
- http://www.pbs.org/kcts/preciouschildren/diversity/read_activities.html
- http://www.drjean.org/html/activityPg.html
- http://globalization-group.com/edge/resources/color-meanings-by-culture/
- *Children Just Like Me,* by Susan Elizabeth Copsey, Barnabas Kindersley, Anabel Kindersley, and Harry Belafonte
- https://www.amazon.com/Children-Just-Like-Me-Celebration/dp/0789402017/ref=sr_1_1?s=books&ie=UTF8&qid=1466791758&sr=1-1&keywords=children+just+like+me

Activity K.1.3
My Family's Favorite Things

  – They ask their family members about their favorite colors and favorite activities and draw their family members wearing these colors and doing these activities. They compare their families with others' families and talk about what they like to do with their families.
  – They read storybooks about families in different places in the world and discuss similarities and differences.
  – They can watch films about families (for example, films about how babies are taken care of in different places).

Resources K.1.3

- http://www.focusfeatures.com/babies
- A list of children's books about family for kindergarteners (http://www.amazon.com/Childrens-books-about-family-Kindergarten/lm/R2SCJ07NE3LZYE)
- *Families: Around the world, One Kid at a Time* by Sophie Furlaud and Pierre Verboudhttp://www.amazon.com/Families-Around-World-One-Time/dp/0789310090)
- A list of books about family diversity (http://www.brighthorizons.com/family-resources/e-family-news/2014-how-to-help-children-understand-diverse-families/)
- *Grandfather's Journey*, by Allen Say

Activity K.1.4
The Clothes I Wear

What am I wearing today? What are you wearing today? What is the weather today, and how does what we're wearing relate to it? What are we doing today, and how does what we're wearing relate to it? Why did you wear this clothing today?

- At the end of the color/family activity, children are asked to come to school wearing a piece of clothing in their favorite color. Students review and identify different articles of clothing (e.g., pants, shirts, skirts, socks, blouses, etc.). They talk about why they chose the clothing they're wearing.
- The students then learn about different weathers and seasons. Using pictures and cutouts, they look at the different items of clothing they wear during the year depending on the season and the weather. This activity introduces the ideas that the same person may look "different" at different times and that there may be change even within one person.
    - http://www.newhavenscience.org/01weather.pdf

- They also learn about different activities/verbs (e.g., activities/verbs that relate to sports, concerts, parties, outdoor activities, etc.) and the different kinds of clothing associated with them. They begin to see, for example, that pants can look different, depending on the weather, the season, or the activity that the wearer is engaged in.
- They begin to form a picture cloud on the classroom walls. A clothing word—
- for example, "pants"—is at the center of it, and they post pictures to show how pants can look different depending on context. They also learn about the different kinds of clothing worn in different cultures and places around the world and also add pictures from other cultures and places to the picture cloud. They also learn about the differences between traditional dress/costumes (e.g., theater costumes) and everyday clothing. They begin to familiarize themselves with differences in appearance and to understand that those differences are a part of living in a diverse world.
- An optional activity would be to learn about different kinds of fabrics (e.g., cotton, silk, wool, etc.), how they feel to the touch, and where they come from (e.g., plants, worms, animals, etc.).

Resources K.1.4

- *Hands Around the World: 365 Creative Ways to Encourage Cultural Awareness and Global Respect*, by Susan Milord from the Williamson Kids Can! series,
- Lesson Plans from the Discovery Channel (http://www. discoveryeducation.com/teachers/free-lesson-plans/around-the-world.cfm)

Unit	K.2
Topic	**Where Do We Live? What Is around Us?**
Theme	**Global risk: environment; arts: other/architecture; and geography**
Region	**India and beyond**
Length	**Six weeks**

Goals and Objectives

1. **Learn** to describe their neighborhood and to identify both man-made (e.g., buildings) and natural (e.g., trees, flowers, animals, etc.) objects. Students learn about the different kinds of houses in which people and animals can live and about how those structures can be influenced be climate and culture.
2. **Inspire** students to be observant and curious about their surroundings.
3. **Act by** starting a collection of different items, both living and non-living (e.g., bugs and rocks), and exchanging those items with children from other schools in the world.

Skills and Knowledge

1. Students will learn to describe their surroundings.
2. Students will describe the basic environmental factors that contribute to construction materials and the types of homes that people live in.
3. Students will use basic vocabulary related to the weather and seasons that contribute to clothing materials and the types of clothing that people wear.

Overview

Children learn to describe their neighborhood and both man-made (e.g., buildings) and natural (e.g., trees, flowers, animals, etc.) objects. They make a collection of different living and nonliving items (e.g., bugs and rocks), and they exchange these items with children from other schools in the world. (They can also build on the previous unit and exchange pictures of clothing and their families, for example.) They continue to realize that food, shelter, water, and clothing may look different in different places. There is also a continued emphasis on climate and weather—for example, on the fact that trees, flowers, buildings, and clothing can differ across cultures because of differences in climate or context.

Activity K.2.1
Homes around the World

- The students are given pictures of houses and rooms from different places around the world, and they are asked to group them according to what they observe as similarities and differences.
- The students also read two photo books, one on clothes and the other on houses around the world. In each case, the students are asked to answer the following questions as part of a group discussion:
  o What do the houses have in common?
  o Why would the houses look different in different places?
  o What is familiar about the houses?
  o What is unfamiliar about the houses?
  o What kind of house do you live in? What do you like about it? What don't you like about it?
- Through these activities, they learn about houses, the different rooms in houses, and the rooms' functions. They learn about different types of buildings where people live (e.g., apartments, houses, condos, cabins, etc.) and how those buildings are different around the world.
  o They can review the alphabet and learn about different types of buildings for each letter (e.g., *a* is for "apartment," *b* is for "boathouses," *c* is for "castle," etc.). See the listings under "Resources" below.

Resources K.2.1

- *Houses and Homes*, by Ann Morris, Ken Heyman (illustrator), and Ken Hayman (photographer) from the Around the World series,
- (http://www.amazon.com/Homes-Around-World-ABC-Alphabet/dp/0736836659/ref=sr_1_2?ie=UTF8&qid=1306891959&sr=8-2)
- A list of other books about homes around the world (http://www.amazon.com/s/ref=pd_lpo_k2_dp_sr_sq_top?ie=UTF8&keywords=homes%20around%20the%20world%20kindergarten%20books&index=blended&pf_rd_p=486539851&pf_rd_s=lpo-top-stripe-1&pf_rd_t=201&pf_rd_i=0736836659&pf_rd_m=ATVPDKIKX0DER&pf_rd_r=0Q6BD6H5MHM87K5JEAAP)
- *The Three Little Pigs*
- *Wonderful Houses Around the World,* by Yoshio Komatsu
- *Imagine a House*, by Angela Gustafson
- *Homes in Many Cultures*, by Heather Adamson *Clothes in Many Cultures*, by Heather Adamson
- *Children Just Like Me: A Celebration of Children Around the World,* by Anabel Kindersley and Barnabas Kindersley
- A list other sets of lessons on houses tied to story books (http://www.homeschoolshare.com/houses_and_homes.php)
- Building Museum of Washington, DC

Activity K.2.2
Oh, Give Me a Home

- They learn how the climate impacts the shapes and materials used in different places around the world.
- They can follow the following lesson plan from *National Geographic*: http://www.nationalgeographic.com/xpeditions/lessons/15/g35/givemehome.html. Here is a description of it: "Just as humans need oxygen, food, and water, they also need shelter. This need for shelter

is satisfied in a variety of ways. This lesson will explore ways in which the environment influences the design and construction of homes around the world":

Activity K.2.3
Making House Models

- As part of this unit, students review and learn about simple shapes (e.g., circles, rectangles, squares, etc.) and learn to use these shapes to make representations of where they live. For example, they may make construction-paper representations of their home; use different shapes made out of gingerbread to make a gingerbread house; or use clay, straw, cardboard, and other materials to build a model of their home. Ideally, they should make a few different types of houses from the same part of the world.

Activity K.2.4
Animals, Plants, and Their Houses

- As part of this unit, students also learn about animals and their habitats and learn to identify the animals that live in their region of the world.
- It would be a good idea to include a trip to a zoo in this unit.
- They also learn about the different kinds of flowers and plants found in their neighborhood.
- They begin to learn about greenhouses and about how a "house" or shelter can enable plants to live under different circumstances than those of their natural habitat.
- The students then partner with older students and take pictures. They collect some items that are around them and exchange them with children in other places. A platform that enables such

student-to-student exchanges is touchable earth (http://www.touchableearth.org/).

Resources K.2.4

- http://www.education.com/activity/article/Animal_Habitat_Game/
- *I See a Kookaburra! Discovering Animal Habitat Around the World*, by Steve
- Jenkins and Robin Page
- *In A Small, Small Pond*, by Denise Fleming
- *Magic School Bus Hops Home: A Book About Animal Habitats*, by Joanna Cole
- http://www.amazon.com/Wanna-Take-Me-Picture-Photography/dp/0807031410
- http://www.42explore2.com/sheltr.htm
- *Children from Australia to Zimbabwe: A Photographic Journey Around the World*,
- by Maya Ajmera, Anna Rhesa Versola, and Marian Wright Edelman

Unit	K.3
Topic	**Where Do We Live? How Do We Move Around?**
Theme	**Geography; arts: music and literature; and ICC: interpersonal (work in teams)**
Region	**All/any**
Length	**Six weeks**

Goals and Objectives

1. **Learn** that transportation can take on different forms (e.g., transportation via land, water, or air) depending on function, one's region, and other factors.
2. **Inspire** students to appreciate the inventiveness of people in moving and carrying people and things and to want to try to experience as many different forms of transportation as they can (now and in the future).
3. **Act** by working together with others to create models and collages of different forms of transportation.

Skills and Knowledge

1. Students will identify various forms of transportation (e.g., land, water, and air).
2. Students will recognize that forms of transportation vary by function, region, culture, and other factors.
3. Students will learn the meaning behind different types of road signs (including how they may vary by region, country, and language but also how these signs can be helpful even when they don't know the language of the country the signs are in).

Overview

The children learn about different forms of transportation around the world and learn to identify how they vary by purpose and context. They are also introduced to the concept of symbolism by learning about different types of road signs and how they are similar and different across cultures.

Activity K.3.1

- Students are asked to share how they get to school (e.g., bus, car, subway, walking, biking, etc.). For homework, they ask their parents how they get to work, and then they report back to the class what they learned.
- The students read books about transportation (see the resources listed below) and learn to sing songs about movement (e.g., "The Wheels on the Bus").
- They read books such as *Transportation in Many* Cultures, by Martha E.H. Rustad, and Ann Morris's *On the Go* from the Around the World series to make the global connection that, for example, "boats" can look different in different parts of the world but can have similar functions.
- Various activities can be incorporated into the lessons to facilitate learning and community.
  - ○ For example, each child draws a car of a train, and then they link the train cars together to make a model train as a class.
  - ○ Each child selects a favorite mode of transportation. The children who share the same favorite form of transportation can work together to make a collage about that particular form of transportation by finding and cutting out as many different pictures as they can (so those who choose cars could cut out pictures of sports cars, vans, electric cars, race cars, limousines, etc.). They can then share it with the rest of the class.

Resources K.3.1

- *Sesame Street's* video of Zoe Saldana explaining the word "Transportation" (https://www.google.com/?gws_rd=ssl#q=sesame+street+zoe+saldana+transportation)
- *Transportation in Many Cultures*, by Martha E.H. Rustad
- *On the Go*, by Ann Morris from the Around the World series
- *Red, Stop! Green, Go!*, by P. D. Eastman.
- *Go, Train, Go!* from the Thomas & Friends series, by Rev. W. Awdry
- *The Big Book of Transportation*, by Caroline Bingham
- *On the Go!*, by Teresa Imperato

Activity K.3.2

As they look at the collages, the students begin/continue to ask and learn why we need so many different kinds of transportation.

- They learn about the different purposes that each form of transportation may have (e.g., carrying people, animals, supplies, etc.) and how the purpose of a vehicle may impact its size and shape.
- They also begin to learn about the different types of water (e.g., rivers, lakes, oceans, etc.) and landforms (e.g., deserts, forests, mountains, etc.). They begin to learn that different modes of transportation are good for traveling on different types of terrain. (They can, for example, work with models of various types of wheels on various surfaces as a way to explore which kinds of wheels work better on which types of surfaces.)
- They learn about different words and activities associated with different forms of transportation and moving and about how those words and activities may be different in different parts of the world.

– Again, the theme of differences and similarities is explored by looking at different representations of a similar concept (e.g., by looking at boats across different cultures and uses).

Activity K.3.3

– Children learn about different kinds of transportation, safety signs, and the meaning of the colors in road signs (e.g., red means "stop," yellow means "caution," green means "go," orange indicates construction, and blue indicates information). They can play "red light green light" to reinforce the meanings of red and green.
– They read books such as Tana Hoban's *I Read Signs.*
– They learn basic safety rules, such as those relevant to crossing the street.
– They make signs to communicate what they want to say.
– They may play games like charades or Pictionary to continue the theme of learning to communicate nonverbally with pictures and motions.
– They can also find other nontransportation related signs and explain to the class what they mean (e.g., Do not Disturb or Poison).

Resource K.3.3

• An explanation of road signs from around the world (http://www. elve.net/rcoulst.htm)

Unit	K.4
Topic	**What Do Different People Do in My School and in My Neighborhood? How Do We Help One Another?**
Theme	**Ethics: trust in institutions and humility and respect and interpersonal: etiquette**
Region	**All/any**
Length	**Four weeks**

Goals and Objectives

1. **Learn** about the different jobs that people perform in the neighborhood and the school and how those jobs may be similar or different depending on the context and one's place the world.
2. **Inspire** students to appreciate the roles that others play in the community.
3. **Act** by taking a role in their classroom and helping with the everyday functioning of the classroom.

Skills and Knowledge

1. Students will know the different roles that people play in the community (e.g., firefighter, policeman, teacher, mayor, etc.).
2. Students will recognize that it takes many people to help a community function.
3. Students will learn basic etiquette that is helpful for interacting with others.

Overview

At the end of the previous transportation unit, children learn about fire trucks, police cars, trash trucks, ambulances, taxicabs, subway cars, and other forms of transportation that they may see often on the streets of New York City (or the city of their residence). In this current unit, they learn more about the people who drive and ride those forms of transportation and about how they help the city. The students also learn and review basic interview skills and social etiquette, and they listen and ask questions to guest speakers (e.g., firefighters, policemen, parents who come in to talk about their jobs, etc.). To connect these concepts to the idea of global citizenship, they can invite a guest speaker who has traveled to a different part of the world for humanitarian aid (e.g., as a Peace Corps volunteer) to speak to them about how he or she helped a community abroad. They also learn about the different roles that different people play around the school (e.g., the head of the school, custodians, technology support staff, etc.) and list the different jobs that make the classroom function (e.g., passing out papers and picking up papers).

Activity K.4.1

    – Children review the forms of transportation that help the community, like fire trucks, police cars, trash trucks, ambulances, taxicabs, and subway cars, for example.

    – They learn about the basic duties of the people who drive these vehicles and how they help the city.

    – They learn to ask questions for an interview and then pose them to guest speakers (whom to ask, including parents, is within the teacher's discretion).

Resources K.4.1

    • There are songs and activity sheets available online (http://www.amazon.com/Big-Book-Neighborhood-vecindario-Foundations/dp/193139881X/ref=sr_1_3?s=books&ie=UTF8&qid=1306 892652&sr=1-3 and http://www.first-school.ws/theme/commhelpers.htm).

Activity K.4.2

- The teacher can take the class through a series of relevant Peace Corps lesson plans (https://sharemylesson.com/partner/peace-corps-world-wise-schools), including the following:
  1) "The following lesson engages young children in ideas and concepts surrounding community with an exploration of the varied factors that influence how people live, the roles of adults and children, and the interaction of people who live and work within a community."
  2) "Asha, a young girl living in India, takes the reader on a virtual journey through her village. She offers a glimpse into aspects of her culture and daily life while introducing a variety of words in Hindi. By seeing components of a village in India, students can compare and contrast daily life in India with their own. In doing so, they can see that although people may have differences in country of origin, foods, or language, we are more alike than different."
- The teacher then invites a former Peace Corps volunteer to come and be a guest speaker for the class. Children ask the volunteer questions that they have brainstormed together as a class based on these lessons and on the particular volunteer's background and experience.

Activity K.4.3

- The students brainstorm a list of all of the adults they know in the school, including what they think the adults' roles are. With the teacher's help, they identify three to five people and take a mini–field trip to where the different staff members work (e.g., the cafeteria or the school's administrative offices). They take a "tour" of the spaces and learn how these people help the school community and how they are relevant to the students' own learning.

- The students then learn how these functions may look similar or different in a different part of the world. Consider using the following lesson plan from the Peace Corps: "The following lesson engages young children in exploring the concept of school and education with an exploration of the varied factors that influence children's access to formal schooling, the subjects taught and learned, and children's role in their classroom."

Activity K.4.4

- Students learn about the different ways they can help their own classroom become a place where they take responsibility for each other's well being and learning and help one another. With the teacher's help, they create a list of roles and take on tasks on a rotating basis.
- They then link with another kindergarten classroom in a different part of the world and compare notes on the kinds of roles that students play in the classroom.

Unit	**K.5**
Topic	**What, When, Whom, How, and Why Do We Celebrate?**
Theme	**ICC: interpersonal; culture: arts and music; and ethics: religious diversity**
Region	**Various**
Length	**Four weeks**

Goals and Objectives

1. **Learn** to recognize the different ways and occasions in which people celebrate around the world.
2. **Inspire** students to have joy and gratitude as a part of their lives.
3. **Act** by creating a holiday for someone or a group of people they would like to celebrate, writing a thank-you card, and celebrating that person or group in other ways.

Skills and Knowledge

1. Students will know that common holidays (e.g., New Year's Day) can be celebrated differently and similarly in different regions and cultures
2. Students will be able to say common forms of greeting and celebration in different languages.

Overview

As a way to transition from the previous unit, the students learn about citywide celebrations (e.g., family-friendly summer celebrations) that help to build a sense of community. They may talk about the Fourth of July if they're in the United States (or about national holidays of their school's country if they aren't) and also about how and what their own family celebrates. They talk about what they feel when they're part of a birthday party and also identify a person or a group of people they want to celebrate (and explain why). They write a thank-you/celebratory card and create other ways to celebrate that person or group (this celebration can be linked to Father's Day or Mother's Day, for example). The class can also study how Children's Day is celebrated in different parts of the world and have its own Children's Day celebration.

Activity K.5.1

- Throughout the year, the class may participate in celebrating different holidays and special occasions.
- Children can draw and talk about the different things they celebrate within the classroom and with their families (e.g., the birth of a brother or sister, good work, holidays, religious celebrations, etc.).
- They read about different common celebrations around the world (e.g., New Year's Day celebrations, birthdays, weddings, births of children, etc.).

Activity K.5.2

- They learn simple greetings and celebratory messages in different languages. They can learn to speak, read, or write these messages and even learn the alphabet in different languages.
- Peace Corps challenge game—Traditional Greetings:

Activity K.5.3

- They learn different celebratory songs (e.g., birthday songs or holiday songs) and dances and play with different instruments, examining the different sounds that each instrument makes. They can learn about orchestras, listen to music, and learn how each different instrument contributes to making a larger, grander sound as a group. They can then learn about different musical instruments from different cultures.

Activity K.5.4

- They learn how Children's Day is celebrated around the world (http://en.wikipedia.org/wiki/Children's_Day).
- They can design their own Children's Day celebration and/or identify a person or a group of people they want to celebrate. They then explain why they want to celebrate that person or group and create a thank-you card and/or other forms of celebration. Grandparents and parents are easy candidates for celebration and thanks, as are the people they met during the tour of the school and the guest speakers (people who serve the community) they met in the previous unit.

Resources K.5

- An explanation of New Year's Eve (http://en.wikipedia.org/wiki/New_Year%27s_Eve)
- http://www.lessonplanspage.com/NewYears.htm
- *Celebrations Around the World: A Multicultural Handbook*, by Carole S. Angell
- *Children Just Like Me: Celebrations!*, by Anabel Kindersley (contributor) and Barnabas Kindersley (photographer) (http://www.amazon.com/Children-Just-Like-Me-Celebrations/dp/0789420279/ref=sr_1_1?s=books&ie=UTF8&qid=1306523549&sr=1-1)
- http://www.amazon.com/DK-Readers-Holiday-Celebration-Beginning/dp/0789457113

- http://www.tarleton.edu/Faculty/boucher/Elementary%20 Music%20Resources.htm
- The Kindergarten around the World Malay dance (http://www. youtube.com/watch?v=1ZZL3Ynujxs&feature=related)
- https://www.putumayo.com/shop/
- A list of a variety of lesson plans on holidays
- (http://www.cloudnet.com/~edrbsass/edholiday.htm)

Unit	K.6
Topic	If Things Look Different, How Can We Be Fair?
Theme	Arts: literature and drama and creative communication
Region	All/any
Length	Five weeks

Goals and Objectives

1. **Learn** to become familiar with different fairy tales and folktales around the world.
2. **Inspire** students to treat people fairly.
3. **Act** by creating their own fairy tales on the theme of fairness.

Skills and Knowledge

1. Students will learn the components of common fairy tales and folktales around the world.
2. Students will talk about their thoughts about fairness and why it is important.
3. Students will write and illustrate original fairy tales.

Overview

Children read folktales and fairy tales whose theme is fairness from around the world; the folktales also serve as a review of the different kinds of differences and similarities learned earlier in the year (e.g., differences and similarities in clothing, buildings, climates, contexts, animals, celebrations, families, houses, etc.). The students then write and illustrate their own fairy tales. They learn about different puppets from around the world and compose a puppet show with puppets and props that they make to represent what they've learned about different clothing, shelters, animals, musical instruments, and folktales from around the world.

Activities and Resources

Lessons can be taken from the following resources on recognizing the components of fairy tales from around the world and on creating their own fairy tales:

- – http://edsitement.neh.gov/lesson-plan/fairy-tales-around-world
- • Resources on puppets from around the world (https://makingvisualnarratives.com/)
- • A list of links to sites that describe puppetry in Japan, Vietnam, and Indonesia (http://score.rims.k12.ca.us/activity/puppets/)
- • One World, One Sky: Big Bird's Adventure (https://www.youtube.com/watch?v=E1D7xXLO8yk)
- • http://contentdev.sesameworkshop.org/web/street/parents/topicsandactivities/toolkits/oneworldonesky
- • The *Global Grover* series (aimed for preschool children)
  - o https://www.youtube.com/watch?v=cX750lVbI_s
  - o https://www.youtube.com/watch?v=H-XJV9feNOI
  - o https://www.youtube.com/watch?v=DAburU-d__s
  - o https://www.youtube.com/watch?v=qdFgpMj9o0o
  - o https://www.youtube.com/watch?v=5XTtrwnPPcA
  - o https://www.youtube.com/watch?v=gqPaWJe99PY
  - o https://www.youtube.com/watch?v=xJvkmcyC2uo
  - o https://www.youtube.com/watch?v=TMYzKA4Es-I
  - o https://www.youtube.com/watch?v=VC5HDLvrNGY
  - o https://www.youtube.com/watch?v=VgCVh7e4E5Y
  - o https://www.youtube.com/watch?v=F3WMks6MotE
  - o https://www.youtube.com/watch?v=tPVgxbmOhbs
  - o https://www.youtube.com/watch?v=NWP42HDsV2M

- o https://www.youtube.com/watch?v=CwDN2hF2bmU
- o https://www.youtube.com/watch?v=Rjr2A9jLRGQ
- o https://www.youtube.com/watch?v=FCMTvep1_A4
- o https://www.youtube.com/watch?v=rqz7nFiyAw8
- o https://www.youtube.com/watch?v=wRjl6T_n0Ds
- Diversity activities for elementary schools (http://www. diversitycouncil.org/elActivities.shtml)

The World Course
First Grade: We Are One People with Universal Human Needs

Theme

Understanding common humanity across various cultural differences and common needs of all people.

Description

This year establishes the oneness of all human life through an investigation of a few universal human needs. Students learn about what food, water, clothing, shelter, and respectful relationships look like around the world, with a special focus on India. Their understanding of what it means to care for one another and to meet basic needs is deepened by activities involving taking care of plants and classroom pets. At the beginning of the year, students are also given a blank map that they will fill in over the course of the year with the geographical, historical, and cultural information they learn about. The year ends with a project in which students create a "Book of Me" that includes photos, poems, and essays about themselves, their homes, the foods they eat, their clothes, their families, and their other needs and wants.

Looking Back

Our world is diverse and beautiful, and we can learn about it different ways.

Looking Forward:

Who are we, where do we come from, what do we have in common, and how do we differ from others? Exploring people, culture, and the world.

Overview of the Units

1) Human Needs
2) Food and Water
3) Clothing and Shelter
4) Respectful Relationships

Capstone

The students create a "Book of Me" (a scrapbook) about themselves that mirrors the "snapshots" of the children in Oxfam's "My World, Your World." They include photos of themselves, their families, their homes, the foods they eat, their clothes, and other items that they determine are needs and wants. The book will also double as a portfolio of the work that the students will create over the course of the year, such as poems, drawings, and other materials.

(Note that for all Oxfam activities in this year, the United Kingdom should be replaced with the country where the course is been taught.)

Unit   1.1
Topic   **Human Needs**
Theme   **ICC: interpersonal (diverse cultural perspectives, one's own identity and culture, and others' identities and culture); ethics: common values; work and mind habits: innovation and creativity; culture: geography; arts: literature and visual; and investigation and analytical skills: local-global link and creative communication**
Region **Brazil, India, Russia, Ethiopia**
Length **Two Weeks**

Goals and Objectives

1. **Learn** about a few of the things that unite humans—such as the need for food, water, clothing, shelter, and respectful relationships—while at the same time learning about their own and others' cultural perspectives.
2. **Inspire** students to reflect on how plants and animals need many of the same things that humans need.
3. **Act** by identifying some of the key ways in which all humans are the same.

Skills and Knowledge

1. Students will be able to locate Brazil, India, Russia, and Ethiopia on a map and to name the continent that each is on.
2. Students will identify at least four basic human needs that reflect common values.
3. Students will describe themselves (their own identities) and see connections between themselves and others (others' identities), thus gaining interpersonal skills.

4. Students will discuss the meaning of their names and the importance of names, thereby deepening their understanding of common values.
5. Students will make comparisons between two things that may initially seem unfamiliar and different, thereby developing perspective-taking skills.
6. Students will write their own poetry and make visual art that they then share with children in other parts of the world.

Overview

In this unit, students learn about those needs that unite all of humanity, as well as the difference between needs and wants. They begin by getting introduced to children from different parts of the world in the Oxfam curriculum, "Your World, My World." They examine the topic of human needs through the arts, as well as through poetry.

Activity 1.1.1
Your World, My World

Students complete this series of activities from Oxfam, paying particular attention to what the photos/stories tell the class about what people around the world need. They plot the cities and countries mentioned on their maps. After completing the lessons, the students create a similar "snapshot" and a collection of photographs oft themselves. In this way, the students will learn about the others in the class. This series of lessons can also extend throughout the year. (http://www.oxfam.org.uk/education/resources/your-world-my-world)

Activity 1.1.2
Wants and Needs

Students complete this activity (or one like it) on the differences between wants and needs(https://educators.brainpop.com/bp-jr-topic/needs-and-wants/).

They will come up with the following: 1) water, 2) food, 3) clothing, 4) shelter, 5) air, 6) education, and 7) love/respectful relationships.

Activity 1.1.3
Six Billion People, Six Billion Possibilities

Students are instructed to find one object that represents each of the seven universal human needs that they found and to make something out of the object. For example, a student may collect a water bottle (water), an empty cereal box (food), an old sock (clothing), a few Lego bricks (shelter), a balloon (air), a paper clip (education), and a photo of his or her family (love). He or she then creates a sculpture out of the objects. Each child shares his or her sculpture, and the teacher leads the class in a discussion of how even though we all need the same things, those things look different for every person.

Activity 1.1.4
What Makes a Good Friend

The teacher asks the students to think about what a good friend is and what a good friend does. The students write an acrostic poem using a word and descriptions of friendship. Consider the following example:

Friends are nice
Really great to have
In sunny skies
Especially to play
Never to hurt
Don't say mean things
So good to have a friend

They will revisit these poems later in the year.

Resources 1.1.4

- iEARN (www.iearn.org)
- Oxfam Educational Resources (www.oxfam.org.uk/education)
- Useful maps (http://education.nationalgeographic.com/education/mapping/outline-map/?map=Africa)
- Stories of children around the world http://www.oxfam.org.uk/education/resources/your-world-my-world

Unit	1.2
Topic	**Water and Food**
	ICC: interpersonal (diverse cultural perspectives, one's own identity and culture, others' identities and cultures, and working in intercultural teams); ICC: intrapersonal (minimization of the effects of prejudice; ethics: common values, commitment to equality, the value of human potential, and the importance of global compacts); work and mind habits: cross-cultural perspective taking; culture: geography; global risk: environment; arts: literature and visual; and investigation and analytical skills: local-global link and creative communication
Region	**Ghana, India, Uganda, and Mexico**
Length	**Eight weeks**

Goals and Objectives

1. **Learn** about water and food around the world.
2. **Inspire** students to think about how all forms of life, both human and other, need water and food.
3. **Act by** describing what water is needed for and how to access it.

Skills and Knowledge

1. Students will learn the difference between salt water and freshwater (geography).
2. Students will learn the oceans and place them on a map (geography).
3. Students will be able to place India, Ghana, and Uganda on a map (geography).

4. Students will learn about the many uses of water (common values).
5. Students will study water-related poetry (arts) and write their own.
6. Students will learn about the foods that people eat around the world, both those that are different and those that are similar (diverse cultural perspectives).
7. Students will learn about the needs of plants (and maybe animals) and how they differ from human needs (common values).
8. Students will read versions of the story "Stone Soup" from many different countries and cultures.

Overview

In this unit, students learn about two of the universal human needs: water and food. They learn about geography and the difference between salt water and freshwater, about how other cultures access water, and about what foods other people eat. They will compare the foods that they eat with the foods that others eat, with the goal of making "foreign" foods seem less foreign. Finally, they will examine different versions of the story "Stone Soup."

(In science class, students can learn about the makeup of water, the water cycle, and other information about water. In order to learn about the water cycle, students can use the following experiment: https://www3.epa.gov/safewater/kids/.)

Activity 1.2.1
Freshwater versus Salt Water

The teacher asks students about the differences between oceans, rivers, and lakes. On their maps, students color salt water dark blue and freshwater light blue. They talk about the parts of the world that have less freshwater than others. Students label the oceans on their maps.

Activity 1.2.2
Water Has Many Uses

Students reflect on the ways that they use water, how others in their family use water, and why water is important, using section 4 of the following curriculum: http://static.water.org/docs/curriculums/WaterOrg%20ElemCurricFULL.pdf.

Activity 1.2.3
Water Is Life, Water Is Poetry

Students illustrate poems about water from around the world and then write their own poem about water.
(http://static.water.org/docs/curriculums/WaterOrg%20ElemCurricFULL.pdf.)

Activity 1.2.4
Hungry Planet

Students look at *Hungry Planet*, a book by Peter Menzel that shows the foods that a family eats in a week. They then compare the quantity and types of foods that the families from all over the world eat. They look for similarities and differences between what they eat. They may be asked to find at least one food that both they and each family eat.

Activity 1.2.5
Our Own Hungry Planet

Students pair with a classroom in another part of the world, and each class records what they ate for a day or a week (whichever the teacher prefers). They must ask their parents/caretakers what is in the food and make note of who prepared the food. Consider the following example

Food Eaten	Who Prepared It?
Spaghetti	Mom
Potato Chips	Packaged
Ice Cream	Packaged

First the students will compare what they ate with what other members of the class ate. Then they will compare the types of foods they ate with the types of foods their partners from another country ate. They will also place the country that their partners are from on their map.

Activity 1.2.6
"Stone Soup"

Students read several different versions of the folktale "Stone Soup." They compare each version and think about why they might be different and how they are the similar. They mark on their map the origin of each version of the folktale.

We recommend the following versions of the story:

o   Marcia Brown's 1947 Caldecott Award–winning "Stone Soup"
o   Jon J. Muth's 2003 "Stone Soup," which is set in China
o   The versions listed on the University of Pittsburgh's website: http://www.pitt.edu/~dash/type1548.html

Activity 1.2.7
Our Food, Our World

Students complete the "Our Food, Our World" series of lessons from Oxfam. They learn about what foods children in India and Mexico eat and also learn about what they have in common with children in those countries. They add information that they learn from Yamini and Luis, two characters in the lessons, to their maps.

http://www.oxfam.org.uk/education/resources/our_food_our_world/

Activity 1.2.8
Our Global Garden

At the beginning of the year, the students will plant plants from some of the countries they're studying. The students will evaluate what conditions exist in the country each plant is from in order to see what it needs to survive. They will be introduced to the concept of native plants and non-native plants. They will monitor the plants' progress in class. If possible, students in another school in another country will do the same, and the two classes will share notes on the progress of their plants. Each student can have one plant that he or she must take care of all year, or the students can take turns being responsible for a plant. Each should keep a journal about what the plant needs to thrive, how he or she is meeting the needs of the plant, and the reasons that the plant is or isn't thriving.

(Note that the class may also want to investigate adopting a pet indigenous to one or more of the countries being studied. They can research what kind of habitat the animal needs, what kinds of things the animal eats, and names for the animal. They can then also reflect on what the pet needs to thrive and on whether the things the pet needs are the same as or different from what the plants need and what humans need. Chickens may be an ideal choice for this project.)

Optional Activity
Drip Calculator

Students use this drip calculator to find out about water wastage: http://www.awwa.org/resources-tools/public-affairs/public-information/dripcalculator.aspx.

Optional Activity
Home Water-Use Calculator

Student use this form to calculate the amount of water used in their homes:
http://www.waterbudgets.com/ConserVision/CUWCC/DataInput.htm

Resources

- The Environmental Protection Agency (water.epa.gov)
- WaterAid (www.wateraid.org)
- iEARN (www.iearn.org)

Unit   1.3
Topic   **Clothing and Shelter**
Theme   **ICC: interpersonal (one's own identity and culture and oth-
           ers' identities and cultures); ethics: common values; work
           and mind habits: innovation and creativity; and arts: litera-
           ture and visual**
Region   **India and Beyond**
Length   **Eight weeks**

Goals and Objectives

1. **Learn** about the clothes people wear around the world and the
   houses in which they live.
2. **Inspire** students to reflect on the cultural meaning behind different
   clothing choices and types of houses.
3. **Act** by identifying cultures based on the types of clothing and
   houses.

Skills and Knowledge

1. Students learn about the types of houses people live in around the
   world.
2. Students are able to describe the basic environmental factors that contribute to the construction materials and types of homes people live in.
3. Students learn about the types of clothing that people around the
   world wear.
4. Students are able to describe the basic environmental factors that
   contribute to the types of clothing that people wear and the materials they're made from.
5. Students are able to think reflectively about the type of house they
   live in and about which aspects of their home reflect their family's
   wants and which reflect their family's needs.

Overview

In this unit students learn about more human needs: clothing and shelter. They learn about what clothes and houses around the world have in common with their clothes and houses, respectively.

Activity 1.3.1
Books about Clothes and Houses

The students read two photo books, one on clothes and the other on houses around the world. In each case, the students are asked to answer the following questions as part of a group discussion:

1. What do the houses/clothes have in common?
2. Why do the houses/clothes look different in different places?
3. What is familiar about the houses/clothes?
4. What is unfamiliar about the houses/clothes?
5. What kind of clothes do they themselves wear? Why?
6. What kind of houses do they themselves live in? Why?
7. Do they wear only one type of clothes, or do they wear more than one style or type? Why?
8. Do they think that children in other countries only wear one style or type of clothes every day? Why or why not?

The teacher can also use this guide to lead a lesson about Morris and Heyman's *Houses and Homes*.

Recommended Books

- Morris and Heyman's *Houses and Homes* (ISBN 978-0688135782)
- Komatsu's *Wonderful Houses Around the World* (ISBN 978-0936070346)
- Gustafson's *Imagine a House* (ISBN 978-0972684903)
- Adamson's *Homes in Many Cultures"* (ISBN: 978-1429633802)

- Adamson's *"Clothes in Many Cultures"* (ISBN: 978-1429633826)
- Kindersley's *"Children Just Like Me: A Celebration of Children around the World"* (ISBN: 978-0789402011)

Activity 1.3.2
Oh, Give Me a Home

This lesson is summarized by *National Geographic* in the following way: "Just as humans need oxygen, food, and water, they also need shelter. This need for shelter is satisfied in a variety of ways. This lesson will explore ways in which the environment influences the design and construction of homes around the world."
(http://www.nationalgeographic.com/xpeditions/lessons/15/g35/giveme-home.html.)

Activity 1.3.3
Making House Models

Students make models of houses from different parts of the world using clay, straw, cardboard, and other materials. Ideally, they should make a few different types of houses from the same part of the world.

Resources

- Others sets of lessons on houses tied to storybooks: (http://www.homeschoolshare.com/houses_and_homes.php)
- Building Museum of Washington, DC

Unit	1.4
Topic	**Respectful Relationships**
Theme	**ICC: interpersonal (diverse cultural perspectives, one's own identity and culture, and others' identities and cultures); ICC: intrapersonal (conflict-resolution skills); ethics: common values and commitment to equality; work and mind habits: cross-cultural perspective taking; arts: literature; and investigation and analytical skills: local-global link and creative communication**
Region	**India**
Length	**Eight weeks**

Goals and Objectives

1. **Learn** how all people need respectful relationships and families of some sort.
2. **Inspire** students to reflect on the facts that not all families interact in the same way and that not all respectful relationships involve people who are blood relations.
3. **Act** by treating one another with the respect that all people deserve and need.

Skills and Knowledge

1. Students will learn about the diverse cultural perspectives that influence literature through different retellings of the story "Cinderella."
2. Students will learn about their own cultures and others' cultures by reflecting on their families and the family and friends of Muluken, a character who lives in India. This also develops their cross-cultural perspective taking.
3. Students will link the local (their own families and friends) to the global—the fact that all people around the world need respectful

relationships. This also develops their commitment to equality by establishing a universal human need.

4. Students will use creative communication to write their own versions of "Cinderella" and to add to their "Book of Me."

5. Students will learn conflict-resolution skills by thinking about how all people need respectful relationships and by reflecting on what constitutes a respectful relationship.

Overview

Students examine the need of all people for respectful relationships. They examine the life of Muluken, who lives in India, and her description of her family. They revisit their friendship poems from the beginning of the year and think about what changes they would like to make to them. They also read and write poetry about their families. They also do an extended comparison of different versions of "Cinderella."

Activity 1.4.1
Revisiting Muluken

Students go back to Oxfam's "Your World, My World" series of lessons and focus on the lesson on families. They learn about Muluken's family and use her story to reflect on their own family (http://www.oxfam.org.uk/education/resources/your_world_my_world/files/lesson5_exploring_family.pdf.).

Activity 1.4.2
Revisiting Friendships

Students revisit the section on friends in Oxfam's "Your World, My World" and contrast their answers with what they said and thought at the beginning of the year. They will also look at their acrostic poems on friendship and make new ones based on their current understandings of friendship

(http://www.oxfam.org.uk/education/resources/your_world_my_world/
files/lesson6_our_friends_and_us.pdf.).

Activity 1.4.3
Myself

Students help one another make life-size cutouts of themselves out of butcher paper. One child will lie down on the paper, and another will trace his or her outline. The students talk to one another about their features and help one another draw paper versions of themselves on the paper. They can mix paint to make a shade similar to their skin color and see how people are all just varieties of a few shades.

Activity 1.4.4
Family Poetry

Students create their own poetry about caring relationships and families modeled after poems like this one

> Our family comes
> From many homes,
> Our hair is straight,
> Our hair is brown,
> Our hair is curled,
> Our eyes are blue,
> Our skins are different
> Colors, too.
> We're girls and boys,
> We're big and small,
> We're young and old,
> We're short and tall.
> We're everything
> That we can be

And still we are
A family.
We laugh and cry,
We work and play,
We help each other
Every day.
The world's a lovely
Place to be
Because we are
A family.

or this one

What is a family?
Who is a family?
One and another makes two is a family!
Baby and father and mother: a family!
Parents and sister and brother: a family!
All kinds of people can make up a family
All kinds of mixtures can make up a family
What is a family?
Who is a family?
The children that lived in a shoe is a family!
A pair like a kanga and roo is a family!
A calf and a cow that go moo is a family!
All kinds of creatures can make up a family
All kinds of numbers can make up a family
What is a family?
Who is a family?
Either a lot or a few is a family;
But whether there's ten or there's two in your family,
All of your family plus you is a family!
(Mary Ann Hoberman)

These poems are taken from the following website: http://www.canteach.ca/elementary/songspoems3.html.

Activity 1.4.5
"Cinderella" Around the World

Students will read and discuss "Cinderella." Then they will read variations of the folktale from different parts of the world. They will compare and contrast the stories, discussing why and how the elements of the story are different. They will also write their own version of "Cinderella," keeping the essential components of it but changing other elements to reflect the fact that they understand how the same story can be presented in different ways.

Recommended "Cinderella" Resources:

- http://edsitement.neh.gov/lesson-plan/cinderella-folk-tales-variations-plot-and-setting#sect-introduction
- http://learningtogive.org/lessons/unit205/lesson1.html

Optional Activity
Family Interactions

Have each student pick two or three dolls, puppets, or stuffed animals—one to represent the student and a few others to represent his or her family members. They can also make paper dolls or puppets. Students then pretend that an alarm clock is going off and start their day. Using their dolls, puppets, or stuffed animals, students act out the sequence of events and the role of each family member during their morning ritual. This can be expanded, and students can act out other parts of the day, family celebrations of holidays, or to the process of helping their family members. Consider asking students the following questions: How is each family member's role important, including your own? How are the roles that people play in your family similar to and different from those that people play in other families (e.g., many children in other countries take a more active role in caring for their siblings than do children in the United States)?

Resources

- An optional activity on children's roles around the world (http://www.discoveryeducation.com/teachers/free-lesson-plans/children-around-the-world.cfm)
- Lessons on children around the world, with many references to diverse families
  https://sharemylesson.com/partner/peace-corps-world-wise-schools
- Another unit using children's literature to inspire students to reflect on the idea of family (http://www.halcyon.com/marcs/theme.html)
- A review of children's literature on families of different types (http://www.carolhurst.com/newsletters/23bnewsletters.html)
- The Mosaic Project (on conflict resolution)
- All families are special by Norma Simon
- The family book paperback by Todd Parr
- Mommy, Mama, and Me board book by Leslea Newman
- It's Okay to be different by Todd Parr

The World Course
Second Grade: Ourselves and Others

Theme

Who are we, where do we come from, what do we have in common, and how do we differ from others and what needs to we have in common? Exploring people, culture, and the world.

Description

In this grade students explore cultural differences with a special focus on how childhood is experienced in different parts of the world. They read stories about children, forms of play, customs, and myths; study literature and music from around the world; and learn about different places around the world. They also examine the way in which children can make a significant difference in the world around them and collaborate in a project to improve the educational opportunities of other children. Students are introduced to the SDGs.

This year students work with peers in at least one other second grade in another country. Periodically, students check in with their peers in their sister school to compare notes on what they're learning, to obtain information, and to make presentations.

The year places a special emphasis on having the children observe their own experiences and surroundings as well as the experiences of others. The children then analyze those experiences as they relate to specific cultures and present reports of their observations to other children in a different country using varied technologies.

The curriculum is structured in four units, thirteen activities, and thirty-eight sessions that take place over thirty weeks.

Looking Back
We are one people with universal human needs

Looking Forward
Understanding global interdependence through economic production.

Overview of the Units

1. Similarities and Differences Across Cultures
2. Growing Up in Different Cultures
3. Comparing Literature and Music from Different Cultures
4. How Children Make a Difference

Capstone
The capstone project, which is modest in scope, encourages children to contribute to the education of other children.

Unit	**2.1**
Topic	**Similarities and Differences Across Cultures**
Theme	**Diverse cultural perspectives, empathy, variations within cultural groups, curiosity about global affairs, geography, common values, the use of evidence, and the use of technology**
Region	**Any/all, with more emphasis on the countries represented by the children's parents and on the countries in which partner schools are located. It would be helpful if various sections of the same grade covered different countries and attempted to have representation of various world regions (e.g., Africa, Asia, Europe, and Latin America)**
Length	**Eight weeks (six activities and twelve sessions)**

Goals and Objectives

1. **Learn** similarities and differences in how children play in different cultures and understand the limitations of representing an entire culture or country with ideal types or averages, understanding that within every culture, there is variation.

2. **Inspire** students to take interest in various cultures, cultural differences, and the ways children live in different cultures. Spark their desire to communicate with children in other countries with the use of modern telecommunication technologies.

3. **Act** by describing the games children play in different cultures and sharing those observations with students in other parts of the world.

Skills and Knowledge

1. Students will describe the games that they and other children in their school play and then present those descriptions in a poster.

2. Students will analyze and compare various games played by children in their school.

3. Students will narrate the games they play, produce simple videos and pictures of those games, and share those observations with peers in other countries using Internet-based communication technologies

4. Students will analyze reports produced by peers in a school in another country describing the games they play.

Overview

This unit engages students in the analysis of their direct experience with the games they play, and that analysis is then extended to analyses of the games played by their parents and their peers in other countries. The activities involves collecting evidence, using observation skills, studying interviews and documentary sources, elaborating a framework creating categories to analyze games, and presenting analyses to peers and teachers in their school and to peers in other countries. The unit offers an introduction to maps and to countries and students around the world. Students use technology to communicate with peers in other countries.

Activity 2.1.1
What Games Do We Play?

This teacher-led activity is an analysis of the games that students in the class play. Students take turns describing one game they play. In groups, some students then play the game while other students observe them. The teacher then leads an analysis of the game, focusing the conversation on, for example, the following questions:

1. What is the name of the game?
2. What is the aim of the game?
3. How many students play it?
4. How does the game foster cooperation?

5. How does the game foster competition?
6. What kind of skill is required to play the game?
7. What resources are necessary to play the game?
8. In what way is the game fun?
9. Where did the game originate? Do we know what country the game is originally from?
10. In what countries is this game played?

After the conversation in which the games are analyzed, the teacher and students jointly prepare posters for several games. Some students might write, while others might draw. These posters are then placed side by side, and students engage in a conversation in which they compare and contrast the various games.

Students then decide as a group which of the games they would like to play by taking turns making a case for their favorite game, participating in a conversation about which game they should choose, and finally taking a vote. As some students play the game, others act as recorders, taking pictures and filming a short video. Students then watch the video, look at the pictures, and reflect on their experience playing the game. They go back to the poster describing the game and revise the description of it if necessary.

Activity 2.1.2What Games Did Our Parents Play When They Were Children?
Homework

Following lesson 2.1.1, students interview their parents about the games they played as children. They prepare a poster similar to the posters prepared in class, with assistance from their parents if necessary. They use the following interview rubric:

1. What is the name of the game?
2. What is the aim of the game?

3. How would you describe the game?
4. How many students play?
5. How does the game foster cooperation?
6. How does the game foster competition?
7. What kind of skill is required to play the game?
8. What resources are necessary to play the game?
9. In what way is the game fun?
10. Where did the game originate? Do we know what country is the game originally from?
11. In what countries is this game played?

Using the posters that the students prepared as homework, the teacher leads a discussion in which the students in class compare and contrast the various games they learned about. They compare the games played by their parents with the games they themselves play. They count repeated occurrences of the same games and examine variations of those games. On a world map, they color-code the countries in which the games discussed in class are played.

Activity 2.1.3 Observing Children Play

In small groups during recess, students observe students in other classes in the school as they play games. They take pictures and videos. Using the rubric they've used so far to analyze games, they interview the other children about the games they play. In class, they report their observations and produce posters to systematically compare the various games they've observed. They discuss the differences in age and gender composition of the groups they've observed and which games those groups play.

Activity 2.1.4 Talking about Games with Children in Other Parts of the World

Students examine and analyze how children play in various countries and regions, beginning with the countries and cultures represented in the class and extending into those represented by students in their partner school. In this unit students are also introduced to their peers in their partner school in another country, and they collaborate to describe the games that children play in their school and in their sister school.

The teacher and the students communicate with second graders in a school in at least one other country—and if possible, in two or three other countries. The purpose of this activity is to have students introduce themselves to their peers, exchange greetings, and then share descriptions of the games they play. Each student will introduce him or herself by stating his or her name, age, number of siblings, and favorite game.

This activity could be supported by the following Coverdell lesson plan, which was designed to help students think about themselves and how they are similar to and different from children in other countries: https://share-mylesson.com/partner/peace-corps-world-wise-schools.

If possible, the students will communicate with one another in real time by using Skype to hold a videoconference. If a time difference precludes that, they will exchange a series of PowerPoint slides with videos and pictures in them to present the games they've examined in class. They will receive a similar presentation from their peers, and they'll then discuss in class how those games are similar to or different from the games they themselves play. Students will explore possible connections between the games they've learned about from their peers in another country and the games they themselves play and those that their parents played.

Activity 2.1.5 Understanding Maps

This unit expands on the brief introduction to maps in the previous activity, focusing on the study of what a map is, what a globe is, where the students' school is located, and where their sister schools are located. If possible, they may be encouraged to draw a map of their route from their home to the school and asked to label it with landmarks relevant their interests (e.g., flowers or buildings). They learn about different countries and their flags and basic characteristics of those countries (e.g., their climate, animals, plants, etc.).

— Students learn how to make a map of their classroom, noting where things are located.
— Students are then given a map of the school and are taken to different places using the map; some places will not be on the map, and they will learn how to fill it in.
— They are then given a map of the neighborhood, and they label where they live.
— They use building blocks to make a "map" of their route from their home to the school, and they label landmarks.
— They locate bodies of water (e.g., rivers, lakes, and oceans) and learn to identify them on the globe.

Resources

• Panwapa from *Sesame Street* (https://www.youtube.com/watch?v=YVyPHSHnMsM and http://www.panwapa.com/)
• *The Journey of Oliver K. Woodman*, by Darcy Pattison
• *My Granny Went to Market: A Round-the-World Counting Rhyme*, by Stella Blackstone
• *How to Make an Apple Pie and See the World*, by Marjorie Priceman
• *How to Make a Cherry Pie and See the U.S.A.*, by Marjorie Priceman
• *Tulip Sees America*, by Cynthia Rylant
• *My Sister's Rusty Bike*, by Jim Aylesworth
• *Me on the Map*, by Joan Sweeney
• *Zigby Hunts for Treasure*, by Brian Paterson
• Pirate Treasure Map: A Fairytale Adventure
• *X* Marks the Spot

- The Good Night Our World series, by Adam Gamble (http://www. amazon.com/gp/search/ref=sr_nr_p_n_age_range_mrr_1?rh=n%3 A283155%2Cp_27%3AAdam+Gamble%2Cn%3A%211000%2 Cn%3A4%2Cp_n_age_range%3A673422011&bbn=4&sort=rele vancerank&ie=UTF8&qid=1306892573&rnid=673420011)

Students then locate their partner schools on a map of the world. They focus on the countries where those partner schools are located and learn about them and their flags and perhaps about their basic characteristics (e.g., climate, animals, plants, etc.).

Optional Activity

A possible activity would be for students to divide into groups, each of which would be responsible for one country and for making a display with pictures and other items from that country. The students then carry around a "passport" and fill it in with pictures or stamps as they "visit" each country/ station. Parents can be asked to help with this activity.

Activity 2.1.6 (Four Sessions)
Learning about Games in Other Countries

Using the games described in the following resources, the teacher will teach a lesson about games played in different countries. Students will label those games and the countries in which they're played on a world map, and in small groups, they'll study one particular game. The small groups will then apply the rubric used throughout these activities to prepare a poster analyzing the game and will present that poster to the class. If feasible, students will bring home handouts with information about the game they're studying and discuss this game with siblings and parents.

As part of this lesson, students learn to locate on a map all of the continents and the regions or countries from which they, their parents or guardians, their grandparents, and other relatives or ancestors came. They also learn to locate the oceans of the world, five major rivers, and major mountain ranges.

Resources

- http://www.amazon.com/Kids-Around-World-Play-Games/dp/0471409847#reader_0471409847
- http://www.amazon.com/Multicultural-Game-Book-Grades-1-6/dp/0590494090/ref=sr_1_1?ie=UTF8&qid=1306514348&sr=8-1#reader_0590494090
- http://www.clintrogersonline.com/blog/2008/06/20/games-people-play-in-different-countries-and-cultures/
- http://www.gameskidsplay.net/games/foreign_indexes/index.htm
- http://www.streetplay.com/playfulworld/
- http://www.amazon.com/Children-Just-Like-Me-Celebration/dp/0789402017/ref=sr_1_1?ie=UTF8&qid=1306513644&sr=8-1#reader_0789402017

Unit	2.2
Topic	**Growing Up in Different Cultures**
Theme	**Diverse cultural perspectives, curiosity about global affairs, cross-cultural perspective taking, empathy, commitment to equality, variation within cultural groups, poverty, the use of evidence, and the use of technology**
Region	**India, Japan, and the world (as reflected in the countries represented by partner schools)**
Length	**Ten weeks (four activities and fourteen sessions)**

Students examine how children grow up in various parts of the world, including the rights and responsibilities that children have. Beginning with themselves and with their peers in their partner school, students examine how children spend their time and their rights and responsibilities at home and in school. They also define and give examples of some of the rights and responsibilities that students as citizens have in school (e.g., students have the right to vote in class elections and have the responsibility to follow rules). Students then learn about growing up in various cultures and learn about how different demands and opportunities influence school attendance.

Goals and Objectives

1. **Learn:** Learn similarities and differences in how children live in different cultures
2. **Inspire** students to take interest in various cultures, in how children live and grow up in different cultures, and in communicating with them using modern telecommunication technologies
3. **Act** by describing the rights and responsibilities of children in different cultures and by sharing those descriptions with students in other parts of the world.

Skills and Knowledge

1. Students will describe the rights and responsibilities of children in different countries.
2. Students will analyze and compare childhood in different countries.
3. Students will begin to learn about child labor and the concept of educational opportunity.
4. Students will, using Internet-based communication technologies, exchange presentations on how children spend their time (specifically, a week) with peers in other countries.

Overview

This unit builds on the students' analysis of the games children play in different countries and parts of the world and helps students analyze the lives of children in different cultures. Students observe and record how they spend their time and compare and contrast those observations with those of their peers as well as with those of their peers in partner schools around the world. They learn the concepts of rights and responsibilities and use those as categories to examine how they and other children spend time. They prepare presentations that they will share in class and with peers in other countries using telecommunication technologies. They then study childhood in urban and rural areas and examine school attendance and the education experience of students in different countries and regions. This unit also introduces the concept of child labor around the world.

Activity 2.2.1 A Typical Week in Several Countries

Students maintain a record of how they spend their time in a given week. In class they examine those observations and classify their activities using various categories (e.g., time alone and time with others; time with other children and time with adults; time with relatives and time with nonrelatives; and time at home, in school, or outdoors). They examine variations in how different children in the class spend their time and discuss, for example, how they help in school and how they help at home. Students also discuss the rights and responsibilities that they have at home and in school. Students then prepare a presentation—using text, pictures, and PowerPoint slides—that summarizes how most of them spend their time, how they help, their rights and responsibilities, and variations within the class.

They then share that presentation with peers in their sister school abroad. Students exchange ideas about the reasons for the differences in how they spend their time, in how they help at home and in school, and in their rights and responsibilities at home and in school.

Activity 2.2.2Growing Up in India and Japan and Going to School in Different Countries

This lesson introduces how children grow up in urban and rural areas in Japan and in rural areas in India. It also introduces some of the different approaches to education in use in various countries.

Students discuss selected segments of the following Discovery DVD: http://store.discoveryeducation.com/product/show/51900.

Students read and discuss the book *I Live in Tokyo*, by Mari Takabayashi. In this book the main character, seven-year-old Mimiko, describes special dates throughout the year.

The teacher leads the students through the lesson "Asha's Village in India," which was developed by the Peace Corps' Coverdell Program.

Students then watch selected segments of this video series and discuss differences in school characteristics and in opportunities to attend school in various countries: http://www.pbs.org/wnet/wideangle/episodes/time-for-school-series/introduction/4340/.

Activity 2.2.3
Growing Up Around the World

Using a library of books that describe growing up in different countries, students in small teams select a country whose children they want to learn more about. They read a book, and with the assistance of the teacher, who will draw from the *Greenwood Encyclopedia of Children's Issues Worldwide*, they prepare a presentation for their peers on how children grow up in the country they selected. That presentation focuses on analyses of what percentage of the children in that country attend elementary school and secondary school and of what forms of child labor exist in the country. Students place on a world map the country they are studying.

Students will also develop activities, reflective essays, drawings, and discussions.

Teacher Resources

- *The Greenwood Encyclopedia of Children's Issues Worldwide*, which has very complete summary chapters describing basic characteristics of childhood in most countries.
- A list of literature about growing up in various countries. Ideally, the school library will have all of these titles; if not, the teacher can select a subset of them specifically for this activity. (http://www.ala.org/ala/mgrps/divs/alsc/compubs/booklists/growingupwrld/GrowingUpAroundWorld.cfm.)

Activity 2.2.4
Access to School and Child Labor around the World

In this lesson the teacher explains how access to school around the world varies and introduces the topic of child labor. The children read selected chapters in the book *Facing the Lion*, by Joseph Lekuton, and discuss in class the different responsibilities and opportunities that children have in different parts of the world. They also watch selected segments of the series *Time for School*. To introduce the discussion of the factors that influence access to school, the teacher uses lessons from the Coverdell program.

Resources

- *Facing the Lion: Growing up Maasai on the African Savanna*, by Joseph Lekuton (http://www.amazon.com/Facing-Lion-Growing-African-Savanna/dp/0792251253)
- http://news.nationalgeographic.com/news/2003/09/0917_030917_lekuton.html
- http://www.pbs.org/wnet/wideangle/episodes/time-for-school-series/introduction/4340/

Unit   2.3
Topic   **Comparing Literature and Music from Different Cultures**
Theme   **Arts: literature and music; one's own and others' identities, common values, empathy, curiosity about global affairs, cross-cultural perspective taking, and geography**
Region **Any/all**
Length **Six weeks (two activities and eight sessions)**

In this unit students examine literature and music from different cultures and countries. They situate the stories and songs on a map and a time line and discuss the themes that those creations focus on, comparing and contrasting them.

Goals and Objectives

1. **Learn** similarities and differences in children's literature and myths and in songs from different cultures
2. **Inspire** students to take in interest and appreciate literature and music as cultural expressions.
3. **Act** by analyzing the values reflected in literature and myths and by assessing the potential of music to promote global understanding.

Skills and Knowledge

1. Students will recognize the similarities and differences in various myths and literature from different countries.
2. Students will identify responses to songs and music and recognize the impact of music on other children.

Overview

Building on the analysis of similarities and differences in direct experiences with play and games and on the analysis of how children spend their time, students explore music and literature from different countries and analyze the similarities and differences in music and literature across cultures and over time.

Activity 2.3.1
Folktales and Myths from around the World

Students read and discuss folktales and myths from around the world. They discuss the aspects of the human experience and the values conveyed by those stories and their similarities and differences. If possible, students then place the origin of those stories on a time line and a map.

Resources

- http://homeschooling.gomilpitas.com/explore/myths.htm
- http://www.amazon.com/Beginning-Creation-Stories-Around-World/dp/0152387420

Activity 2.3.2 Music and Songs from around the World

Students explore music and songs from around the world as well as how songs can highlight commonalities of the human experience. Students learn a few short songs in several foreign languages and learn basic greetings in Arabic, Chinese, French, Japanese, and Spanish. Students explore songs that celebrate cultural diversity and are introduced to the project "Playing for Change," which brings together musicians from around the world in a collaborative project promoting global understanding.

Parents are invited to submit songs appropriate for second graders that convey significant meaning. These songs are played in class, and the children discuss the themes addressed in these songs. They compare these themes.

The teacher then introduces and plays additional songs, and students share what emotions those songs evoke and what themes they think are addressed in those songs. Students learn a few of these songs and situate their origin on a world map and a time line.

Students are then introduced to projects in which musicians from around the world collaborate to promote global understanding through music.

Resources

- http://www.mamalisa.com/?t=e_atoz
- http://en.wikipedia.org/wiki/Jessi_Colter_Sings_Just_for_Kids:_ Songs_from_Around_the_World
- Playing for Change project (http://www.amazon.com/PFC-Songs-Around-World-Combo/dp/B003TJ4YUQ/ref=amb_link_356415782_3?pf_ rd_m=ATVPDKIKX0DER&pf_rd_s=hero-quick-promo&pf_ rd_r=1SDMQ9GY4MQ2GKXP801N&pf_rd_t=201&pf_rd_ p=1299285482&pf_rd_i=B001QOOCTE)

Unit	2.4.
Topic	How Children Make a Difference
Theme	Empathy, ethical frameworks, common values, commitment to equality, innovation, creativity, the value of human potential, creative communication, and the use of technology
Region	Any/all and countries in partner school
Length	Six weeks (two activities and five sessions)

This unit will examine how children around the world make a difference by helping others, improving their communities, and collaborating to address global needs. It will conclude with children in the school taking on a project to make a contribution to the education of other children. The project will be of a modest scale, and it could be as simple as making a financial contribution to an existing organization that supports education. The project could also be more complex, and students could work with their peers in the sister classroom with which they have collaborated throughout the year to find age-appropriate ways to jointly address a global challenge.

Goals and Objectives

1. **Learn** that people, and especially children, have the ability to influence others positively through their actions in a significant way and the ability to question the barriers that limit opportunities for children to exercise agency in improving the conditions in their communities. Identify the SDGs.
2. **Inspire** students to develop an appreciation for those who contribute to solving important global challenges.
3. **Act** by analyzing various ways to improve educational opportunity and by evaluating their own capacity to contribute to those improvements.

Skills and Knowledge

1. Students will learn the characteristics that children change makers share.
2. Students will recognize their own capacity to be change makers.
3. Students will develop the skills to collaborate with others in order to make a tangible contribution to the education of other children.

Overview

In the concluding unit for the grade, students build on the previous analyses of similarities and differences in how children grow up around the world and in their opportunity to be educated and analyze the ways in which children can express their agency in positive ways that make a difference. Students engage in a small project in which they make a contribution to the education of other children in some part of the world.

Activity 2.4.1 How Do We Help Others?

The teacher will discuss examples of how the students help others at home, in their community, and beyond. The teacher will then discuss examples of children who have helped others on a larger scale—for example, the founders of the World Children Organization or some of the children featured in Scholastic's Kids Make a Difference series (see below). Students in the class will then be asked to read a story about one of those children and to create a painting or write a song, paragraph, or poem that explains how that child is making a difference and why that difference is important. The teacher will then introduce the SDGs using the lesson plans developed by UNICEF.

Resources

1. Kids Make a Difference articles from Scholastic http://www2.scholastic.com/browse/collection.jsp?id=504)
2. UNICEF's lesson plan on introducing the SDGs (https://teachunicef.org/teaching-materials/topic/sustainable-development-goals)
3. The iEARN projects created for the purpose of introducing the SDGs (https://iearn.org/news/iearn-projects-align-to-the-un-sustainable-development-goals)

Activity 2.4.2
What Can We Do Together to Help Other Children Get an Education?

In class the teacher will lead a discussion of how students can help with the education of other children. The teacher will present some of the organizations that are involved in supporting education, explain the ways they do it, and suggest ways that the students in the class could make a contribution. The students in the class will decide which other children they want to help and how and implement a plan to help in a concrete way. The teacher may do this activity in collaboration with the partner school.

The World Course
Third Grade: Understanding Global Interdependence through Entrepreneurship in Chocolate Manufacturing

Theme

Exploring and experimenting with social entrepreneurship to address global issues, especially around child labor; Understanding and addressing social and global issues from an inter-disciplinary lens using the perspectives of multiple stakeholders such as individuals, businesses, and NGOs.

Description

In this year, students learn about entrepreneurship and managing a business. They start with knowing that they have to make their own kind of chocolate but based on the multiple processes that underpin chocolate manufacturing as it moves from raw material to a finished product. Students also examine the growth of chocolate as a global phenomenon through a historical perspective. The students work in groups and imagine that they are the owners of a chocolate business that they want to expand into three different countries. Students are introduced to a pen pal from each of those countries and learn about those countries' cultural values and norms and begin to recognize some of the stereotypes about them. Throughout the year, students "manage" a business by monitoring the associated expenses, developing a business strategy, and creating a prototype. Students learn about different physical markets in the world, focusing specifically in three countries they study, and are informed that they can sell their chocolate in those markets. Based on what they've learned through discussions with their pen pals about the culture, lifestyles, and preferences in their countries, students create their final prototype, a logo, and their own advertising campaign for the chocolate. At the same time, they question key business-related concepts such as free trade, child labor, and creating products that are ethical, and they learn to acknowledge, appreciate, and value diversity across the world.

Looking Back
Exploring similarities, commonalities and differences between people and cultures across the world

Looking Forward
Understanding the formation, maintenance, governance and the decline of ancient and modern civilizations across time

Overview of the Units

1) Setting the Stage for the Life of a Chocolate
2) The Life of a Chocolate and Its History
3) Let's Make Our Own Chocolate
4) Understanding the Culture of My Market
5) Marketing My Chocolate in School
6) Child Labor
7) Taking My Chocolate to the Market
8) Beyond Chocolate

Capstone
A Yearlong project in which students develop a business plan and manage a business of selling chocolate.

Unit   3.1
Topic   **Setting the Stage for the Life of a Chocolate**
Theme   **Geography; globalization; ICC; and work and mind habits:**
          innovation and creativity
Region   **Cocoa-producing areas (West Africa: Ivory Coast, Ghana,**
          Nigeria, Cameroon, Togo; Mexico; Brazil; Malaysia, and
          Indonesia)
Length   **One to two weeks**

Goals and Objectives

1. **Learn** a story in a classic children's book (*Charlie and the Chocolate Factory*) and begin to see chocolate as a global product.
2. **Inspire** students to take interest in examining some of the global interdependencies in the creation of chocolate.
3. **Act** by demonstrating an understanding of the fact that the main ingredient in chocolate and its production are confined to very few parts of the world.

Skills and Knowledge

1. Students will become familiar with the plot of a classic children's literary piece: Charlie and the Chocolate Factory.
2. Students will understand how the actions of individuals impact eventual outcomes, as in the case of *Charlie and the Chocolate Factory.*
3. Students will plot on a map the countries where cocoa is grown across the world and also understand that the sites for growth, processing, and exporting don't necessarily have to be the same.

Overview

In this unit, students are introduced to the movie - *Charlie and the Chocolate Factory, an adaptation of Roald Dahl's classic book, first published in 1964.* The story not only serves as a primer to the year and creates excitement around the theme of chocolate production but also gives students an opportunity to examine some of the decisions made by the characters and the ways those decisions influence eventual outcomes. Through a mapping exercise, students will identify the countries that are the largest producers of cocoa in the world today and understand that while the critical ingredient (cocoa) might be grown in one part of the world, its production might take place in another part of the world. In that way, the students will draw out some of the global interdependencies involved in the production of the product.

Activity 3.1.1
Charlie and the Chocolate Factory

As the students walk into class, they are welcomed with a piece of chocolate. The teacher provides students with the wrappers of the chocolates and asks them to list out the first few natural ingredients. This will elicit responses from the students about, for example, what they think the ingredients of chocolate are, what forms they think those ingredients might be in (solid/liquid), and whether they think those ingredients come from plants or animals.

The students subsequently watch *Charlie and the Chocolate Factory*, a movie released in 2005 and based on Roald Dahl's original book. After viewing the movie, the teacher asks them the following questions:

1. How do they think the gold wrapper got into the chocolate in the first place?
2. What did they learn about how chocolate is made from the film? What is unique about each of the rooms in the factory?

3. Why do the characters in the film make some of the choices that they make?

(Note that students may also read Roald Dahl's original book alternatively, instead of watching the movie, and it could be assigned as summer reading leading up to third grade.)

For homework, students are provided with a Hershey's Kiss and are asked to answer the following question and complete the following tasks:

1. What is the main ingredient in chocolate? (The main ingredient is cocoa.)
2. Mark on a world map any five countries where cocoa is grown, and also mark the world's largest manufacturer of cocoa.
3. Mark on a world map three countries where Hershey has a chocolate manufacturing unit. (There are Hershey manufacturing units in Mexico, Brazil, the United States, and, thanks to a recent partnership with Lotte, a South Korean candy manufacturer, China.) For more information about Hershey's consult the resources list.
4. Conduct background research to find out if chocolate is a modern phenomenon or if it has a history.

Resources

- Roald Dahl's book *Charlie and the Chocolate Factory* (http://www.roalddahl.com/roald-dahl/stories/1960s/charlie-and-the-chocolate-factory) and (https://www.amazon.com/Charlie-Chocolate-Factory-Roald-Dahl/dp/0142410314/ref=sr_1_1?ie=UTF8&qid=1466877499&sr=8-1&keywords=charlie+and+the+chocolate+factory)
- A sample lesson plan and games associated with *Charlie and the Chocolate Factory*

- (http://www.teachingideas.co.uk/library/books/ charlie-and-the-chocolate-factory)
- A teaching-unit CD on *Charlie and the Chocolate Factory* (http:// www.amazon.com/Charlie-Chocolate-Factory-Teaching-Unit/dp/ B0018XVLVA_
- Information regarding Hershey is available at (http://en.wikipedia. org/wiki/The_Hershey_Company   http://www.reuters.com/ article/2007/01/26/idUSSEO13926420070126)

Unit   3.2
Topic   **The Life of a Chocolate and Its History**
Theme   **Geography, globalization, world history, and ICC: interpersonal (others' identities and cultures)**
Region   **Any/all**
Length   **Three weeks**

Goals and Objectives

1. **Learn** about the global interdependencies in manufacturing using the example of chocolate.
2. **Inspire** students to be excited by the fact that the foods people eat have had a long history and have evolved over time through the interactions of people and culture.
3. **Act** by demonstrating an understanding of the important milestones in the evolution of the product.

Skills and Knowledge

1. Students will understand the geographical reasons for processes entailed in chocolate production and understand the value-addition process in manufacturing across different geographies.
2. Students will describe the important milestones in the development and evolution of chocolate and understand that its form has changed over the years.
3. Students will create time lines that chart the process through which chocolate became a global product.

Overview

In this unit, students get a better understanding of why cocoa production is limited to certain parts of the world and of its importance in the chocolate-manufacturing process. Students get an overview of the processes involved in manufacturing chocolate. They also realize that chocolate isn't a modern phenomenon but has evolved over time through the interactions of societies, cultures, and peoples.

Activity 3.2.1
The Chocolate-Manufacturing Process

Students begin by presenting their findings from their homework to the class. The teacher marks all of the places where chocolate is produced on a world map (West Africa: Ivory Coast, Ghana, Nigeria, Cameroon, Togo; Mexico; Brazil; Malaysia, and Indonesia). The teacher should ask the students the following questions:

1. Which part of the cacao plant does the chocolate come from?
2. Does the plant have a chocolaty smell? A chocolaty taste?
3. Why is cocoa grown only in the countries they listed on the map? Are there special climatic conditions necessary for the growth of the plant? Can they grow the plant in their backyard?

Resources

- A lesson plan on the anatomy of the cacao plant and on how it's cultivated (http://www.rainforest-alliance.org/curriculum/fourth/lesson2)
- A lesson plan concerning ecological connections, the environment, and chocolate (a highly recommended resource) (http://www.rainforestalliance.org/curriculum/third/lesson1)
- Virtual tours of chocolate factories that include explanations of the chocolate-manufacturing process (http://manufacturing.stanford.edu/hetm.html)

(Note that this unit can also be connected to the science curriculum, and specifically to the unit on states of matter. The teacher can explain how chocolate comes from a solid cocoa pod, is subsequently converted to a liquid, and is finally sold as a solid product as well as how this conversion from one state of matter to another could take place.)

Activity 3.2.2
Is Chocolate a Modern or Historical Phenomenon?

The students can read a book about the history of chocolate and about how it spread from the Mayan civilization to Europe and the Americas. Students can create a time line showing the history of chocolate, and the teacher can help them plot on a map the spread of chocolate across the world over time.

Through these activities, the students should also be able to produce a list of the important developments in the history of chocolate (e.g., the Europeans' addition of sugar, the Aztecs' use of cacao as a currency, and the cultivation of the cacao tree).

Resources

- A lesson plan on how chocolate has changed through the ages (http://www.teachingideas.co.uk/themes/chocolate)
- Reading material on the story of chocolate (http://www.amazon.co.uk/Story-Chocolate-DK-Readers-Level/dp/1405303875/ref=pd_bxgy_b_text_b)
- A quick overview of the history of chocolate (https://en.wikipedia.org/wiki/History_of_chocolate)
- A second overview of the history of chocolate (http://www.history.com/news/hungry-history/the-sweet-history-of-chocolate)

Teacher Resources

- A book based on archaeological and ethno-historical research on the significance of chocolate across several millennia (http://www. amazon.com/True-History-Chocolate-Sophie-Coe/dp/0500282293)
- Another book on the history of chocolate
http://www.amazon.com/Chocolate-Pathway-Meredith-L-Dreiss/ dp/0816524645/ref=pd_sim_b_5)

Unit   3.3
Topic   Let's Make Our Own Chocolate
Theme   ICC: interpersonal (one's own identity and culture and others' identities and cultures); work and mind habits: innovation and creativity; geography; and economics
Region   Any/all
Length   Four weeks

Goals and Objectives

1. **Learn** about some of the decisions involved in establishing a business and about how distance and geography play a role in value-addition processes.
2. **Inspire** students to learn more about these underlying interdependencies and about how different pieces of information are required to understand product markets in a holistic way.
3. **Act** by describing where to get the main raw ingredient from and plot on a map the locations of the countries that grow it and their target-market countries.

Skills and Knowledge

1. Students will describe some of the important pieces of information that they need before they can create a product.
2. Students will understand the concepts of export, import, markups, different modes of transportation, and distance as it relates to manufacturing decisions.
3. Students will demonstrate an understanding of the use of budgets and the ability to stick to one while planning a trip.

Overview

Students are introduced to some of the intricacies of starting consumer-goods manufacturing units and to the underlying factors that influence pricing decisions, such as demand, supply, competition, availability of ingredients and raw materials, costs of production and distribution. Students begin to understand that their decisions must be based on factors relating to the raw materials as well as to the end product itself. Students are familiarized with data exploration, markups, and price fluctuations. Through a mapping exercise, students plan a trip to the markets they will sell their product in. Students use a budget to plan the trip and collect the background information necessary to prepare for it.

Activity 3.3.1, Option A
Manufacturing My Own Chocolate

(Note that there are two options for this activity, option A and option B. Option A can serve as a stand-alone activity, and if time and interest permit it, option B can be added to the unit.)

The teacher informs the students that they will start their own chocolate-manufacturing companies and that through the year, they will work to create their own unique type of chocolate. Students are divided into three teams and informed that each team is a competitor. They are also informed that they have to manufacture their chocolate in New York City and sell their chocolate to children of their age in one specific country. (Each team will be assigned one country in Asia, Africa, or South America.)

(Note that the teacher should help the students pick these target-market countries. They should be developing countries and should be a mix of countries that are close to and farther away from cocoa-exporting countries. Also, if the teacher feels comfortable with it, the students may actually use the kitchen in the school and try to produce their own chocolate. Even though the process of chocolate production in the school will be hugely oversimplified, it will still serve to generate excitement and interest around the activities of the year.)

Once each team has been assigned the country in which it will sell chocolate, the team will be asked to create a list of questions about what it needs to know about that country. Consider the following potential list of questions:

Which part of the world will the team get its cocoa from? (The eight largest cocoa-producing countries at present are Côte d'Ivoire, Ghana, Indonesia, Nigeria, Cameroon, Brazil, Ecuador, and Malaysia. These countries produce 90 percent of the world's supply of cocoa.) This question has several subquestions that need to be addressed:

1. What is the cost of exporting cocoa from these cocoa-manufacturing countries?
2. Where have these countries been exporting cocoa to?
3. How would one plot a simple trend of cocoa production in these countries across different years? Does the trend stay more or less the same, or does it fluctuate over time?
4. How much does it cost to import and export cocoa?
5. Are there frequent price fluctuations? How might price fluctuations impact the decision to buy cocoa from a particular country?
6. What are the possible expenses involved in manufacturing chocolate in New York City and, further, in selling it in another country? (Note that students may need to budget for expenses of other raw materials—for example, milk or nuts. Since they will be producing their chocolate in New York City, they can obtain these prices from a supermarket, or the teacher can provide them.)
7. What are markups in the manufacturing process? Are there overhead costs, and if so, how can buying in bulk affect those overheads? (Note that the teacher may connect this idea to the math curriculum to help students learn about profit, loss, and markups.)

The teacher should consult the International Cocoa Organization (http://www.icco.org/) for statistics on cocoa production across the world since 1960. He or she will have to modify this data set before presenting it to the students, though, since there are a lot of data points that could confuse children at this age.

Students should consider the following questions while selling their chocolate (the finished product):

1. What is the climate of the country in which they will be selling their chocolate?
2. Where will they sell their chocolate to children?
3. What kind of food do people in that country eat?
4. When do they eat chocolate (before their meal, after their meal, or in between meals as a snack)? What kinds of chocolate do they eat? (This question can also introduce students to the different kinds and forms of chocolate—for example, dark chocolate, milk chocolate, and hot-chocolate powder.)
5. How much do people pay for chocolate in these countries? Based on this information and on the financial information already discussed (e.g., markups), how much should they sell their chocolate for?

(Note that the teacher should clarify that they don't need to answer all of these questions immediately and that they will discover many of the answers as they proceed through the year. He or she should also mention that much of the research and groundwork will have to be done by the teams themselves.)

Activity 3.3.1, Option B
Examining the Cocoa Market Closely
(This activity can be used in addition to option A if time permits, or the teacher can skip it and move on to activity 3.3.2.)

The students have passports that they update as they visit their cocoa markets and examine the factors below. They also maintain a video journal or a scrapbook and answer the following questions in it:

1. How would they get to those countries?
2. How far will the cocoa have to travel to get to their site of manufacturing (New York City)?
3. In what climates does cocoa grow?
4. What are the fields and farmers of the countries like? How do people live in those countries?

Activity 3.3.2
Planning my trip to my market!

The teams of students are informed that they will have to virtually travel to the countries they will be selling their chocolate in. The teams are provided with a budget for travel and have to stick to it. Using online travel websites and interactive world maps, students will do the following activities:

1. Identify the mode of transportation they will use.
2. Plot their journey on a map.
3. Decide how they will break up their journey if they need to.
4. Identify how much it will cost to get to these countries and figure out whether they've stuck to their budget.
5. Identify other alternative modes of transportation and discuss whether it's better to save time or money.
6. Discuss what they will need to pack for their trip.
7. Make a list of any other background information that they think they might need.

Unit	**3.4**
Topic	**Understanding the Culture of My Market**
Theme	**ICC: interpersonal (one's own identity and culture, others' identities and cultures, and etiquette); ethics: humility, respect, and common values; and work and mind habits: cross-cultural perspective taking**
Region	**Any/all**
Length	**Two weeks at first and then throughout the semester**

Goals and Objectives

1. **Learn** about the day-to-day life and the culture in their target countries and learn to interact with another student in a different part of the world using technology.
2. **Inspire** students to appreciate cultural nuances and differences and to draw comparisons in order to examine how life differs across the world.
3. **Act** by using technology to regularly communicate effectively and respectfully with someone very different in another country.

Skills and Knowledge

1. Use technology to communicate with their pen pal on an ongoing basis and become comfortable doing so even though they haven't seen or met their pen pals in person.
2. Share details of their own culture and contrast it with the cultures of their pen pals.
3. Describe daily lifestyles of other children in different parts of the world.
4. Appreciate literature from different parts of the world.
5. Reflect on their own practices and readily express their apprehensions and excitement about communicating with people from different parts of the world.

Overview

In this unit, students form pen-pal relationships with students in the countries where their chocolate will be sold. Through these interactions, students develop a better understanding of the culture of their market, of how people in it interact with one another, and of the food preferences of those people. Students will also form their own discussion questions based on the assigned books, which will serve to provide them with background information on and insight into the culture of their markets. As these interactions with their pen pal continue, students will also reflect on their thoughts about the cultures of their target markets, on the stereotypes they initially had about them, and on how those thoughts and stereotypes have changed over time.

(Note that while the suggested length for this unit is about two weeks, it could also be made into a semester-long, ongoing activity where their pen pals serve as consultants as the students further explore the market where they will sell their chocolate.)

Activity 3.4.1
Getting to Know the Other

In this unit, the students are introduced to pen pals in their sister schools. The aim of this activity is for students to know more about the background and preferences of the children who will be the teams' customers. Each student will be paired with a pen pal. Each student will exchange information with his or her pen pal by asking and answer the following questions:

1. What languages are spoken in the country?
2. How do people greet one another, and what is the common etiquette in this country?
3. What food preferences do children have?
4. Are children commonly given pocket money?
5. What does daily life look like?
6. Does the student have a large or small family?

7. Who makes the decision to buy things in the house? Where do they buy things?

8. Does the student work at home and help with daily chores, or is someone else responsible for chores?

Each team will be assigned a children's book based on the country it picked. The following are databases of age-appropriate books and stories from across the world that the students may pick a book from:

o   http://www.unc.edu/~rwilkers/title.htm,
o   http://resources.primarysource.org/content.php?pid=53344&sid=390913
o   http://www.eslstation.net/theREALWF/Folktale%20Links.htm

After the very first interaction with their pen pals, the teams will maintain a video journal and answer the following questions:

1. What are their expectations about how this person looks or behaves?

2. What were their responses to their first encounter with this new person? Were they scared, excited, happy, or indifferent? Why or why not?

3. What were their beliefs about people in that part of the world, and what are their beliefs now?

4. How are their lives and the lives of children in those countries similar or different?

At the very end of the activity (or maybe even later in the year, depending on whether these interactions continue or are terminated after two weeks), students will look back at some of their reflections on their interactions with people from other cultures and seek to understand whether their perceptions have changed. (Note that this could be a very powerful learning experience for the students and thus could require scaffolding from the teacher.)

Alternatively, students could also maintain a portfolio of pictures and important items that represent the day-to-day life in the countries of their pen pals, and those portfolios could be exchanged with students' pen pals at this point in time. This portfolio would be similar to the one they created and exchanged in second grade (if implemented at that time), or they could even do it at this stage in the event that students and pen pals did not exchange the same during the second grade.

(Note that students are asked to keep a video journal so that they can become familiar with technology from the start and also because many activities in the middle school rely heavily on written tasks. A video journal would also provide a form of documentation that could eventually be shared with stakeholders.)

Unit	3.5
Topic	**Marketing My Chocolate in School**
Theme	**ICC: interpersonal (empathy and diverse cultural perspectives); ICC: intrapersonal (curiosity about global affairs); ethics: commitment to equality; and poverty**
Region	**Developing world**
Length	**Four weeks**

Goals and Objectives

1. **Learn** about the different entry points for a product and about what school life in different parts of the world looks like.
2. **Inspire** students to develop a better understanding of the differences in schooling experiences.
3. **Act** by describing schooling experiences in various places, analyze differences and provide possible reasons and hypotheses for those differences, and realizing how schools are used as target markets for products.

Skills and Knowledge

1. Students will become comfortable using interviews and field observations as data-collection techniques.
2. Students will identify cases of product differentiation within the school.
3. Students will describe differences in the schooling experiences of children of similar ages in different parts of the world.
4. Students will understand and articulate the differences and similarities in the relative valuations and expectations placed on schooling across the world.

Overview

In this unit, students see the school as a potential market for their chocolate. Students observe their own school cafeteria, taking note of the products that are sold there and the various forms of product differentiation. Students may also test prototypes of the chocolate they've produced and give out samples in the school so that other students can provide them with feedback. They extend this further to an examination of schools and school life in different parts of the world. Students also examine some of the motivations behind attending school and explore trends related to, for example, school enrollment and dropout rates.

Activity 3.5.1
The School as a Market and Testing My Prototype

The students take a tour of their school and their cafeteria and are asked to take field notes and to interview students buying goods from the vending machines and the cafeteria. Alternatively, students can create samples of different kinds of chocolates in their school kitchen and then use their school cafeteria as a site in which to get feedback on their products. Students can collect and collate data and learn to take polls and to organize their data in percentages. (Note that these concepts can be linked with the math curriculum at this stage.) Based on the data they've collected, they will answer the following questions in their teams and then present their analyses to the class:

1. What goods and candy did they find in their school vending machines and cafeteria?

2. Do these products look the same as they do in regular markets? What is different or similar? (For example, are there packages or contents different?) What might be the reasons for these similarities and differences?

3. Why do they think people purchase more of one type of product than another? What attracts them to a product?

4. Would students still buy this product if it were located a little far-ther away in another part of the building? How much does location matter?

Activity 3.5.2
School Life across the World

Students are then asked to think about how they might want to sell their chocolates in their target-market countries. But before that, the teacher asks the students if they indeed can reach all children by selling their products in schools—what if there are children who don't go to school?

The students are then asked to find out more information from their pen pals by asking them the following questions:

1. What percentage of children attend school in these countries? (Note that students may also find this information in reports, such as the *UNESCO Education for All: Global Monitoring Report.*)
2. Why do they think that some children in these countries don't go to school?
3. What does a regular school life look like across the world? Is it the same as their school life, or are there differences?
4. Why do their pen pals go to school?

The teacher also shows the students excerpts from the PBS Series *Time for School*

(http://www.pbs.org/show/time-school/) and (http://www.thirteen.org/programs/time-for-school/)

In a video journal, the students reflect upon why they themselves go to school and on the relative value that is placed on schooling in different parts of the world. Students also may reflect on the ways their schooling experi-ences differ from others' schooling experiences. Students reflect on those similarities and differences and consider their interactions with their pen pals and what they've seen in the PBS series.

(Note that this could be an important time for the students to realize how different their schooling experiences might be from those in other parts of the world.)

Unit	3.6
Topic	Child Labor
Theme	ICC: intrapersonal (curiosity about global affairs); ethics (trust in institutions, commitment to equality, importance of global compacts, and commitment to supporting human rights); work and mind habits: cross-cultural perspective taking and innovation and creativity; economic development; and poverty
Region	Developing world, especially West African cocoa-producing countries
Length	Four weeks

Goals and Objectives

1. **Learn** about the issues related to child labor.
2. **Inspire** students to examine the nuances of child labor and to understand its complexities in depth.
3. **Act** by describing some differences in childhood experiences and by formulating a call to action for addressing the issue.

Skills and Knowledge

1. Students will become aware of the complexities of child labor and describe the issues related to child labor in cocoa plantations and thus in chocolate manufacturing.
2. Students will be informed about the different forms of child labor across the world and the different ways in which they impact children.
3. Students will articulate stakeholders' different approaches to tackling child-labor issues and debate and defend their own stances on the issue.
4. Students will be aware of concepts such as organic production and fair trade certification.

5. Students will be confident about their agency and efficacy in addressing the issue.

Overview

Beginning with the cocoa-plantation industry, students are familiarized with the issue of child labor, which is then discussed in the context of other industries. Through the use of literature and stories about child labor in different industries, students will analyze some of the complexities of child labor as well as its moral- economic-, and development-related causes and effects Students also learn about the International Labour Organization and its efforts to eliminate child labor globally. Since students will be involved in creating their own chocolate, they will collectively seek to discover the most effective way to combat child labor in the chocolate-manufacturing industry and discuss how they'd like to tackle the issue.

Activity 3.6.1
Understanding Child Labor

The teams present their findings concerning the different valuations placed on schooling and the proportion of out-of-school children in each of the countries to the class.

All of the students are introduced to the issues of child labor in cocoa plantations and in the chocolate-manufacturing industry.

Use the following link to learn facts about child labor in cocoa plantations and to study advocacy materials that advocacy-based organizations have used when advocating with chocolate-manufacturing companies: http://www.stopthetraffik.org/resources/chocolate/#1.

Each team reads a book that deals with child labor in different industries.

Resources

- A story about a 12-year old boy and his organization, Free the Children, fighting against Child Labor and international human rights (http://www.amazon.com/Free-Children-Fights-Against-Proves/dp/0060930659)
- A story about a boy working in a carpet-manufacturing factory in Pakistan (http://www.reachandteach.com/s/20050831122910561)

Based on what they read/learn, students can conduct background research and then discuss the following questions:

1. What is the role of education in addressing child labor?
2. Why do they think the children who they read/learned about don't go to school?
3. What can be done to support families to ensure that they don't send their children to work but to school?
4. Are there some types of work that seem more dangerous than others?
5. Should all forms of child labor be banned? Or should only the more dangerous types be banned?
6. Does helping at home with household chores count as child labor?
7. What can children do to help other children?

Students are then introduced to Craig Kielburger, who, at the age of twelve, founded Free the Children and traveled to South Asia to understand child labor in the region (http://www.reachandteach.com/content/article.php/20050831122910561/2).

Activity 3.6.2
Tackling Child Labor

The teacher introduces the concept of stakeholders to the students and helps them identify three important stakeholder positions that are part of a civil society: businesses (e.g., chocolate-manufacturing companies), consumers, and NGOs.

Students are provided with a challenge that concerns tackling child labor in their own chocolate-manufacturing businesses. As a class, they have to find a solution to the child-labor issue, and each group of stakeholders has to take its own approach to the issue.

The aim is for students to understand the different approaches that may be adopted.

Each group is then introduced to the different approaches that the other stakeholder groups have decided to adopt.

Resources

- Approaches chocolate manufacturers have adapted to prevent child labor —fair-trade cocoa and chocolate and manufacturing organic cocoa (http://www.icco.org/about/chocolate.aspx). (Note that an executive of a chocolate-manufacturing company can be brought into the class as a guest speaker and that the students can interview him or her about fair wages and child labor in the industry.)
- Approaches NGOs have used to advocate with chocolate manu-facturers around issues of fair trade and child labor (http://www.worldcocoafoundation.org/index.html).

The teacher introduces to the students the International Labour Organization (ILO) and explains its role in advocating against child labor. (See the resources listed at the end of unit.)

In the end, the groups debate the solutions to child labor, making a case for the solutions that they believe would be the most effective in addressing child labor, especially in the context of the chocolate-manufacturing industry.

As teams, students discuss how they can make chocolates without the use of child labor. They should answer the following questions:

1. Will they donate their profits to help combat child labor and promote education of children in countries where cocoa is produced?
2. Will they avoid buying cocoa from exporting countries that have a history of child labor?
3. Will they ensure that their chocolate is certified as child labor–free?

Each team presents its own case and stand, and the teams collectively debate the best course of action for their manufacturing processes.

Resources

- Background reading for teachers (http://www.independent.co.uk/life-style/food-and-drink/features/chocolate-worth-its-weight-in-gold-2127874.html)
- Introduction to the ILO (http://www.ilo.org/global/topics/child-labour/lang--en/index.htm)
- ILO-designed activities and advocacy material for learning about child labor (http://www.ilo.org/ipec/Campaignandadvocacy/Youthinaction/C182-Youth-orientated/lang--en/index.htm)

Unit   3.7
Topic   **Taking My Chocolate to the Market**
Theme: **Economics; work and mind habits: innovation and creativity and cross-cultural perspective taking; ethics: ethical frameworks, importance of global compacts, and commitment to equality; and ICC: interpersonal (diverse cultural perspectives)**
Region **Any/all (based on the countries the students picked to sell their chocolate in)**
Length **Four to six weeks (based on interest)**

Goals and Objectives

1. **Learn** about different forms of physical markets across the world and about creating a marketing strategy.
2. **Inspire** students to further understand how different companies use leveraged product differentiation to market their products.
3. **Act** by creating a marketing strategy and an advertising jingle.

Skills and Knowledge

1. Students will become familiar with the interactions between markets and organizations and with how organizations tap into markets based on the characteristics of those markets.
2. Students will articulate the role of markets in creating profits and in economic development.
3. Students will demonstrate an understanding of the process of creating a sound and locally relevant marketing strategy.
4. Students will develop a brand that represents the team's ethos.

Overview

In this unit, students learn about the ways different markets of the world appear, they ways they're organized, and they ways their organization might influence the sales of products. Students work toward creating a marketing campaign around their chocolate and examine some of the intricacies behind their final decisions about how they'll price and market their end product in fair and ethical ways. Students also pick a brand ambassador and a logo for their chocolate.

(Note that based on time availability and interest, this could be the culminating activity of this year, or the teacher could proceed to the next unit. The last activity in this unit should be fun, competitive, and collaborative.)

Activity 3.7.1
Markets of the World

Each team has to conduct background research on the way the markets in their country look. Using pictures, videos, and articles, they create a profile of markets in their target countries. These profiles can answer the following questions:

- Are the markets open or covered?
- Are the markets crowded?
- Who shops at these markets? Do children come to these markets?
- What is sold at these markets? Are goods cheap or expensive?

Each team also reads a book about the markets of the world. For some suggestions, see the resources below.

Resources

- This may be a little childish, but it could be used in earlier grades as an interesting read (http://www.amazon.com/Market-Day-Story-

Told-Folk/dp/0152168206/ref=sr_1_19?s=books&ie=UTF8&qid=
1310112472&sr=1-19).

- Two illustrated books for children about markets across the world
  (http://www.amazon.com/Market-Days-Around-World/dp/
  0816735050/ref=sr_1_5?s=books&ie=UTF8&qid=1310112449&
  sr=1-5) and (http://www.amazon.com/Markets-Global-Community-
  Cassie-Mayer/dp/1403494134/ref=sr_1_13?s=books&ie=UTF8&qi
  d=1310112472&sr=1-13)

(Note that if the markets that are listed in the books are not the ones the
students will sell their chocolate in, a parent from one of the target-market
countries may be called to make an audiovisual presentation about the market in that particular country.)

Activity 3.7.2
May the Best Chocolate Win

After learning about their target markets, the students are informed that
they have been given a chocolate stand at a market and that they have to sell
their chocolate there.

Based on what they've learned thus far regarding the culture and lifestyles
in these other countries, students have to design a marketing campaign for
their products. To do so, they should answer the following questions:

1. What differentiates their product from other products? (The answer
    could be its content, packaging, or price.) What makes their prod-
    uct unique and distinct?
2. How will they price it? Why will it be priced that way?
3. Besides schools and sporting events, where else could they sell their
    product?
4. Has the chocolate been culturally adapted? (Note that to help stu-
    dents with this question, the teacher can draw from pictures and

menus of a fast-food chain with restaurants around the world—for example, McDonalds—to give students examples of how similar foods undergo a series of adaptations based on the markets they serve.)

5. How, if at all, will they incorporate aspects of free trade into their market strategy and combat child labor?

6. What will the jingle for their product be? (The students will then record it.)

7. What logo will they choose, and how will they design it? What will their logo represent?

8. If they had to choose a brand ambassador for their product, who would they choose? Why?

Unit   3.8
Topic   **Beyond Chocolate**
Theme   **Globalization; ICC: intrapersonal (curiosity about global affairs); work and mind habits: innovation and creativity; and geography**
Region   **Any/all**
Length   **Remaining time (time and interest permitting)**

Goals and Objectives

1. **Learn** about global interdependencies in manufacturing for other food products. Extend the discussion of interdependencies to the achievement of the SDGs.
2. **Inspire** students to undertake a comparative study across different products based on the framework they've been introduced to.
3. **Act** by being smart consumers of different products and by understanding the process of value addition across different food products and the controversies associated with it.

Skills and Knowledge

1. Students will become aware of and familiar with value addition in different food products.
2. Students will compare and contrast similarities and differences in value addition in different food products.
3. Students will articulate how different stakeholders have addressed the controversies associated with value addition and free trade in different food products.

Overview

The aim of this unit is for students to understand the global interdependencies and linkages in different food products beyond chocolate. Using the framework they used to examine the interdependencies and associated controversies in chocolate manufacturing, students can analyze the value-addition process in the manufacturing of food products such as bananas, milk, or coffee.

(Note that the teacher can decide whether this unit is necessary based on the amount of time left in the year.)

Activity 3.8.1
Understanding Value Addition and Controversies in Other Food Products

The teacher informs the students that many of the issues they confronted around chocolate manufacturing and cocoa processing (such as child labor, free trade, and rising prices) are common in the manufacturing of several other food products.

The class is once again divided into groups, and each group is given a food product to research. They will use their research on chocolate and cocoa as a model for this research. The food products can include bananas, milk, cotton, or coffee. (Note that students may have a hard time relating to coffee, as they probably don't drink it. Thus, it's only a suggestion, and the first three options might be more appropriate.) The students could then answer the following list of questions, and possibly even trace some of them using a map:

1. Where are these products grown and manufactured?
2. Where are they are exported to?
3. Historically, what trends have there been in production levels and prices?

4. What does consumption over the past ten years look like?

5. What does superimposing consumption and production on the same graph reveal?

6. If certain countries stop producing or consuming these products, what impact will those changes have on the children in those countries?

7. Is there any form of product differentiation based on where the product is exported?

8. What fair-trade and child labor–related controversies have concerned the product?

9. How have these controversies been addressed?

10. In a supermarket or a department store, can one find versions of these products that are organically produced or free-trade certified?

Activity 3.8.2
Introduce Design for Change in the context of the SDGs

Using the lesson plans on designing for change offered by UNICEF, engage students in a discussion around the generation of innovative solutions that students may use to address one and/or several of the SDGs (https://teachunicef.org/teaching-materials/topic/sustainable-development-goals).

The World Course
Fourth Grade: The Rise (and Fall) of Ancient and Modern Civilizations

Theme

How civilizations evolve over time, and how understanding the past is helpful to make sense of current events.

Description

In this year, students learn how and why civilizations are formed and examine how humans interact with the environment, studying two civilizations with enduring influences on modern times: Egypt and China. Concepts that are central to this year include how ancient humans conceived of nature, as evidenced by mythology; how human settlements and ancient civilizations were built around the essential natural resources of water and arable land; how social hierarchy was established and power was distributed; and how varying systems of governance arose and with that, how various groups conceived citizenship and the relationship of varying classes of people to the state. Each area will be studied both as an ancient civilization and as a modern civilization. The learning in this unit will be activity based throughout and will focus on understanding, not simply recalling, facts. Through this study, students will link the modern with the historical and gain an appreciation of the science of archaeology as well as of the study of modern cultures unlike their own. Furthermore, in the study of both the ancient and the modern, they will gain critical and analytic skills.

Looking Back
Understanding Global Interdependence through Entrepreneurship in Chocolate Manufacturing

Looking Forward
Freedom and the Rights of Individuals: Social Change around the Rights of Individuals

Overview of the Units

1) Archaeology Today
2) Ancient China and Modern China
3) Ancient Egypt and Modern Egypt

Capstone
Students design a game in small groups that represents components of Chinese and Egyptian civilization (government, religion, economy, arts, technology, settlement, and system of writing).

Unit   4.1
Topic   **Archaeology Today**
Themes **ICC: interpersonal; investigation and analytical skills; and history**
Region **All, focus New York City**
Length **Three weeks**

Goals and Objectives

1. **Learn about** the skills involved in the science of archaeology, the questions that archaeologists seek to answer, and the study of history through the examination of material remains.
2. **Inspire** in students an appreciation for the links between the ancient past and the modern day.
3. **Act** by participating in several activities concerning the challenges and opportunities of archaeology, by thinking critically about modern culture and how it may be perceived thousands of years from now based on remains, and by learning more about one another at the start of the new school year.

Skills and Knowledge

1. Students will follow the process of an archaeological excavation.
2. Students will use critical-thinking skills to evaluate material remains.

Overview

This unit kicks off the study of the ancient and the modern with an activity that may be messy: a simulated archaeological dig. It is recommended that the teacher partner with the Archaeological Institute of America (http://

www.archaeological.org/about/whoweare), which is based out of Boston University but also has a center in New York City. Students will need to keep an archaeological notebook (a composition book or other notebook) for record keeping in this unit and throughout the year.

Activity 4.1.1
Time Capsules

In this activity, students create time capsules that include artifacts that they would want archaeologists to find many years from now and clues about themselves (e.g., clues about their likes, dislikes, family structure, values, and more). The objects in their time capsule should be placed in a container, and the outside of the container should be decorated to depict their daily life. For containers, consider using small plastic bins, boxes, or coffee cans. (Note that the students should not bring items of value to school. They can take a picture of the items or draw a picture of them to include in their box instead.)

Students should exchange their time capsules with one another. (The teacher should manage this so that the students do not know whose time capsule they receive). Without explaining the time capsules to one another, students should take careful notes and create drawings about them and then come to their own conclusions about the importance and meaning of the objects. They should then share their observations with a partner. Finally, they should try to figure out whose time capsule they have.

Students should get into larger groups (at least groups of six to eight students, although if the groups are larger, the students will have more artifacts to work with) and combine the artifacts from all of the groups. Students should categorize the objects by theme and summarize the contents of the entire group. They should make generalizations about the modern US culture using the artifacts of the group.

Activity 4.1.2
Simulated "Shoebox" Dig

As an activator, the teacher should place a toilet seat in the center of the room and ask the students to pretend that they have no idea of the purpose of the item. The teacher should guide the students and encourage them to think of other uses for the item that archaeologists far into the future might come up with (e.g., a religious object or a game) Students should be guided to understand that archaeology is a science of inference based on artifacts and sites (context). Many of our interpretations of artifacts are shaded by our current culture and beliefs. Suspending our modern beliefs to scientifically uncover the mysteries of the past is an incredibly difficult task, and at best, the conclusions we come to are always inferences.

Students simulate an archaeological dig. See the following resource for detailed information.

Resources

- This resource includes an introductory and explanatory video for teachers. It will also be helpful to remember to encourage less mess and more thinking. (http://www.archaeological.org/education/lessons/simulateddigs)
- http://www.archaeological.org/pdfs/education/digs/Digs_everything.pdf

Note that this activity will require a considerable amount of time to set up. Teachers should solicit help from at least five or six parents. As a modification to the above activity, teachers can create much larger, flatter dig sites using specialized under-the-bed bins (i.e., shallow, wide, large plastic bins on wheels like the ones found here http://www.amazon.com/Sterilite-Under-Wheeled-Storage-Container/dp/B0000CFH7G). This way, students can use string to create grids over the "dig sites," and although the bins will be heavy with layers of soil, the wheels will make them movable. Between four and six students should be assigned to each dig site, and the dig sites should together tell a story of a culture that left artifacts behind. Students should keep meticulous records of their findings in their archaeological notebook. Students should present a summary of their findings to the class, and then the class should come together to discuss and reflect on the project, both in whole-class discussions and through reflection in the student notebooks.

There are quite a few additional lesson plans on the following site: http://www.archaeological.org/education/lessonplans. Of particular interest is the "What Will Survive" lesson plan (http://www.archaeological.org/sites/default/files/files/What%20Will%20Survive-edited.pdf), which allows students to think about what is not left behind (most organic matter, such as food and clothes) and, therefore, the gaps that archaeologists have to fill in.

Activity 4.1.3
Read *Motel of the Mysteries*

Students should read *Motel of the Mysteries*, by David Macaully (ninety-eight pages). In this book, archaeologists from the year 4022 excavate artifacts in the United States that were buried after a catastrophe in 1985. Most of the conclusions are absurd (for example, considering a bathroom to be a religious inner sanctum, which also connects to activity 4.2.2). This book is mainly entertaining, but it also shows the cultural biases often present when one makes inferences about the past.

Activity 4.1.4
Archeology in New York City

The teacher may form a partnership with the New York chapter of the Archaeological Institute of America in order to create a walking tour of archaeological sites in New York City. The teacher can also use the following online tool from the New York State Office of Parks, Recreation, and

Historic Preservation: http://www.nysparks.state.ny.us/shpo/online-tools/. The tool is a Geographic Information System that identifies all of the state's archaeologically sensitive sites (users can zoom in to the New York City level). The students should start with the school building itself and use pictures, videos, and primary documents from the construction of the school—and from before the construction of the school—to try to figure out the prior uses of the building. They can then visit some of the archaeological sites in New York City.

Unit	4.2
Topic	**Ancient China and Modern China**
Themes	**ICC: interpersonal; ICC: intrapersonal; ethics; work and mind habits; economic development; demography; politics; arts; communication; technology; world history; and investigative and analytical skills**
Region	**China**
Length	**Twelve weeks**

Goals and Objectives

1. **Learn** the history of both ancient China and modern China; to apply the components of civilization (government, religion, economy, arts, technology, settlement, and system of writing) to ancient China; to understand the arts and culture of modern China; and to draw comparisons and links between ancient and modern times in the context of China.

2. **Inspire** in students an appreciation for the accomplishments of great ancient and modern civilizations.

3. **Evaluate** ancient and modern China by participating in several activities to develop an understanding of ancient Chinese history and culture as well as of modern culture and by conducting self-guided research projects and class presentations.

Skills and Knowledge

1. Students will understand (as opposed to recall) the components of the major periods of Chinese history, including
   - the Xia dynasty (around 2070 BCE–1600 BCE);
   - the Shang dynasty (around 1600 BCE–1046 BCE);
   - the Qin dynasty, including the unification of China and Shi Huangdi (around 221 BCE); and
   - the Ming dynasty (AD 1368–AD 1644).

2. Students will articulate the role of archaeology in developing an understanding of the past through the close examination of archaeological sites and artifacts.
3. Students will evaluate the link between ancient and modern cultures in China.

Overview

This unit covers the first ancient civilization and modern civilization that will be studied this year, and students will be introduced to the components of a civilization (government, religion, economy, arts, technology, settlement, and system of writing) as a framework for understanding civilizations both ancient and modern. This unit relies heavily upon a partnership with Primary Source, and in particular upon Primary Source's collaboration with the Harvard University Asia Center and the unit "China Source."

Note that there are many additional links that can be made to the art curriculum (e.g., Chinese art and calligraphy), the literacy curriculum (poetry in particular, and tales are included here), the language curriculum, the music curriculum (e.g., Chinese opera and traditional and contemporary music), the math curriculum (e.g., the abacus), and the science curriculum (http://asiasociety.org/education-learning/resources-schools/elementary-lesson-plans/chinese-inventions). Ideally, multiple departments at the school will take part in the study of ancient and modern China as well as in the following unit on Egypt.

Activity 4.2.1
Ancient Bronzes and Bronze Vessels in the Shang and Zhou Dynasties: An Archeologist's Notebook

For this unit, it is recommended that the school purchase a bronze replica (http://www.galleriapangea.com/bronze_vessel_ritual_bronze_vessel_fu_xin_jue/product_details.html) for the students to handle while they make observations.

Using their archaeologist notebooks, students make detailed notes about the bronze and make inferences about its significance and use, for example.

Activity 4.2.2
Understanding Civilizations and Ancient China

The following lesson plan from Primary Source should be used to guide students in developing a framework for understanding that civilizations consist of main components (government, religion, economy, arts, technology, settlement, and system of writing) and applying those components to ancient China: http://resources.primarysource.org/content.php?pid=55748&sid=408002

This activity should take about nine separate forty-five-minute lessons to complete.

Activity 4.2.3
Bringing Ancient Chinese History to Life: A Living Time Line Activity

The students will create a time line of Chinese history, with partners being assigned varying points on the time line to research. They will then present to the class two or three of the major events of their time period in the form of a short drama.

Activity 4.2.4
Leading up to Modern China

In small groups the students will study the following major periods, people, and events by using guided Internet searches: Students will then make presentations to their class on the following topics:

1. The People's Republic of China in 1949, Mao Zedong (the leader of the Communist Party), Mao's Great Leap Forward, and the cultural revolution;
2. Deng Xiaoping (1976–1989);
3. Tiananmen Square (1989); and
4. China regains control of Hong Kong (1997)

Students in each group should create a slogan or a poster about their period, person, or event to share with the class.

Activity 4.2.5
Stories from China and Tibet Come Alive

Students should use *Favorite Children's Stories from China & Tibet* (http://www.amazon.com/Favorite-Childrens-Stories-China-Tibet/dp/0804835861) to create theater scripts for class performances. The tales, many of which involve animals, teach lessons and morals. Students should discuss these lessons and the cultural differences (and similarities) between China, Tibet, and the United States. (Notes that students should be given time for this activity so that they can produce high-quality scripts and performances; also, teachers should be sensitive to the controversies, both current and historical, surrounding Tibet.)

Activity 4.2.6
Modern China (Maps and a Research Project)

The following excellent set of lesson plans developed by Professor Knapp (SUNY) details explorations of modern China using maps: http://afe.easia.columbia.edu/china/geog/maps.htm. The following excellent research project is included in it:

Plan a trip in China so that you can travel by boat, by train, by car, by foot, and by camel. Decide which parts of China would be best for each mode of transport. Imagine what you eat in the different regions you travel through. If you needed to talk with the local inhabitants, how many languages would you need to know? Would you need different clothes in different regions so as not to be too hot or too cold? If you stayed in the homes of the local inhabitants, how would these homes be constructed?

Activity 4.2.7
Chinese Children's Film

Children should watch *Nima's Summer* (http://www.amazon.com/Nimas-Summer/dp/B0043P14SU), a part-anime, part–live action film about a boy who moves from a rural village in Tibet and then attends a middle school in a metropolis. Students should take note of the cultural differences experienced by the boy in the film.

An alternative film to watch is *The Rain in Spring* (http://www.amazon.com/Rain-spring-xiaobin-Zhang/dp/B00480PTQS/ref=sr_1_3?ie=UTF 8&qid=1306900790&sr=1-3-spell), which doesn't have animation and is about a strong relationship between a teacher and his students. It's a very touching story and will provide ample opportunities for discussions regarding Chinese culture and relationships.

Activity 4.2.8
Classroom Connection and Minicapstone:
Documentary Film Project

Students create documentaries about their own classroom and school to share with students in a partner school in China. Students should base their documentaries on either of the two films mentioned above. Students should take care to film the surrounding community, social and geographical context of the school, to discuss its history, and to show its teachers and students. This should be a rigorous media project, and the students should take the time to prepare, plan, and execute a high-quality documentary. Upon receiving a film from the partner school, students should compare the school experience of their peers in their Chinese sister school with their own and the context of their peers' school with that of their own, noting similarities and differences.

Resources

- New York Film Academy (http://www.nyfa.edu/film-school/documentary-filmmaking/?gclid=CKiV5r7flKkCFQl75 Qodk0pDcg)
- American Film Institute (http://www.afi.com/)
- Documentary Film Institute (http://www.docfilm.sfsu.edu/education/)
- Lesson plans and information organized by time period from Columbia University's Asia for Educators (http://afe.easia.columbia.edu/)
- The China section of *Time Life's Lost Civilizations* http://www.amazon.com/Time-Lifes-Lost-Civilizations-DVDs/dp/B00006L942/ref=sr_1_7?s=dvd&ie=UTF8&qid=1306892602&sr=1-7

Unit	4.3
Topic	**Ancient Egypt and Modern Egypt**
Themes	**ICC: interpersonal; ICC: intrapersonal; ethics; work and mind habits; economic development; demography; world history; geography; world religions; comparative government; arts; and investigative and analytical skills**
Region	**Egypt and the Arab world**
Length	**Twelve weeks**

Goals and Objectives:

1. **Learn** the history of both ancient Egypt and modern Egypt; to apply the components of civilization (government, religion, economy, arts, technology, settlement, and system of writing) to ancient Egypt; to understand current events and culture in Egypt; to draw comparisons and links between ancient and modern times in the context of Egypt.

2. **Inspire** in students an appreciation for the accomplishments of great ancient and modern civilizations.

3. **Evaluate** Egypt by participating in several activities to develop an understanding of ancient Egyptian history and culture as well as of modern culture and by conducting self-guided research projects and class presentations.

Skills and Knowledge

1. Students will understand (as opposed to recall) the components of the major periods of Egyptian history.

2. Students will articulate the role of archaeology in developing understanding of the past through the close examination of archaeological sites and artifacts.

3. Students will evaluate the link between ancient and modern cultures in Egypt.

Overview

This unit covers the second ancient civilization and modern civilization that will be studied this year while still applying the components of civilization and the link to modern civilization studied in the previous unit. The students are gaining research experience, so this unit includes more independent research. It also includes a focus on current events, particularly on the protests in Tahrir Square.

Activity 4.3.1
What Are the Meanings behind this Artifact?

The school should purchase the following replica artifact from the Museum Store for classroom use: An offering to Isis and Osiris—Temple of Isis, Philae, Egypt. Dynasty XXVI, 530 BC (http://www.museumstorecompany. com/An-offering-to-Isis-and-Osiris-Temple-of-Isis-Philae-Egypt-Dynasty-XXVI-530-B-C-p5583.html). The artifact itself can serve as a springboard for a discussion of the relationship between the rulers of Egypt and the gods, myths, rituals, and hieroglyphics.

The students should examine the artifact and take careful notes about its physical qualities. As it is a stone relief, students can make paper and wax rubbings of the stone to examine in small groups. Students should then research the site the Temple of Isis in Philae, Egypt, using the following website: http://www.ancientegyptonline.co.uk/isisphilae. html#gate.

The story of Isis and Osiris is told here in language appropriate for fourth graders: http://www.ancientegypt.co.uk/gods/home.html

Students could also depict a scene of importance in their family history and include inscriptions in hieroglyphics around its outer edges.

Also, later in the unit, students can follow the same lesson plan to examine canopic jars.

Activity 4.3.2
Hieroglyphics Tablet Activity

In conjunction with the art department, students create hieroglyphics tablets of messages to one another. The messages need to be one sentence in length and should describe one detail of the Egyptian time line. The tablets are then broken into parts (aim for a manageable number of pieces, as they will need to be reassembled later), placed into a box, and mixed with the parts of another tablet (the more tablets, the more difficult this activity will be) and sand. The students will then trade their boxes and excavate their tablets, working carefully to make detailed notes in their archaeologist notebooks as they go. They must piece the tablets back together to receive the historical message. All of the tablets are read together to review the ancient Egyptian time line.

The book *Fun with Hieroglyphs* is an excellent, child-friendly resource (http://www.amazon.com/Fun-Hieroglyphs-Metropolitan-Museum-Art/dp/1416961143/ref=sr_1_2?s=books&ie=UTF8&qid=1306891614&sr=1-2), as are numerous other children's books on hieroglyphics.

Students should examine the Rosetta stone, the key to understanding the hieroglyphics system. A high-resolution image of the Rosetta stone can be ordered from the British Museum (http://www.britishmuseum.org/research/collection_online/collection_object_details.aspx?objectId=117631&partId=1).

As an extension of this activity, students can consider the controversy around the Rosetta stone (whether the British Museum should keep possession of the stone or whether it should be returned) using the following easily adaptable lesson plan from MacMillan Global: http://www.macmillanglobal.com/elessons/lesson-plan-5-the-rosetta-stone.

Activity 4.3.3
Independent Research Projects

Students will form groups to research the components of civilization established in the previous unit on China (government, religion, economy, arts, technology, settlement, and system of writing) in ancient Egypt. Some achievements of ancient Egyptian civilization, such as shipbuilding, mathematics, medicine, construction techniques, glass, art, and architecture, could also be subjects of independent study within the small groups.

The groups will present their research to the class, and the teacher should guide the students in taking notes in their archaeologist notebooks.

This unit can be supplemented by a field trip to view ancient Egyptian art at the Metropolitan Museum of Art (http://www.metmuseum.org/about-the-met/curatorial-departments/egyptian-art).

Resources

- A lesson plan from *National Geographic* (http://www.nationalgeographic.com/xpeditions/lessons/06/g35/kingtut.html)
- A lesson plan from Discovery Education (http://www.discoveryeducation.com/teachers/free-lesson-plans/ancient-egypt.cfm)
- A lesson plan on mummy masks (http://www.art-rageous.net/MummyMask-LP.html)
- A lesson plan from the Museum of Science, including a "planning for your afterlife" game (http://www.mos.org/quest/teaching.php)
- High school lesson plans that can be adapted from (http://www.pbs.org/empires/egypt/pdf/lesson7.pdf)

- Information on the Nile (http://www.bbc.co.uk/history/ancient/ egyptians/nile_01.shtml#three)
- An accessible, interactive, clickable map of the Valley of the Kings (http://www.thebanmappingproject.com/atlas/index.html)
- A link to purchase replicas of canopic jars, which could be used as an extension of activity 4.3.1 (http://www.museumstorecompany.com/Set-of-Canopic-Jars-Egyptian-Museum-Cairo-650-B-C-p5538.html)
- The Egypt section of *Time Life's Lost Civilizations* (http://www.amazon.com/Time-Lifes-Lost-Civilizations-DVDs/dp/B00006L942/re f=sr_1_7?s=dvd&ie=UTF8&qid=1306892602&sr=1-7)

Activity 4.3.4
Modern Egypt: Protests, Culture, and an Introduction to the Arab World

Students examine maps of Cairo and identify Tahrir Square, the site of protests demanding the removal of Hosni Mubarak from the presidency. Students use current-events articles (http://www.socialstudiesforkids.com/ subjects/currentevents_egyptprotests2011.htm) to determine the reasons for the protest, the forms of the protest, the responses to the protest, and the outcomes of the protest.

Activity 4.3.5
Modern Egyptian Culture

Students will examine modern Egyptian culture through a study of the modern city of Cairo, linking the ancient history with the modern, with Egyptians of today, and with globalizing influences.

- Students will use maps to identify the cultural, historical, and political landmarks of Cairo.
- Students will identify Islam as the majority religion in Egypt and describe the major tenets and sacred texts of the religion. Students

will use maps and primary sources to identify places of worship in Egypt.

— Students will identify evidence of cultural and historical tradition in Cairo, as well as of its globalized nature

— Students will map the geography of Egypt, linking it back to how geography shaped the ancient civilization

— In small groups, students will use what they have learned to create an illustrated tour guide for modern Cairo.

Activity 4.3.6
Classroom Connection and Minicapstone: News Project

Students will create a newscast of current events at the school that covers, for example, what the students are studying, how they are studying, and how they are acting as historians as well as cultural events in New York City and other features. Students will share this newscast with a classroom in Cairo, and that classroom will share a newscast with their school. Teachers should film the students' reactions to the news programs. Students will discuss their reactions and the perspectives of their peers.

Special Activity
Film and Media Festival

Students will hold a film and media festival during which they will show their documentary and the documentary of their partner school from unit 2 and their newscast and their partner school's newscast to parents and the community. Each film will be followed by a brief question-and-answer session with audience members.

Unit   4.4
Topic   **Capstone Activity: Civilization Games**
Themes   **Economic development, demography, world history, geography, world religions, comparative government, arts, and investigative and analytical skills**
Region   **China, Egypt, and All Length**
Length   **Three to four weeks**

Goals and Objectives

1. **Learn** to apply the components of civilization (government, religion, economy, arts, technology, settlement, and system of writing) to both ancient Egypt and China by playing student-created games.
2. **Inspire** in students an appreciation for the complexities of civilizations and the achievements of civilizations.
3. **Evaluate** Egypt and China by creating and playing games that reinforce the learning from the year.

Skills and Knowledge

1. Students will understand the components of civilization (government, religion, economy, arts, technology, settlement, and system of writing).
2. Students will evaluate the components of civilization within two contexts.
3. Students will compare the two contexts in a systematic and logical way.

Overview

In this capstone activity, students review the components of civilization (government, religion, economy, arts, technology, settlement, and system of writing) by creating games in small groups. The fourth grade is divided into groups of students who then create games focusing on Egypt and China. Each group will consist of smaller sub-groups of between two and four students. (The goal is to form ten groups total throughout the fourth grade, so groups will be larger or smaller depending on the student body. See below for more detailed plans.)

Activity 4.4.1
The Creation of the Games

Each group will research one game from ancient China or Egypt (depending on which group they are in) and create a version of the game to be played during the game days. Some examples include dice games, Senet, Mahjongg, and physical games to be played outside.

Each group will also create one board or physical game that illustrates the components of civilization. Students may consider building on existing board games, such as Trivial Pursuit—each pie piece could represent a component of civilization—or the electronic Civilization games; role-playing games; or strategy games.

Note that sufficient time should be given to this activity. It may stretch across several weeks, with the teacher checking in on students' work periodically. Or the teacher may choose to more intensively prepare for these games over a few weeks. Either way, the games should be well developed, with all of the necessary pieces or components made by students and fully functional, and demonstrate a clear understanding of the components of civilization. Students should be given rubrics to evaluate their own games for these quality components, and teachers should also use the rubrics to communicate to students the areas that need improvement before the games are played.

Activity 4.4.2
Let's Play: The World Course Fourth-Grade Game Day (i.e., the Playing of the Games)

Students will divide into groups on two different days. On one day the students will show one another how to play the games at various game "stations," and on another day, they will play the games that the other students created.

Note that this can be set up like a typical elementary school field day across two days, with plenty of parent volunteers to help. Stations can be set up both within the school for the board games and outside of the school for the physical games. Alternatively, the games could be woven throughout several partial days or could be played in the evening. Not all students need to play all games.

Activity 4.4.3
Let's Collaborate: Collaborating for Humanity's Sake

Download the lesson "Working Together to Achieve the Global Goals" and engage the students in the activities outlined in it (https://teachunicef.org/teaching-materials/topic/sustainable-development-goals).

The World Course
Fifth Grade: Freedom and the Rights of Individuals: Social Change around the Rights of Individuals

Theme

Understanding how civic engagement helps people improve themselves and their communities.

Description

In this grade the primary focus is on individual rights and freedoms as well as on social change. It builds from the creation of a classroom community. It then moves into historical explorations of various independence movements (the United States is the primary focus, and the French, Haitian, and South African resistances to oppression are also discussed). In this sense, it is meant to build on immediate concepts and them move back through history, starting with the most familiar contexts and expanding to other global contexts. This unit also stresses nonviolence as a successful path to resistance to oppression and to independence. The MDGs and SDGs and the Universal Declaration of Human Rights provide the foundation for students to identify and examine organizations promoting human rights historically and helping students can organize around issues through the capstone activity. The year ends with a capstone in which the students create their own media documentary about one of the SDGs.

Looking Back
The Rise (and Fall) of Ancient and Modern Civilizations

Looking Forward
How do people in societies organize themselves? Social contracts, individuals and society, and the study of society.

Overview of the Units

1) Creating Classroom Rules and Building a Classroom Community
2) American Revolution (Literature Link: *Johnny Tremain*)
3) French Revolution (Literature Link: *Les Misérables*)
4) Haitian Revolution (Arts Link: Jacob Lawrence and Literature Link: Wordsworth)
5) Universal Declaration of Human Rights and the Poverty SDG
6) South Africa and Resistance to Oppression

Capstone
Create an awareness-raising project on the topic of one of the SDGs using some medium (e.g., a video, a PowerPoint presentation, a dance, a work of art, or a speech).

Unit	5.1
Topic	**Creating Classroom Rules**
Themes	**ICC: intrapersonal; ethics; and scenario building**
Region	**Any/all**
Length	**Two lessons**

Goals and Objectives

1. **Learn** the meaning and the uses of rules by comparing them to possible misuses of rules.
2. **Inspire** students to develop and live by an equitable set of rules for the classroom and to take an interest in the American Revolution.
3. **Act** by demonstrating an understanding of rules and by creating equitable rules.

Skills and Knowledge

1. Students will identify the need for rules and understand why rules are important.
2. Students will compare equitable rules with inequitable rules.
3. Students will judge rules based on their fairness to all and their usefulness in enabling the classroom to work together for the common goal of learning.

Overview

The students and the teacher will collaborate to create a set of rules for the classroom.. Students will be guided in thinking about concepts such as fairness, individual rights and responsibilities, freedom from tyranny, and communication.

Activity 5.1.1
It's Tyranny!

The teacher has a prewritten set of rules for the class and reads them to the class. The list starts out rather reasonably but then gets progressively more tyrannical and unreasonable, such that by the end of the list, the students know that those aren't the real class rules. The following rules are only suggestions. Some of the rules below foreshadow some of the causes of the American Revolution:

1. All students must treat one another with respect applying the golden rule.
2. All students are expected to help one another learn.
3. All students must turn in homework on time, with the proper heading.
4. All students should raise their hand to speak and will wait to be called upon before speaking.
5. Students are not allowed to question the teacher's grading of papers.
6. Students are not allowed to talk among themselves in class if the purpose of the discussion is to question the authority of the teacher.
7. Students must bring the teacher ten dollars every day and give the teacher half of any money that they are given or earn.
8. Students will not be a part of the process of making rules and must abide by all rules.

The teacher should notice some surprise when the last rules are read and then should lead a discussion. The teacher should ask the students whether these rules are like the rules they had in previous classrooms. Are they fair? Which ones aren't fair? Why not? The teacher made these rules, so would another rule-making process result in rules that were more fair? Why do we need rules?

Activity 5.1.2
The Veil of Ignorance[2]

The teacher separates the class into two teams. The teacher tells the students that each team will create two rules that are specific to their team. Note that these rules should be completely unfair and clearly advantage one team over the other. Write this example on the board: "All members of team A get credit for turning in their homework whether they turn it in or not." Allow the teams to come up with two rules like this one.

The teacher has a bag with yellow and green slips of paper in it (there should be an equal number of each and one for each student). The teacher goes around the classroom, and the students close their eyes and pull out one slip of paper. Once everyone has their paper, the teachers says, "If you have a green slip of paper, you are a member of team A. If you have a yellow slip of paper, you are a member of team B."

Some students become members of the other team (that is, they switch teams), which will place them at a disadvantage because of the rules that they themselves created. Ask them for their response to this change. Those who haven't switched teams will still be advantaged; ask them for their response.

The teacher explains the "veil of ignorance" and the idea that the rules should be fair to all regardless of which team they're on. One can determine if a rule is fair by imagining one's self making that rule from behind the veil of ignorance—that is, without knowing to which groups others belong (e.g., others' gender, age, race, creed, or religion). The rule maker should then consider whether the rule would still be fair if he or she were a member of a different group.

The students should free write about this experience in the journals they keep in class. For those students who have trouble getting started, the following prompt can be used: How did you feel when the rules that were

---

2   This is based on the philosophy of John Rawls in *A Theory of Justice*.

added either advantaged you or disadvantaged you? Did you want to keep those rules? Why or why not?

Activity 5.1.3
Classroom-Rule Creation

What are the goals of this classroom? What rules would help us achieve those goals?

Through discussions in small groups and sharing, the classroom will develop a statement of the goals of the classroom (or a mission statement) and develop a shared set of classroom rules.

If necessary, use the following prompt: Think back to one of the days or lessons when you learned a lot in school. What made it so successful? Think back to a time when you didn't learn anything or felt frustrated in school. What made that experience so unsuccessful? What do you need others to do to help you learn as well as you can?

Unit	5.2
Topic	**From Colonialism to Democracy: The US Revolution**
Themes	**ICC: interpersonal; ethics; work and mind habits; economic development; world history; geography; comparative government; arts: literature, visual, and drama; analyze and assess; the use of technology**
Region	**United States**
Length	**Nine weeks**

Goals and Objectives

1. **Learn** to describe the key events leading up to the American Revolution and the causes of the Revolution; to identify the philosophical tradition of the Enlightenment and its relation to the Revolution; and to describe the formation of a democratic nation.

2. **Inspire** in students an appreciation for a momentous historical event that set in motion many of the modern systems of governance used today.

3. **Act** by demonstrating an understanding of the historical time line and philosophical underpinnings of the American Revolution.

Skills and Knowledge

1. Students will describe the key events leading up to the American Revolution and the causes of the Revolution and identify the philosophical tradition of the Enlightenment and its relation to the Revolution.

2. Students will describe the formation of a democratic nation.

3. Students will evaluate the vision of the founders, using many sources to identify varying perspectives.

Overview

In this unit, students will study the American Revolution with a focus on the rights of the individual and on the organizations for social change concerning these rights. They will begin with a story from literature, *Johnny Tremain*, and move into a close reading of the Declaration of Independence. They will then build a historical understanding of the reasons for settlement in the New World, the causes of the American War of Independence, and the outcomes of the war. They will also examine Benjamin Franklin as a unique personage with tremendous personal agency in the social movement. Several optional enrichment activities as well as a field trip are suggested.

Resources

*https://books.google.com/books?id=mZd6bUoNwNIC&pg=PA246&lpg=PA24
6&dq=oxford+university+press+history+of+american+revolution+for+fifth+gr
aders&source=bl&ots=5uMfxGVLXG&sig=cSFu_zU54w38E0UE94B4k_We
hcQ&hl=en&sa=X&ved=0ahUKEwjD7rmkzonNAhUDGD4KHST2AMM
Q6AEIJTAC#v=onepage&q=oxford%20university%20press%20history%20
of%20american%20revolution%20for%20fifth%20graders&f=false
https://global.oup.com/academic/product/the-american-revolution-
9780199324224?cc=us&lang=en&*

Activity 5.2.1
Johnny Tremain

Ideas for this unit are taken from the following site: http://www.lengel.net/ hebron/5ssunit1.html.

Students will read *Johnny Tremain* as homework during the American Revolution unit, and then they will spend one day a week discussing it. (Or the teacher may incorporate the book into the core historical study of the

Revolution in any other variety of ways.) Students will read approximately forty pages each week.

Each Friday (for example), short journal entries told from the perspective of Johnny will be due. The journal entries will discuss the problems and issues that are important to him and reflect on them. The teacher will give the students some journal prompts that will tie together the historical themes and the socioemotional themes.

The purpose of this section of the unit is to personalize and personify historical understanding from the perspective of a (fictional) fourteen-year-old main character who is imperfect (arrogant and a bully at the beginning of the story) and then changes during the course of the story as he meets adversity. As Johnny "meets" important figures of the American Revolution, the "history" comes alive.

Activity 5.2.2
The Declaration of Independence

Note that this lesson starts with one part of the document itself. One of the concluding activities of this unit is to read the entire document.

Start with this text: "We hold these truths to be self-evident, that all men are created equal, that they are endowed by their Creator with certain unalienable rights, that among these are life, liberty and the pursuit of happiness."

Many of the revolutionary ideas are right here in this one sentence. The teacher will direct a discussion on the meaning of each part of it. Model close reading and thought about the meaning of each phrase as well as the sentence as a whole.

Use the following statements to extend the lesson. Divide the class into four small groups and give each group one of the two sentences. In their small groups, the students follow the same process to closely read and think about the sentence, about what each phrase means, and about what the sentence means. After they've had a chance to evaluate the sentence, have the groups get together according to which sentence they worked on to compare their evaluations of it. Later, regroup, and have the students compare the sentences. Use the following sentences:

1. That to secure these rights, governments are instituted among men, deriving their just powers from the consent of the governed.
2. That whenever any form of government becomes destructive to these ends, it is the right of the people to alter or to abolish it, and to institute new government, laying its foundation on such principles and organizing its powers in such form, as to them shall seem most likely to effect their safety and happiness.

Activity 5.2.2b
In English, Please!
The students can work individually or in groups to write a paragraph that explains the three sentences they examined in modern English.

As an extension of the activity, students can compare the passage of the Declaration of Independence to this section of John Locke's 1690 *Second Treatise of Government*:

> The natural liberty of man is to be free from any superior power on earth, and not to be under the will or legislative authority of man, but to have only the law of Nature for his rule. The liberty of man in society is to be under no other legislative power but that established by consent in the commonwealth, nor under the dominion of any will, or restraint of any law, but what that legislative shall enact according to the trust put in it.

Activity 5.2.3
Who Were the Colonists? Where Did They Come from and Why? A Comparison of the Jamestown and Massachusetts Settlements
(Consider including New York in this activity as an extension.)

In a guided research activity, students research the Jamestown settlement.

The students could complete a table, placing information about Jamestown on one side and information about Massachusetts on the other side. Guide the students in finding the following information about Jamestown:

1. the date of the first settlement
2. the purposes of the settlement
3. what life was like in the colony
4. how the colony was governed
5. the relationship between the colonists and the Native Americans who were there

In a computer lab, the students should work in pairs to find information about the Massachusetts settlement. Back in class, groups should get together to discuss their answers and to make sure that all of the important information is included.

The teacher leads a discussion on the two colonies' similarities and differences. The major topics that should be included are religious freedom and economic opportunity (both for the colonists and the English).

As an extension of this activity, students should research the other Eastern Seaboard colonies, either in class or as homework. The students pretending to be colonists should then hold a mock meeting to discuss the challenges and opportunities they have found in the New World. Note that this could also be developed into an activity that simulates the First Continental Congress, but if it is, it should be included later in the unit.

Activity 5.2.4
Growing Discontent: An Exploration of the Causes of the American War of Independence

(Note that the recommended approach is to have the students use the sources to determine the causes of the war.)

Through reading texts, primary sources, and other historical documents and sources of information, students create a time line of events leading up to the American War of Independence. From this activity, they should develop a sense of the several causes of the war. The teacher should split the class into four groups. Each group should create a tableau for one of the causes of the war. The tableau should include objects that represent the particular cause of the war. Each group should explain its tableau to the class. The tableaux can include the students themselves if they want to get into character. Assign the following main causes of the war to the students: taxation, representation, a reaction against acts seen as unjust, and a will for independence (self-rule).

Resources

- http://www.pbs.org/ktca/liberty/
- http://www.discoveryeducation.com/teachers/free-lesson-plans/the-american-revolution-causes.cfm

Optional Activity
The Printing Press: A Closer Look

In this activity, students use a scaled time line to show how quickly history changed after the development of literacy (visual and written) and, more importantly to the Revolution, after the invention of the printing press. The following points in time are given to the students:

1. Earliest cave paintings (about 30,000 BCE)
2. Earliest writings (pictorial) from Ancient Sumer (about 4000 BCE)
3. Hammurabi's Code (about 700 BCE)
4. Signing of the Magna Carta (AD 1215)
5. Invention of the printing press (AD 1465)
6. Publication of Thomas Paine's *Common Sense*, which became the most widely sold and circulated book in American history to that point (AD 1776)
7. Invention of the silicon chip, the basis of personal computers, by Jack Kilby and Robert Noyce (AD 1961)
8. Invention of the World Wide Web by Tim Berners-Lee (AD 1991)

Students should create a drawing and a brief description of their assigned event to be posted in the classroom.

The teacher and students create a scaled time line. This needs to be done along a long hallway or outside. The teacher needs to determine the amount of available space ahead of time. Once that is determined, the period between 30,000 BCE and AD 2000 (32,000 years will be scaled in more compressed form than the rest of the timeline. If you have one hundred feet of space, then each foot will represent 320 years, for example. The students assigned the cave paintings will stand at the far end of it. Then the students assigned the earliest writings will stand at the appropriate distance from them. In the end, the first few events will be very far away from one another and very widely spaced out. Then after the signing of Magna Carta or the invention of the printing press, the students will stand very close to one another. They will learn that the development of the written word and the development of technology that can spread the written word quickly have led to many rapid developments.

(Note that the Morgan Library in New York City is an excellent resource for printing history and printed resources.)

Activity 5.2.5
The Life of Benjamin Franklin

After a brief introduction, the students should research the life of Benjamin Franklin. This research should focus on the following topics:

1. His life as a thinker and an inventor
2. His role in the expansion of the printing press as a popular medium
3. His role in gaining support for the American War of Independence from the French and his role as the first American ambassador to France
4. His use of wit and comedy

Resources

-   http://www.pbs.org/benfranklin/
-   http://www.webenglishteacher.com/franklin.html

Optional Activity
The *Colonial Times* Newspaper: An Exploration of the Ideas of and Motivations for the War
(See appendix A for detailed instructions.)

Activity 5.2.6
Propaganda and Imagery in the American Revolution
First, the teacher should introduce the class to the following slogans (additional slogans can be used):

- "Give me liberty, or give me death!"
- "We must, indeed, all hang together, or assuredly we shall all hang separately."
- "No taxation without representation!"
- "These are the times that try men's souls."

The teacher could print these slogans on separate pieces of paper and then cut them up into jigsaw pieces. Students are then each given one "puzzle" piece, and they have to find the other students whose pieces fit with theirs to form the slogan. They then discuss the possible meaning of the slogan and record their thoughts in their notebook. Each group shares its slogan and thoughts with the class.

Second, the teacher can collect images from the Revolution (example, a sign saying "Don't Tread On Me") and from art. Students should discuss the symbolism and meanings of the images.

Activity 5.2.7
The Declaration of Independence: A Second Look

The teacher should prepare the students to read the document by explaining its parts: the introduction and thesis statement, the list of grievances, and the resolutions of the colonies. The students review the causes of the war, the philosophy of the age of reason, and many aspects of the unit as a whole through this reading. It is not expected that the students will master the document.

Consider showing students this YouTube video of a reading of the document by famous actors and actresses: http://www.youtube.com/watch?v=ZxTvS-kyHzs.

Activity 5.2.8
Field Trip
The students may take a field trip to Philadelphia, Colonial Williamsburg, the Jamestown settlement, and the Yorktown Victory Center.

Resources

- Colonial Williamsburg's electronic field trip (http://www.history.org/history/teaching/eft/index.cfm.)
- Jamestown and Yorktown (http://www.historyisfun.org/jamestown-settlement.htm)
- Oxford University Press's series A History of US (https://global.oup.com/academic/content/series/h/a-history-of-us-hus/?cc=us&lang=en&)
- "Teaching with Documents," from the National Archives: (http://www.archives.gov/education/lessons/revolution-images/)
- Colonial history (http://www.pbs.org/ktca/liberty/tguide_2.html)
- Archiving Early America
- (http://www.earlyamerica.com/earlyamerica/freedom/doi/)
- Brain Pop video on the causes of the American Revolution (http://www.brainpop.com/socialstudies/ushistory/causesoftheamerican-revolution/preview.weml)

Unit	5.3
Topic	**French Revolution**
Theme	**ICC: interpersonal; ethics; work and mind habits; poverty; world history; geography; comparative government; arts: literature and drama; and analyze and assess**
Region	**France**
Length	**Eight weeks**

Goals and Objectives

1. **Learn** about the injustices that led to the French Revolution and the links and differences between the French Revolution and other revolutions.
2. **Inspire** students to think about injustice and how it can be remedied.
3. **Act** by evaluating what makes a democratic movement successful.

Skills and Knowledge

1. Students will learn about the three estates.
2. Students will learn about absolute monarchies and government symbols.
3. Students will learn about art and how it can portray historical events.
4. Students will practice independent research skills.
5. Students will continue developing comparative skills.
6. Students will examine the French Revolution using the same criteria that will be used to examine South Africa later in the year.

Overview

The students will expand their understanding of social movements around the rights of individuals from the American Revolution to the French Revolution. The same frameworks for understanding the causes, events, and outcomes of the war should be carried over to this unit to aid in understanding. Students will again begin with literature and then take a deeper look into social hierarchy and poverty as well into issues of fairness and human rights.

Activity 5.3.1
French Revolution and Art: Les Misérables

The teacher assigns an abridged student version of Victor Hugo's *Les Misérables*[3] at the beginning of this unit. Periodically over the course of this unit, the teacher asks the students to write in a journal on the topics highlighted by the scenes listed below:

1) Jean Valjean's imprisonment after stealing bread for his nephews and nieces
   a. Hunger
   b. Law versus justice
2) The scene between the priest and Jean Valjean after he's been captured for stealing from the priest
   a. Major concepts in Christianity (forgiveness, grace, mercy, redemption, and rebirth)
3) Jean Valjean's role as mayor and how he helps Fantine and Cosette
   a. The use of power
   b. The notion of caring for others and taking responsibility
4) Marius's role as a student in the Revolution
   a. The role of ordinary people in the Revolution

(Note that later on in the year, when the students are studying SDG 1, poverty; SDG 2, hunger; and the UDHR—especially articles 11 and 25, which deal with law and justice—it may be useful to refer back to these topics.)

---

3 Hugo, V. & Kulling, M. (1995). *Les Misérables*. New York, NY: Random House Books for Young Readers. [ISBN 978-0679866688]

Once the students have completed the book, the class watches the musical film adaptation of *Les Misérables*. The teacher asks the students to take note of the clothing of the period, the symbols of the revolution (on both sides), and the architecture. They will look at contemporary pictures of French clothing, symbols (including currency—both the now-defunct Franc and the Euro), and architecture and note how they have changed, how they reflect current and historical French beliefs, and how certain aspects of the French Revolution have been incorporated into modern French culture.

Next, the students will be given a copy of the lyrics of some of the songs in *Les Misérables* (chosen at the discretion of the teacher). They will discuss the accuracy of the songs in portraying the Revolution and how effective they are in creating an emotional response, such as sympathy, for the characters or cause. The teacher will lead the class in a discussion of how both novels and songs can be used to convey emotion, build a movement, and share history.

Resources

- Currencies of France over time (Banknotes.com)
- *What Your Fifth Grader Needs to Know: Fundamentals of a Good Fifth-Grade Education.* (ISBN 978-0385411196)
- Hugo, V. & Kulling, M. (1995). *Les Misérables.* New York, NY: Random House Books for Young Readers. (ISBN 978-0679866688)
- "Those who have and those who have not" (http://www.learnnc.org/lp/pages/3432)
- Information on Marie Antoinette from PBS (http://www.pbs.org/marieantoinette/)

Activity 5.3.2
The Three Estates
(This activity is adapted from Kevin Huntley's "The French Revolution: Those who have and those who have not": http://www.learnnc.org/lp/pages/3432.)

Prior to class, the teacher sets up different stations around the room with articles from French culture and history. These items should reflect France as it is/was and should not simply be clichéd symbols of France. The purpose of this is to orient students in the French context so that their study of France is not out of context.

Once the stations are prepared, the teacher should fill the classroom with the smell of freshly popped popcorn. After the students arrive and while they are getting settled, the teacher explains that they will be taking a tour of France. She tells them each to visit all of the stations and to makes notes about what the stations say about France. While they are doing that, the teacher shares popcorn with around 6 percent of the class (just a few students) without saying why or saying anything to the students who don't get popcorn. Students will no doubt begin to complain, and the teacher will observe their reactions.

Once the students have finished touring "France," the teacher initiates a discussion with the students about injustice, how they felt about getting/not getting popcorn, and why they should have all gotten popcorn. The teacher will introduce the three estates (clergy, nobility, and the rest), explaining what percentage each group was of the total population, the percentage of wealth that each group held, and the amount of power that each group held in eighteenth-century French society. The teacher then explains that this social and economic inequality was one of the primary reasons for the unrest that led to the French Revolution. The teacher should point out the connections between the cases that the students are making for equality and the Universal Declaration of Human Rights. The teacher should also help the students make comparisons between the context of the American Revolution and the context of the French Revolution, and students should note the fact that the French were revolting against their own government rather than against a colonial government. It is important that the connections to the previous unit on the American Revolution be made clear to the students in preparation for the rest of the unit on the French Revolution.

Activity 5.3.3
"L'Etat, C'est Moi!"

In this activity, students will learn about Louis XIV. They will read pages 156–158 of *What Your Fifth Grader Needs to Know.*[4] Once they have read these pages, the teacher will ask the class what Louis XIV did that was good for France. They may say, "He built a magnificent palace," "He made France powerful," and "He commissioned plays and concerts," for example. The teacher lists these in a column on the board. Next the teacher asks what Louis XIV did that angered the people. They may say, "He made France poor," "He spent money on plays but not on his people," and "He did not share any power or wealth with anyone, including the third estate." Next, they will talk about the role of government in people's lives, how government can help people, and how it can hurt people. The class will create a third list of the things that they would want their government to do for them.

They will next analyze the symbol of the sun and the saying "L'état, c'est moi" and compare those to the symbols and slogans of the Revolution—for example, the Bastille, *La Marseillaise* (national anthem), and the saying "Liberty, Equality, and Fraternity." This connects to the previous unit on the American Revolution, particularly to lesson 5.2.6. They will next look at other governmental figures' symbols (e.g., symbols from Obama's 2008 campaign and the US national anthem). Finally, each student (or pairs of students) will be tasked with making a symbol for their ideal government and writing a paragraph about what the symbol represents to them.

---

4 Hirsch, E.D. Jr. (ed.) (1993). What Your Fifth Grader Needs to Know: Fundamentals of a Good Fifth-Grade Education. New York, NY: Dell Publishing. [ISBN 978-0385411196]

Unit   5.4
Topic   The Haitian Revolution
Theme   ICC: interpersonal; ethics; work and mind habits; poverty;
          world history; geography; comparative government; arts:
          literature and visual; and analyze and assess
Region   Haiti and the Caribbean
Length   Six weeks

Goals and Objectives

1. **Learn** about the Haitian Revolution, why it is important, and how it has been represented in art.
2. **Inspire** students to reflect on how the French Declaration of the Rights of Man and of the Citizen not only influenced Haitian history but also developed the framework for the Universal Declaration of Human Rights.
3. **Evaluate** art not only for its aesthetics but also for deeper historical and cultural meaning.

Skills and Knowledge

1. Students will learn about Toussaint Louverture and the Haitian Revolution.
2. Students will make comparisons between the UDHR, the Declaration of the Rights of Man and of the Citizen, and the US Declaration of Independence.
3. Students will learn about the power of art to share history.
4. Students will learn about how historical "facts" are often a matter of perspective.
5. Students will practice using intercultural skills to work with a class of students in Haiti.

Overview

The students will again extend their understanding of social movements around the rights of individuals by looking at a less commonly understood revolution, the Haitian Revolution.

Activity 5.4.1
The Declaration of the Rights of Man and of the Citizen versus the Universal Declaration of Human Rights and the Declaration of Independence

The teacher explains to the class that the Haitian Revolution began, in large part, because France did not extend the rights listed in the Declaration of the Rights of Man and of the Citizen[5] to Haitians. During the French Revolution, the assembly that was created during the reign of Louis XVI drafted a document that outlined the equal rights of all citizens. The class begins a discussion on the freedoms that French people were seeking during the Revolution, the freedoms that Americans were seeking during the Revolution, and the freedoms that Haitians were seeking. Next, the students, with the help of the teacher, discuss the similarities and differences between the Declaration of the Rights of Man and of the Citizen, the US Declaration of Independence, and the Universal Declaration of Human Rights,[6] using close-reading methods to study selections of text from these primary documents.

Activity 5.4.2
Art and Toussaint Louverture[7]

The teacher begins the class by explaining that, just as the French Revolution did, the Haitian Revolution inspired people all over the world, including artists. Haiti was the first colony of blacks that gained independence, and

---

5   Available here: http://www.pbs.org/wgbh/aia/part3/3h1577t.html

6   http://www.un.org/en/documents/udhr/index.shtml

7   An alternate spelling is "L'Ouverture."

unlike many African nations, they fought for it, rather than had it bestowed upon them. For this reason, the Haitian Revolution remains a very important piece of history that has been commemorated through art.

The charismatic yet controversial figure of Toussaint Louverture has been a particularly rich subject for art and poetry. The teacher first reads William Wordsworth's poem "To Toussaint L'Ouverture." (Note that this poem can be very difficult for young learners to understand, so the teacher should take care to explain the complex language and to focus the learning on how Louverture was unhappy because he was not free.)

The class is paired with a class of students in Haiti so that they can learn about how Haitian students learn about the Haitian Revolution. The teachers of each class collaborate to show their students the paintings of Jacob Lawrence,[8] which tell the story of Louverture's life and Haiti's struggle for independence. The teachers show their classes one painting at a time and asks the classes to describe the story each painting tells. The American teacher then shares biographical information about Louverture from a source like The Louverture Project (see resources below). The Haitian teacher asks his or her students to use what they have learned previously about the Haitian Revolution to caption the paintings. Next, the students break into pairs and share how they interpreted the paintings and their thoughts on the similarities and differences in the stories they tell. Ideally, the students will talk about how Louverture is represented and about what devices the artist used to convey information and feeling.

(Note that the teachers should both take care to explain to the students that while these particular paintings tell a particular story, there is no "right" way to interpret art.)

A possible student-level resource for the Haitian Revolution is a leveled reader (the sixth-grade reader is available below, on, above grade level) from

McGraw-Hill MacMillian (https://www.mheonline.com/) called *Timelinks: The Haitian Revolution* (2009).

Resources

- Frederick Douglass's 1893 lecture on Haiti (http://www.americaslibrary.gov/jb/progress/jb_progress_douglass_1.html)
- The Louverture Project (http://thelouvertureproject.org/index.php?title=Main_Page)
- National History Day Essay Winner Jim Thomson's "The Haitian Revolution and the Forging of America" (http://www.historycooperative.org/journals/ht/34.1/thomson.html)
- Africans in America's "Declaration of the Rights of Man" from PBS (http://www.pbs.org/wgbh/aia/part3/3h1577t.html)
- Teaching for Change's "Teaching About Haiti" (http://www.teachingforchange.org/publications/haiti)
- Teaching History's "Teaching About Haiti" (http://teachinghistory.org/nhec-blog/23787)
- The UN's Universal Declaration of Human Rights (http://www.un.org/en/documents/udhr/index.shtml

Unit	5.5
Topic	**UDHR and Poverty and Hunger**
Theme	**ICC: interpersonal; ICC: intrapersonal; ethics; work and mind habits; economic development; poverty; geography; comparative government; global risk: economic; arts: literature and drama; and analyze and assess**
Region	**United States, India, and Africa**
Length	**Four weeks**

Goals and Objectives

1. **Learn** about the representation of rights and needs in the UDHR and the SDGs and understand the centrality of SDG 1 and SDG 2 to the other SDGs.

2. **Inspire** students to reflect on the causes of poverty, its consequences for different groups in society, and the stigmas associated with it; to understand that it's a dynamic concept that can affect anyone disproportionately at a given point in time; and to undertake action and contribute in the best possible way

3. **Act** in informed ways while trying to understand the issues associated with poverty and by treating poor people in respectful and dignified ways without stigmatizing them.

Skills and Knowledge

1. Students will increase awareness of the UDHR, of its value as a normative framework in articulating the rights and freedoms of all individuals, and of how it came into being.

2. Students will express thoughts and opinions regarding these human rights, and understand and exhibit the behavioral competencies associated with the UDHR.

3. Students will examine the complexities of poverty and understand it as an evolving concept over time that can disproportionately affect different groups of people for reasons that may not even be in their control.
4. Students will draw clear links between the SDGs and the UDHR.
5. Students will differentiate between hunger, starvation, malnutrition, and overeating.
6. Students will understand that statistics concerning the poor and hunger are based upon measurements that are variable, and see the links between poverty and hunger
7. Students will increase awareness of the different stakeholders involved in addressing SDG 1 and SDG 2.
8. Students will understand the stereotypes associated with poverty and also the importance of treating everyone equally with dignity and respect, even if they're poor.

Overview

The following unit takes the principles of the revolutions, human rights, freedom, and the social movement around human rights and applies them to the modern global compacts of the SDGs and the UDHR. It begins with concrete explorations and then links to the document of the UDHR. It applies the principles to poverty, and although there may not be any (or many) students in the school living in poverty, the students will be well aware of the realities of poverty that it addresses. The capstone at the end of this year allows the students to raise awareness about an SDG that they care about. The ability to raise awareness provides students with a sense of agency, which is fundamental to the World Course.

Activity 5.5.1
What do I need to function?

In this activity, students are divided into groups and provided with large poster-size paper on which the shape and form of an individual has been drawn. The teacher asks each students to imagine that he or she is that individual and asks what each needs to function on a day-to-day basis. While most students may say basic things such as food or water, the teacher should push the boundaries of their thinking further by asking leading questions about security and safety, rules and norms, and health-care services.

The teacher then shows them pictures of children from across the world. He or she should show a good mix of children from different parts of the world, of different ethnicities and races, and from different socioeconomic backgrounds. The teacher asks the students to define what these children in particular might need and to make comparisons between what they said they needed and what they said those other children needed. The purpose of this is for children to be able to see the universality of needs.

The teacher then proceeds to introduce students to the Universal Declaration of Human Rights (UDHR), a global value framework granted to all human beings in the world.

Activity 5.5.2
What's the UDHR?

In this activity, the teacher shares a copy of a child-friendly version of the UDHR, and the children read it together in class. The class is once again split into groups, and those groups are given name cards belonging to a fictitious nation or to a certain society. The teacher then informs the students that they will be given particular situations and that they have to decide what they would do in those situations using the texts they've been provided with.

The teacher introduces "violations"—that is, actions that would violate the UDHR and that may not be used to solve the situations they students have been given:

1. They may not blame a particular group without proof that that group is guilty.
2. They may not take away the students' right to a nationality.
3. They may not treat a group unfairly and discriminate against it on the basis of race, color, or sex.

The teacher then asks the students to defend themselves by drawing on certain specific portions of the text. Through this activity, the teacher introduces the concept of the UDHR as a normative framework that is holistic and that grants individual rights.

Resources

- http://www.guardian.co.uk/books/gallery/2008/oct/17/amnesty-declaration-human-rights-children#/?picture=338702813&index=6
- http://www1.umn.edu/humanrts/edumat/hreduseries/TB3/appendices/kidsversion.htm

Activity 5.5.3
Human Rights Day: Every Day or One Day?

Using technology, students communicate with other students in different schools in different parts of the world and work to examine how HR day is celebrated in each of the countries. Do the countries do certain symbolic things? Is the day even marked or observed?

The students then present their findings and talk about Human Rights Day. The teacher asks the students how they would celebrate HR Day in class. She then pushes the discussion further by asking how they would celebrate the day in class if every day were Human Rights day. The purpose of this activity is for students to draw out a list of the guiding values and principles that govern their own actions in class. The list should include the essentials related to treating everyone with equality, respect, and dignity.

Activity 5.5.4
What Did I See on My Way Back Home Today?

Students are shown a short clip: http://www.agarota.com/e_mk_release.html.

The teacher then asks the students to carefully observe what they see on their way back home from school that day. They should then answer the following questions:

1. Did you see poor people?
2. What makes you think that those people are poor?
3. Why do you think those people are poor?
4. Were those people doing something in particular that classified them as poor?
5. Were they wearing certain kinds of clothes?
6. What kinds of homes might those people live in?

Stereotypes will emerge from this discussion. The teacher should allow the students to record the stereotypes and their reactions to them in their journals. They can them form partnerships to share the stereotypes and their reactions to them, highlighting the similarities and differences in the stereotypes and reactions. Students can then lead a class discussion about each of these questions, and the reasons behind what they saw,. through the lens of poverty, articulating the many complex reasons that influence poverty at an individual and household level.

The aim of the activity that follows is for students to examine the underlying causes of poverty and for the teacher to address some of the stereotypes that emerge.

Activity 5.5.5
The Web of Poverty

In this activity, students are provided with name cards that represent ficti-tious people of different ages in different roles and occupations. Students are informed that collectively, these cards mirror a society in which the old people are not working, some of the young people are in school or don't have jobs, some of the people are earning lots of money, and some are earning less. The teacher informs the students that he or she will gradually introduce cer-tain situations that some people will have to alter their behavior to address. The teacher should introduce this as a dynamic game in which each group of people responds to the others group. The teacher gradually begins introduc-ing different situations. The following is a suggested list of situations:

1. The costs of health care and education rise, or certain individuals don't have access to health-care facilities when they need care.
2. Some students drop out of school or don't have access to learning opportunities.
3. There is a disaster in the country, and all of the family's assets are lost.
4. The price of food increases owing to less agricultural output.
5. Some people lose their current jobs, and thus, their families don't have money.

The teacher should stress the importance of finding a solution to the is-sue despite the constraints at hand. The aim of this is to bring to light the agency of ordinary people who may be poor.

Based on this activity, the teacher helps the students draw various intercon-nections between poverty, education, livelihoods, and access to health care and realize that poverty is a dynamic concept that evolves over time owing to the complexity of the issue at hand.

The students write a blog post about what they learned and reflect on one particular instance that influenced their way of thinking about poverty.

Note that in this simulation, the teacher should be especially careful to ensure that the students understand that anyone can become poor for reasons outside of their control and to address any emotions associated with feeling superior or "helping the poor." It's important that the students understand the complexities of poverty. The teacher can help them understand those complexities by imposing two simultaneous constraints (e.g., some people have lost their jobs, and the prices of food are escalating simultaneously, and thus, poverty impacts those without jobs even more severely).

Activity 5.5.6
The SDGs from the UDHR

For homework, the teacher asks the students if there's anything about the simulations that draws students' attention to human rights that are not being fulfilled, as articulated within the UDHR. The teacher asks the students to present their thoughts in class.

The teacher introduces the students to the SDGs, the seventeen goals of the world until 2030. Through visuals and graphics, the teacher showcases each of the seventeen goals and speaks about them.

The teacher then gives the students a sheet that lists the UDHR and the SDGs side by side and asks the children to match the two and to see which parts of the UDHR the SDGs draw from.

Use the lesson "A Global Goals Assembly" to remind the students of the SDGs (https://www.tes.com/worldslargestlesson/).

Activity 5.5.7
Children in Poverty

Here the teacher introduces SDG 1, poverty, and SDG 2, hunger. The students are asked to monitor what they eat for the next two days. During these two days, the teacher shows the children the foods that children in different parts of the world eat. (Pick a good mix from across the world and across different SES). The teacher presents a fictitious dietary chart and uses that to count the calorie counts of foods (http://www.thecaloriecounter.com/), to discuss the concept of a minimum calorie requirement, and to examine issues related to nutrition and poverty.

The students are asked to answer the following questions:

1. How long can they go without food?
2. Why is food important to them?
3. What would they do if they couldn't access food?
4. What could they not do if they didn't have access to food?

The teacher draws links between food, school attendance, learning, livelihoods, and, most importantly, good health. The teacher further elaborates on the concepts of calories, food for energy, undernourishment. Through this activity, the teacher helps the students distinguish between concepts associated with hunger, overeating, malnutrition, and starvation.

Activity 5.5.8
Escalating Food Prices and Who's Affected the Most

The teacher then divides the students into two groups, one of which will live on $1.25 a day and one of which will have a higher budget. He or she presents a scenario in which students have a defined budget, but the prices of food are escalating. The students are provided with food costs and are asked to cut out food items from their budget. They should be asked what they will choose and why. The teacher compares what the two groups can afford and what they will cut out and highlights the fact that those with a budget of $1.25 a day can barely afford anything.

Activity 5.5.9
Relation between Poverty and Hunger

The teacher then presents students with a poverty map of the world and a hunger map of the world and asks students to overlay one on the other. The students are asked to list countries that appear on both maps. The students should identify three countries that appear on both maps. The teacher will then divide the class into three groups, and each group will research one country to figure out why poverty and hunger are linked in that context. They will then share their understandings with the class. During the class discussion, the following extension questions may be asked:

1. If poverty was defined in another way, would this situation change?
2. If hunger were defined in an alternate way, how would it change?

Activity 5.5.10
What Did I See Today on My Way Home, and How Should We Treat the Poor?

In this activity, the students go back to some of the thoughts they had about the poor in activity 5. The teacher may also ask the students to re-examine their thoughts and observations in light of what they've learned thus far.

The next day in class, the teacher addresses some of these concerns and attempts to trash the stereotypes that the students have about being poor and about who they believe to be poor. The teacher then asks the students the following questions:

1. How do they think the poor should be treated?
2. What does the UDHR say about how to treat people?
3. What do respect and dignity mean in our interactions with people?

This could possibly result in a debate about different perspectives, but the teacher's aim should be to ensure that the students understand that all human beings must be treated with respect and dignity.

Unit	5.6
Topic	**Developments in South Africa**
Themes	**ICC; ethics; work and mind habits; economic development; poverty; world history; geography; comparative government; arts: literature; and analyze and assess**
Region	**South Africa**
Length	**Six weeks**

Goals and Objectives

1. **Learn** about the different methods and approaches that individuals have used to resist oppression.
2. **Inspire students** to develop an in-depth understanding of how history has shaped the current processes and forms that one sees in certain parts of the world.
3. **Act** in informed ways when referring to Africa and understand the diversity of experiences and events of South Africa in particular.

Skills and Knowledge

1. Students will understand the importance of looking at the past to examine the present.
2. Students will become aware of the different ways that individual and collective rights and freedoms can be gained.
3. Students will be well versed in the historical context of the oppressions in South Africa.
4. Students will become aware of Nelson Mandela and of his influential role in shaping the agenda for reform in South Africa.
5. Students will relate to the experiences of others, develop empathy, and articulate emotions.

Overview

This unit on South Africa is a case study on human rights, and it is particularly important to include because the social movement around human rights is based on nonviolent protest rather than on war. It is critical that students receive this alternative message within the context of the concepts of this year.

[Note that this is not a unit on African history. Important turning events in the history of South Africa have specifically been addressed so as to frame this discussion within the context of the larger theme for this year.]

Activity 5.6.1
South Africa Today

The teacher introduces this unit by showing students a map of Africa and South Africa. The teacher then shows the students some pictures of South Africa and discusses its flag, its national anthem, and some interesting facts about the country. [See http://kids.nationalgeographic.com/kids/places/find/south-africa/.) The teacher proceeds to talk about the SDGs (which students were already introduced to earlier in the year). For each of the SDGs, the students are presented with data tables and asked to answer follow-up. The following is a list of possible follow-up questions:

1. What percentage of the students are boys? What percentage of the students are girls?
2. What is the percentage of malnourished children in South Africa?
3. What is the poverty rate in South Africa?

The aim of this activity is to get students interested in and curious about South Africa. The teacher informs the students that to understand the current situation in the country, they must examine what was happening in South Africa many years ago (fifty years ago).

Activity 5.6.2
Making One's Self Heard: The Defiance Campaign of 1952, Sharpeville, and the 1960 Arrest of Mandela

The students write a petition or protest in nonviolent ways to change the situation explored in the above activity. Through this activity, the teacher introduces the students to the 1952 Defiance Campaign, in which eight thousand volunteers defied the laws by entering places that they were forbidden to enter and by not carrying their registration passes. Nelson Mandela is introduced as one of the pioneers and leaders of the movement driven forward by the African National Congress.

Activity 5.6.3
Sharpeville and the Arrest of Mandela

The students are introduced to the events that took place in Sharpeville in 1960, when sixty-seven Africans were killed while protesting against apartheid, and to the arrest of Nelson Mandela in 1961 for creating trouble in the country.

Activity 5.6.4
Collectivism versus Individualism

Students are introduced to the following lines from Mandela's speech from the dock in 1964:

> During my lifetime I have dedicated myself to the struggle of the African people. I have fought against white domination, and I have fought against black domination. I have cherished the ideal of a democratic and free society in which all persons live together in harmony and with equal opportunities. It is an ideal which I hope to live for and to achieve. But if needs be, it is an ideal for which I am prepared to die.

Using these lines, the students compare and contrast what they've learned about Africa with what they learned in the units on the American Revolution, the French Revolution, and the Haitian Revolution, which were revolutions for rights. The students are asked to post online their reflections on what these lines mean and how they differ from what they learned earlier. The teacher uses this as an opportunity to discuss with the students the ideologies of collectivism and individualism, the latter of which is represented by South Africa's struggle.

Activity 5.6.5
Twenty More Years of Apartheid[9]

Students can read one of the following two texts:

- *Journey to Jo'Burg*, which is about Mma, a character who lives and works in Johannesburg, far from the village that thirteen-year-old Naledi and her younger brother, Tiro, call home. When their baby sister suddenly becomes very sick, Naledi and Tiro know deep down that only one person can save her. Bravely, they set off alone on a journey to find Mma and to bring her back. It isn't until they reach the city that they come to understand the dangers of their country and the painful struggle for freedom and dignity that is taking place all around them (http://www.harpercollins.com/books/Journey-Joburg/?isbn=9780064402378).

Out of Bounds, which tells stories set in different decades during the last half of the twentieth century and the beginning of the twenty-first century. It features fictional characters caught up in very real events. Included is a time line across apartheid that recounts some of the restrictive laws passed during the era, the events leading up to South Africa's first free democratic

---

9 Note that details about the Soweto uprising have been deliberately removed since the uprising involved the massacre of seventy schoolchildren, which could possibly frighten fifth graders. The teacher should use discretion when deciding whether to talk about it.

elections, and the establishment of the new "rainbow government" that still leads the country today http://www.amazon.com/Out-Bounds-Seven-Stories-Conflict/dp/0060508019?ie=UTF8&*Version*=1&*entries*=0). Using the backdrop of this story and facts, students should maintain a first-person journal entry or write a blog post about what they see happening around them and how it makes them feel.

Activity 5.6.6
The Release of Nelson Mandela and the 2005 World Rugby Cup

The teacher shows the students pictures and clips from 1990, when Nelson Mandela was released after twenty-seven years of imprisonment. Students collect newspaper clippings and articles from that period, and, acting as reporters for a newspaper, trace the developments leading up 1994, when Nelson Mandela became the first black president of South Africa. Students are given the text of Nelson Mandela's momentous speech on hope and glory and are asked to pay special attentionto the last line of his speech:

> We must therefore act together as a united people, for national reconciliation, for nation building, for the birth of a new world. Let there be justice for all. Let there be peace for all. Let there be work, bread, water and salt for all. Let each know that for each the body, the mind and the soul have been freed to fulfill themselves. Never, never and never again shall it be that this beautiful land will again experience the oppression of one by another and suffer the indignity of being the skunk of the world.
> Let freedom reign.
>
> The sun shall never set on so glorious a human achievement!
>
> God bless Africa!

Time permitting, the teacher could lead a discussion about how Mandela used sports as a strategy for nation building, and selected scenes from the movie *Invictus* can be shown to the students.

Optional Activity Wavin' Flag: The FIFA 2010 World Cup

Time permitting, students are then shown K'Naan's "Wavin' Flag" song and video clips about the hype created around the FIFA World Cup in Africa. In groups, students analyze the symbolism behind each of these songs and discuss why these matter for Africa (and for South Africa in particular).

Unit	5.7
Topic	Capstone: What Can I Do?
Theme	ICC: interpersonal; ethics; work and mind habits; economic development; poverty; analyze and assess; creative communication; and the use of technology
Region	Not applicable
Length	Three weeks

Goals and Objectives

1. **Learn** that they have personal agency and can make a difference by raising awareness of an SDG that they care about and to communicate effectively and creatively.
2. **Inspire** students to see themselves as having personal agency.
3. **Act** to raise awareness of an SDG.

Skills and Knowledge

1. Students will express their thoughts and opinions regarding these human rights and understand and exhibit the behavioral competencies associated with the UDHR.
2. Students will assimilate information across various sources to communicate effectively about poverty and poverty reduction.
3. Students will create a video documentary to raise awareness of the issue of poverty and of possible solutions to it.

Overview

The students create awareness-raising projects (documentaries) to promote awareness of an SDG that they care about. They will share their work with a partner school in India or South Africa.

Activity 5.7.1
What Can I Do?

The teacher throws out a challenge to the students. The teacher says, "The poor are helpless, and I don't think I can do anything to change the situation." The teacher asks the students to challenge that statement and to pick one country as a class and one thing that they would like to focus on as they challenge the teacher's statement. The students create documentaries (shorts) to promote awareness of poverty and of their challenge. These documentaries should be shared with a sister school in India or South Africa whose students will create similar documentaries. The teacher introduces the notion of designing for change using the lesson plan on the following web page and engages students in the design of innovative approaches to tackling poverty: https://www.tes.com/worldslargestlesson/taking-action/.

Resources

- A short video on how different people will spend USD 10 (http://www.youtube.com/watch?v=M0XTPSYdP08)
- What have different people done? (http://www.youtube.com/inmyname)
- Free Rice (http://www.wfp.org/students-and-teachers/teachers)
- Publications and media resources designed for human rights education purposes (http://www.ohchr.org/EN/PublicationsResources/Pages/TrainingEducation.aspx)
- Resources for educators to teach about poverty (http://www.make-povertyhistory.org/schools/index.shtml)

Because the documentary will be shared with a sister school in India or Africa, an important component of this capstone is a study of what good communication looks like across cultures.

During the year, students looked at how people communicated ideas through songs, art, and other means during various revolutions. In particular, during the SDG unit, they looked for and researched different examples of good communication about topics relevant to the SDGs.

They now make the connection between what worked then—that is, how people were able to communicate ideas effectively during revolutions—and the new tools available and what good communication looks like today.

In this culminating unit, they examine ways to communicate about topics of interest to them by studying modern examples of communication and advocacy, including Bono's ONE Campaign, other groups' efforts, documentaries, and movies.

Guest speakers and workshops can include people working in the film, media, documentary and advocacy, videos, communication, and marketing industries in New York City.

Resources

A collection of lesson plans on this topic (this is just a short selection of the many that are available on the subject):

- http://www.educationworld.com/a_lesson/lesson/lesson158.shtml
- http://propaganda.mrdonn.org/lessonplans.html
- http://www.brighthub.com/education/k-12/articles/39376.aspx

Appendix A *Colonial Times* Instructions

This activity consists of fifty-two assignments designed to produce a newspaper in 1775.

The following are four news-story prompts to be written by twelve students (four groups of three reporters):

1. Write an article about the Stamp Act riots, explaining why the Stamp Act is not being enforced. Explain how tempers are rising as a result of the passing of the Quartering Act and the Stamp Act. Include interviews with the Massachusetts governor, Thomas Hutchinson; Andrew Oliver; and Patrick Henry. Ask the following questions (among others): Is it ever right to break the law? When you intimidate a tax collector, is that a crime? Isn't it inhumane to tar and feather someone? Do tax collectors deserve such punishment? (The important personages are Thomas Hutchinson, Andrew Oliver, and Patrick Henry.)

2. British Parliament Debates the Repeal of the Stamp Act
Based on your interviews with Benjamin Franklin and Samuel Adams, explain why the British Parliament is likely to repeal the Stamp Act. Interview Lord Dunmore about what a terrible mistake it will be for the king to display weakness toward the colonies. Interview Benjamin Franklin about what's going on in Britain. Interview Samuel Adams to find out why repealing the Stamp Act won't be enough to quell the colonial desire for independence.

(The important personages are Lord Dunmore, Benjamin Franklin, and Samuel Adams.)

3. Write a news story about the Boston massacre. Interview Captain Thomas Preston, Paul Revere, and John Adams. Write an investigative report titled "The Truth About the Boston Massacre." Discuss whether the popular Paul Revere is exaggerating what really happened and whether Preston is trying to escape blame for "losing America." You will find the truth!

(There are a few important personages. You will need to look at British sources to tell the story of the skirmish from Preston's point of view and to explain why he feels that he did nothing wrong. As John Adams, explain why you defended the soldiers in court. As Paul Revere, tell the reporter the colonists' version of events. Be prepared to talk about your famous etching and to explain why your etching isn't historically accurate.)

4. Write an account of the Boston Tea Party. Interview a colonist who wants to tell you everything about the Boston Tea Party but won't allow you to print his name because he's afraid that if you do, the British will arrest him. You can print his quotes but not his name. Also talk to Samuel Adams, find out if he's taking credit for the raid, and learn whether any Sons of Liberty have been arrested by the British.

(The important personages are your anonymous-source colonist and Samuel Adams.)

The following are two news-story prompts to be written by six students (two groups of three reporters):

1. Profile of Governor Thomas Hutchinson: Loyalist or Toady?
Write a profile about the life, times, character, and political beliefs of Hutchinson. Interview Hutchinson himself. Talk to the Reverend Jonathan Boucher about Hutchinson. Ask Boucher whether Hutchinson is being unfairly smeared, and give Boucher a

chance to defend Hutchinson. Then interview Thomas Paine about Hutchinson.

(The important persons are Hutchinson, Jonathan Boucher, and Thomas Paine. You will have to use British sources to find material sympathetic to Hutchinson for this assignment.)

2. Profile of George Washington: The Most Admired Man in America
Who is George Washington, and is he the best man to lead the fight against the British? Interview people who know him to learn whether George is as honest, brave, and smart as he's cracked up to be. And, in an exclusive interview with George Washington himself, learn his thoughts on where the British are vulnerable.

(The important personages are Augustine Washington, George's father, who can tell you about that cherry-tree story; Virginia Governor Dinwiddie, who gave Washington his first military jobs and saw him through his early successes and failures; and George Washington.)

The following is a list of fourteen historical characters. Note that two students will be assigned to some characters because those characters need to be interviewed by more than one reporter:

1. Thomas Hutchinson (two students)
2. Andrew Oliver
3. Patrick Henry
4. Lord Dunmore
5. Benjamin Franklin
6. Samuel Adams (two students)
7. John Adams
8. Captain Thomas Preston
9. Paul Revere
10. Jonathan Boucher

11. Thomas Paine
12. Anonymous-source colonist
13. Augustine Washington
14. Governor Dinwiddie

Two artists are required. One should make a drawing or a political cartoon about the Boston Tea Party, and one should make a drawing or cartoon about George Washington or Benjamin Franklin.

Four advertisements should be created:

1. A publisher's ad for Thomas Paine's *Common Sense*
2. An ad for Benjamin Franklin's old *Farmer's Almanac*
3. An ad for men's clothing or accessories. What exactly did they wear, and what did it cost? Design your own ad for wigs, boots, or anything else, but make it historically accurate.
4. An ad for women's clothing. What exactly did they wear and what did it cost? Use the guidelines listed for the previous ad.

Write two editorials:

1. "Why It's Time to Declare Independence"
2. "Stop Tarring and Feathering"

Write one op-ed using the following prompt:

Benjamin Franklin writes a first-person account of the Hutchinson Letters Affair: Why I leaked the letters, how I got into trouble with the British, why I confessed, and why I'm now coming home. I'm sorry for all the fuss, dear readers, but I thought you should know the truth.

Write the following obituaries:

1. Nathan Hale
2. Crispus Attucks

Write letters to the editor from the following people:

1. Samuel Adams
2. Patrick Henry
3. An ordinary colonist warning that unless things calm down, the colonists might be headed toward a war with the British. This colonist feels fondly toward Britain and thinks that a war would be a terrible tragedy and must be prevented.

Create an arts page with a theater review, a poetry review, an article covering sports, and an article about food. One reporter should work on each article.

Theater Review

One reporter should write a review of one of Mercy Otis Warren's plays. Tell the readers what the play is about, whether you would recommend that they attend it, and whether readers are likely to feel angry after seeing it. Tell the readers whether the actors and the playwright have received any threats. Please include information about where and when the performances are held and about how much they cost.

Poetry Review

You are the newspaper's poetry editor. Pick a poem by Phillis Wheatley that you would like to print, and write a note to the readers explaining who she is, why she is becoming famous, and why this particular poem is so important that you have decided to publish it. Please comment on the significance of the fact that she's a black woman poet at a time when most black women in the colonies are illiterate slaves.

Sports
Write an account of a rolling-of-the-hoop contest you recently covered.

Food
With all of the tea dumped into the Boston Harbor, what are the colonists drinking instead? Offer some alternate suggestions. Also, offer readers a recipe for a hearty winter meal to enjoy during a cold Boston winter based on the food that is actually available to the colonists.

The World Course
Sixth Grade: How Values and Identities Shape People and Institutions

Theme

Understanding cultural values and their impact in people's lives and in institutions and societies.

Description

In the sixth grade, students move from looking at the fight for the rights of individual people and peoples to looking at the way that values and identity shape people and institutions, including governments. After establishing norms for the classroom, the students first look at their identities and reflect on their complexities. They will read books like *The Light in the Forest* and *The Conch Bearer* to enable them to think about values and identity in another place and/or time. They will then learn about how individual choices and values play a role in the need for government and civic organizations through an examination of commons. After that, they will be introduced to civil society and to different types of civic participation, using their own identity maps as a basis for the concepts. Next, the students will do an extended comparison of governments, focusing on the United States, the United Kingdom, and China. They will read biographies of Thomas Jefferson and Alexander Hamilton to understand how their particular values helped shape American democracy. The final section deals with indigenous peoples and the complex roles they play as members of not only indigenous nations but also nation-states.

Looking Back
Freedom and the Rights of Individuals

Looking Forward
Social Movements and Change Makers

Overview of Units

1) Creating a Classroom Constitution
2) Introduction to Complex Cultural Identities: Identity Mapping
3) World Values: Organization, Respect, and Freedom
4) The Commons
5) Civil Society and Civic Participation
6) Comparative Study of the Three Branches of Government
7) Indigenous Peoples

Capstone:
The capstone is an advocacy project. The students choose a current issue and create an advocacy project around it, working with government and civil society to raise awareness or to influence policy.

Unit   6.1

Topic   Creating a Classroom Constitution

Theme   ICC: interpersonal (one's own identity and culture); ICC: intrapersonal (conflict-resolution skills); ethics: trust in institutions; knowledge: politics (government/politics and comparative government); arts: literature; and skills: global problem solving (scenario building)

Region Not applicable

Length Three lessons

Goals and Objectives

1. **Learn** the purpose of creating constitutions, their functions, and their limitations.
2. **Inspire** students to develop concrete frameworks for creating their own constitutions to help achieve the group's goals.
3. **Act** by demonstrating an understanding of and creating a classroom constitution.

Skills and Knowledge

1. Students will identify the purposes and limits of constitutions.
2. Students will judge current events as they apply to the US Constitution.
3. Students will judge constitutions and their usefulness in enabling the classroom to work together for the common goal of learning.

Overview

The purpose of this unit is to organize the classroom and to define its rules and purpose. The students will also review their summer reading, a book on the American Revolution.

Activity 6.1.1
Simulation

The students are divided into three separate governments. Each group will be given a task, but they need to complete the task under the general governing structure to which they are assigned.

Structure A is a true democracy with majority rule,

Structure B is a representative democracy in which there are five elected representatives who ultimately make the decisions.

Structure C is a monarchy in which one person makes the decision.

In all three structures, there is a constitution that states (among other things) that all people have the right to keep their property and that no property shall be seized by any other citizen or by the governing structure itself.

Now students imagine that there is an extreme shortage of textbooks. While electronic resources are one solution to the textbook shortage, many schools in the area lack computers. There are seven schools and enough books for every student in three schools to have textbooks. The teachers own the textbooks and bought them using his or her salary. How will the government structure ensure that all students can access the textbooks?

The goal is for the students to solve the problem using any one of a variety of solutions. But they must reach a consensus according to their structure, and they must not violate the constitution (unless, perhaps, they are in a monarchy, in which case they must be very careful about the population's reaction).

Students should be guided to learn that

1. A constitution provides some guidance about what one can and cannot do
2. The differing structures have clear strengths and weaknesses

3. The United States is most like structure B
4. The classroom itself might be a mixture of C and A or B (at the discretion of the teacher)

Activity 6.1.2
Summer Reading Discussion

The students discuss their summer reading book in light of the simulation above. The summer reading book should be a novel about the American Revolution, such as *My Brother Sam is Dead*, by James Lincoln Collier; *Chains*, by Laurie Halse Anderson; or *Duel in the Wilderness*, by Karin Clafford Farley. They can also refer to *Johnny Tremain*, which they read in the previous grade. They can talk about the perspectives of the Loyalists and the Patriots in each of the stories and about how their views reflect the structures that the students played out in the simulation.

Activity 6.1.3
Creation of a Classroom Constitution

With guidance from the teacher, the class will create a constitution in which

1. The purposes of the classroom (the mission) is defined
2. The governing structure of the classroom is described
3. The rights of the students and the teacher are defined
4. The obligations of the students and teacher are defined.

Unit	6.2
Topic	**Introduction to Complex Cultural Identities: Identity Mapping**
Theme	**ICC: interpersonal (diverse cultural perspectives, one's own identity and culture, others' identities and cultures, and working in intercultural teams); ICC: intrapersonal (recognizing prejudice and minimizing the effects of prejudice); ethics: religious diversity; work and mind habits: cross-cultural perspective taking, cultural change, and variation within cultural groups; and knowledge: culture (world religions and philosophical traditions)**
Area	**Not applicable**
Length	**Two weeks**

Goals and Objectives

1. **Learn** about complex identities, including the students' own identities and others' identities.
2. **Inspire** the students to reject stereotypes and useless generalizations and to see nuance and complexity in others' identities.
3. **Act** by recognizing the students' myriad roles as well as those of others and by understanding how those roles shape who people are.

Skills and Knowledge

1. Students will think about their roles in their families, their communities, and the world.
2. Students will learn abstract mapping by making identity webs.
3. Students will practice working on an intercultural team.

4. Students will practice reflecting on their own identities and on how they are influenced by (and how they influence) culture and institutions.

Overview

Students will be introduced to the idea that identities are complex, composed of many facets, and can change with context, roles, and perspectives. They will examine how their perspectives might change with different experiences, roles, and knowledge.

Activity 6.2.1
Identity Web

The teacher will model an identity web, drawing him or herself at the center of it, and then list and describe the aspects of it that are important to him or her. For example, the teacher might list his or her

1. Family roles
2. Leisure activities
3. Professional roles
4. Volunteer roles
5. Demographics (e.g., ethnicity and age)
6. Talents
7. Favorites (e.g., music, foods, art, sports teams, etc.)
8. Key experiences (experiences important to his or her identity)
9. Favorite superhero and what his/her superpower and superhero name would be if he or she were a superhero.

Next, students create their own identity webs and then share them with one another in class, commenting on what they have in common and how they differ. They then try to create a class identity web and name those items that they have in common and the ways they differ.

Students then partner with students from different parts of the world (one school from each of the BRIC countries), share their identity webs with one another, compare and contrast the different presentations, and discuss cultural similarities and differences.

Students can continue the interactions by interviewing other students from different countries. They can ask about and compare their roles and responsibilities as

- daughters or sons
- sisters or brothers (elder/younger/middle)
- students in a class
- friends
- teammates (in sports)
- other roles they might have

The students should then ask their partner what those identities mean to him or her and whether or why one means more to him or her than the others.

Unit	6.3
Topic	World Values: Organization, Respect, and Freedom
Theme	ICC: interpersonal (diverse cultural perspectives, one's own identity and culture, others' identities and cultures, working in intercultural teams, and etiquette); ICC: intrapersonal (minimizing the effects of prejudice); ethics: showing humility and respect, religious diversity, ethical frameworks, and common values; work and mind habits: innovation and creativity, cross-cultural perspective taking, cultural change, and variation within cultural groups; knowledge: culture (world religions and philosophical traditions); arts: literature; skills: analytical and investigative skills (local-global link and creative communication); and global problem solving: produce media and the use of technology
Area	India, the United States, and teacher's choice
Length	Two weeks

Goals and Objectives:

1. **Learn** about how individuals and cultures have both different and similar values.
2. **Inspire** students to explore and respect cultural differences.
3. **Act** by becoming aware of the cross-cultural variations in these values.

Skills and Knowledge

1. Students will learn about cultural values in different cultures.
2. Students will learn about how people show respect in different parts of the world.

3. Students will learn about the types of people and things that people show respect for in different parts of the world.
4. Students will practice interacting with other students from different parts of the world.

Overview

Students begin by extrapolating cultural values from the values they see demonstrated in the actions of characters in two novels, and then they try to determine the cultural values present in their own complex identities. They then share the values that they've identified with classmates in another part of the world through a discussion of respect (e.g., who it is given to, how it is given, and why). At the end of the unit, the students create a video showing how to properly greet different types of people in different countries.

Activity 6.3.1
The Conch Bearer and *The Light in the Forest*

Half of the class reads *The Conch Bearer*, by Chitra Banerjee Divakaruni, and the other half reads *The Light in the Forest*, by Conrad Richter. While they are reading the books, they should reflect on what the main characters value, how they come to value those things, and how they show that they value them. The teacher prompts the students to write journal entries using language such as "It is important for [character] to do [action] because [reason]." After each group has finished reading its book (and also periodically throughout), the two groups come together to talk about the motivations of the characters, and what values the books share. In the end, each student should write an essay about what they value most and why and about the people or institutions who shaped their values.

Activity 6.3.2
Cross-Cultural Analysis of Values

The students think not only about their personal values but also about the values that shape their society. They begin by trying to extrapolate from the two books they read the larger societal values of the Lenni-Lenape, the American frontiersmen, and those in modern India. They then conduct research to find out and compare the groups' religious views, major philosophies, and national mottoes as well as other value-based information. The teacher may want to share some of the information from the World Values Survey slides with the class to show the shift from away from religion and toward secular-rationalism as a global trend. They can discuss how the Lenni-Lenape Indians' values are different from today's values in India and how the old man is portrayed in the story about India (and how religion/spirituality can be portrayed as something from the past).
http://www.worldvaluessurvey.org/wvs.jsp

Activity 6.3.3
How Do We Show Respect?

Each student is paired with a student from another culture (an American student attending school in a Native American community, for example, or a student from another country) using a tool such as iEARN.[10] Ideally, they will have access to students from a number of different cultures (that is, the class will not be paired with students from only class but with students from different classes in different countries or cultures).

Each student (in both groups) is instructed to think of one person whom he or she respects. That person could be a politician, a historical figure, a relative, or a celebrity. The students should then write a short essay on what qualities of that person they respect and why. They then share their essays first with their own class and then with their cross-cultural partners. They will discuss similarities and differences in the essays.

Next, each student is instructed to imagine an encounter with the person he or she respects. Each student should write a second essay that describes the encounter and places special emphasis on how the student would dress, behave, and address the person; what the student would say to the person; and how the student would express respect.

Again, the students share their essays with their own class and then with their cross-cultural partners. They will discuss similarities and differences in the essays.

Activity 6.3.4
Greetings around the World

Since a resource describing greetings around the world does not appear to exist, the students will create one themselves! The students gather information

---

10 http://media.iearn.org/

on the proper way to greet someone in another culture. They each pick a culture (some may pick the same one), and they find out the proper ways to greet someone older, someone the same age, and someone very important.

They can use the Internet, travel guides, and family members and friends to collect information. They will then create a video that shows how to greet people in many different cultures.

Resources

- World Values Survey (http://www.worldvaluessurvey.org/wvs/articles/ folder_published/article_base_83)

Unit	6.4
Topic	**The Commons**
Theme	**ICC: intrapersonal (curiosity about global affairs); ethics: trust in institutions, breakdown of trust in institutions, and the importance of global compacts; knowledge: economics, trade, and demography (economic development and demography); politics: government/politics and comparative government; global risk: environment and globalization; skills: analytical and investigative skills (evaluate sources of information and the local-global link); and global problem solving: scenario building and being a critical consumer**
Area:	**Any/all, but specifically the United Kingdom and Canada**
Length:	**Five weeks**

Goals and Objectives

1. **Learn** to bring into focus the complicated and valuable relationship between individuals and their government.
2. **Inspire students to** reflect on the motivations of those who wish to increase or decrease the government's role in individuals' lives.
3. **Act by** understanding that individuals can work with their government to create healthier, more just societies.

Skills and Knowledge

1. Students will learn about the important relationship between individuals and their government by examining commons.
2. Students will learn about the tragedy of the commons and government's role in protecting the environment.

3. Students will learn about the important role that common spaces have played in allowing the free exchange of thought and criticism of governments.

4. Students will reflect on common spaces within their contexts, including on what they are used for, what value they provide, and how they are regulated.

Overview

In this unit, students learn about the commons in two different contexts. First they learn about how competing individuals' choices can result in the need for government and civil society. They will watch a documentary and play a simulation game to learn about global overfishing. Second students learn about how commons can provide a space for individual expression and particularly for demonstrations against governmental policies.

Activity 6.4.1
Film

Show the class a film about the world fisheries crisis. For example, the class can watch *The End of the Line*[11] or *Taking Stock*.[12] Ask the students to take notes on the film and to answer the following questions:

- What is the problem?
- Why is the problem hard to stop or fix?
- Who in the film do you sympathize with the most?
- What role can and should governments, international organizations, and supragovernmental organizations play in regulating commons?

---

11 Rupert, Murray (Dir.) (2009). *The End of the Line*. Arcane Pictures. Eighty-five minutes. http://endoftheline.com/

12 Markham, Nigel (Dir.) (1994). *Taking Stock*. National Film Board of Canada. Forty-seven minutes. http://www.onf-nfb.gc.ca/eng/collection/film/?id=32271

The teacher should then lead a discussion based on the reflections of the students. Ask them to imagine that they are fishermen/fisherwomen, and ask them if they think that they would be a part of the problem.

Activity 6.4.2
The Tragedy of the Commons
(Note that this activity is adapted from Alabama Learning Exchange's "The Tragedy of the Commons," by Kelly Morton.)

Using what they learned from the fisheries film, the students will try to avoid a tragedy of the commons during this simulation. The teacher will need to provide two cups (or, alternatively, two small bowls) of different colors, straws (one for every student), and a large quantity of M&M's or other similar candy. One cup will be "cup 1," and one will be "cup 2." The students are given a lab sheet. They will play several rounds of the simulation.

ROUND 1
Students need to be divided into groups of four. Each person represents the head of a household that must be fed. The only food source is a small pond that can hold only sixteen fish. The pond begins with sixteen fish and is adjusted after each round. After each round of fishing, the fish will double in number (spontaneous reproduction). Each head of a household can take as many fish as he or she wants but must take more than one to keep his or her family alive. Each head of a household can only fish for thirty seconds at a time. Cup 1 is the common pond. The straws are the fishing poles. The students try to suck fish (the M&M's or Skittles) up through the straw until they think they have a fish, and then they take the fish off of the straw (the fishing pole). The pond should be taken to the teacher after each round of fishing so that the fish can "reproduce." (Remember, each fish can double; therefore, three fish become six, and six fish become twelve, etc.). Each student will fish three times. For each round of fishing, the order should be rotated so that each head of a household gets to go first. There is to be no

talking during this round. The students are not permitted to look in the pond in this round. Complete the data table after each round of fishing.

ROUND 2

In this round there will be the common pond (cup 1, with the same rules as last time) and a private pond (cup 2, which will have one pond per student). The students can talk in this round and can look in the pond while they are fishing. It will be possible to see how many fish are available at all times. The private pond can hold only four fish. The common pond still begins with sixteen fish. Each student must take at least one fish from each pond during each round. Each student may remove as many fish as he or she wishes from each pond, as before. The fish will reproduce (they will be taken to the teacher, as they were in the last round) after this round. Complete the data table after this round of fishing. Upon completion of this round, the students should answer the questions in the "analysis" section of the lab sheet. (See the "Tragedy of the Commons" lesson plan.)

After completing this activity, the students should choose an environmental-management issue to which the idea of the tragedy of the commons is relevant. They should research the issue thoroughly, and create a multimedia presentation that is presented to the class in the form of a brochure, PowerPoint, or mock newscast.

Activity 6.4.3
The Opportunities of the Commons

The teacher explains to the students that they are shifting gears from tragedy to opportunity: they will next examine the important role that common spaces have played in history. The class will be divided into groups, and each group will be assigned a common area (e.g., a park, a common, or a square) that was influential in history. These areas could be famous or infamous for the rallies and protests held there, for the military stationed there, or for the executions or public events that occurred there. For example, students may study Boston Common, which has been used as a common grazing ground, as a public park, for public executions, and as housing for British troops during the Revolutionary War.

The students will write research reports on the important role that the space assigned to them played in the history of its region or city.

Activity 6.4.4
Contemporary Commons

This activity instructs students to be amateur anthropologists in their own community. The students are each assigned one common area in their neighborhood. They might be assigned, for example, a sidewalk, a street, a local park, the school cafeteria, or a hallway in school. They are instructed to write an investigative report that answers the following questions:

- What sorts of activities take place there?
- Who is the common area used by?
- What exchanges of culture or ideas takes place there?
- What are some of the threats to the common area? (For examples, threats could include littering, fighting, or noise.)
- Who regulates the common area, and how is that person or group effective?

They must then create some sort of exposé in the style of a nature documentary that shares with the class their assigned common area.

Unit	6.5
Topic	**Civil Society and Civic Participation**
Theme	**ICC: interpersonal (one's own identity and culture and empathy); ICC: intrapersonal (conflict-resolution skills); ethics: trust in institutions, common values, and the value of human potential; and work and mind habits: innovation and creativity**
Area	**Not applicable**
Length	**Two weeks**

Goals and Objectives

1. **Learn** what a civil society is and what social capital is.
2. **Inspire** students to build social capital in their communities and to join voluntary organizations.
3. **Act** by becoming active members of civil society.

Skills and Knowledge

1. Students study the concept of civil society and various civil-society organizations, such as unions, political parties, religious organizations, nongovernmental organizations, and community organizations.
2. Students examine the different forms of social capital.

Overview

In this unit, students will look at the roles they play in organizations and, through their experiences, learn about civil society. They will identify the organizations and groups they belong to and describe how they're governed, how membership is decided, and how differences are resolved. They will learn about different types of social capital and about why it is important.

Activity 6.5.1
What Is Civil Society?

Students turn back to their identity maps. The teacher instructs them to look for the roles they play as members of organizations. They may find that they are members of community sports leagues, churches, or volunteer groups. Once they have made note of all of their membership roles, the teacher leads the class in a discussion of those organizations. He or she asks, for example, about what organizations they belong to, the purposes of those organizations, why those organizations exist, and why the students belong to them.

The teacher then explains that these types of organizations help to form civil societies. The teacher asks the students if they can define "civil society," given the discussion they've had. Ideally, the students will decide that a civil society brings people together to do things that individuals alone cannot do and that the government does not do.

Activity 6.5.2
Student Projects

In small groups students research one organization in a civil society, its history, and its major accomplishments and examine in particular how it is organized and governed, how membership is recruited, and the patterns in the growth of its membership. These projects are then presented to the class as a PowerPoint or through the use of other media, and they lead to a discussion on the collective role of civil society in a democracy.

Activity 6.5.3
What Is Social Capital?

The teacher presents the class with a dilemma that demonstrates how much social capital each student has. The teacher should say the following: "Imagine that you are alone on the corner of Fourteenth Street and Second

Avenue[13] with no money and no cell phone, and you are carrying a large box—one that is too big for you to carry all the way home alone. What do you do?"

The students should brainstorm ideas, like visiting a friend who lives in the neighborhood, asking for help from a safe adult, or asking a cabdriver to take him or her home and to wait for payment from another adult. Once the students have generated a few plans, the teacher asks the class the following questions:

1. How did you come up with the plans?
2. How do you know they would work?
3. Who would you rely on to execute the plans?
4. How do you know that they would help?
5. How likely is it that you'll be in this situation?

After the class discusses these questions, the teacher explains to the students that all of the answers have to do with social capital. The teacher explains that "capital" means "wealth" (like money), and "social" means "having to do with people." As such, having social capital means having resources of people and know-how concerning interacting with people. The teacher refers the students to the main character in *The Light in the Forest* and explains that he has a lot of know-how when he's among the Lenni-Lenape but that he has to build new social capital when he rejoins his original community. To deepen their understanding of social capital, the students write a short essay describing the social capital that they would *miss* if they suddenly found themselves whisked off to an alien community. They may describe the lack of the language skills, the lack of an understanding of the culture, and the lack of friends and family as problems.

---

13 Use any intersection or address that is likely to be familiar to the students.

Activity 6.5.4
Bonding and Bridging Capital at School

The students are instructed to think of a small project that they could each undertake that would build social capital among the school community. For example, a student could create a new club, pledge to invite a different student to eat lunch with him or her each day, or try to get to know his or her classmates' brothers and sisters. The students should write a series of journal entries that describe this experience.

Resources

- Robert D. Putnam. (2000). *Bowling Alone*. Simon & Schuster.

Unit: 6.6
Topic: **Comparative Study of the Three Branches of Government**
Theme: **ICC: interpersonal (one's own identity and culture and others' identities and cultures); ethics: trust in institutions and commitment to equality; knowledge: culture (world history and philosophical traditions); politics: government/politics and comparative government); and arts: literature**
Area   **The United States, the United Kingdom, and China**
Length   **Twelve weeks**

Part 1
The United States

Goals and Objectives

1. **Learn** to describe the three branches of government in the United States and their functions; to describe the Constitution, its purpose, and its content; and to describe the relationship between the three branches of government and the government's relationship with the citizens.

2. **Inspire** in students a desire to reach out to representatives in the US government and to participate in organizations working within the political system.

3. **Act** by demonstrating an understanding of the three branches of government and the Constitution through an in-class assessment as well as through an application of this understanding of the respective role of each branch to a discussion of a current policy issue.

Skills and Knowledge

1. Students will describe the three branches of government in the United States and their function and describe the Constitution, its purpose, and its content.

2. Students will evaluate current events in terms of the branches of government that are involved and in terms of the constitutionality of the decisions that are made.

Overview

Students learn about the three branches of the US government and about the cultures and experiences of the individuals who helped to form the US government by reading biographies of Alexander Hamilton and Thomas Jefferson. They will study the first country case in the extended comparison of the three branches of government: the United States.

Activity 6.6.1.1
Balancing Three Branches at Once: Our System of Checks and Balances

(Note that this activity is taken from the National Endowment for the Humanities' Edsitement!)

With the class, do the four activities concerning the three branches of government listed on the NEH's "Edsitement" page (http://edsitement.neh.gov/lesson-plan/balancing-three-branches-once-our-system-checks-and-balances#sect-activities):

1. "No More King" from *Schoolhouse Rock*
2. The Colonies Complained
3. "Three-Ring Government" from *Schoolhouse Rock*
4. Accounts of Checking and Balancing

Activity 6.6.1.2
Extended Role-Playing of the Three Branches

The teacher divides the class into three groups: the executive branch, the legislative branch, and the judicial branch. Each group receives a description of its role:

The executive branch (three to five students) includes the president of the United States, the vice president, and the major departments of the government, such as the Labor Department, the Department of Defense, the State Department, and the Department of the Treasury. Each department has a leader appointed by the president. Together, all of the leaders, along with the president, the vice president, and a few other people, make up the cabinet. The job of the executive branch is to enforce the laws.

The judicial branch (three or five students—it must be an odd number) is made up of the Supreme Court and other courts, and its job is to interpret the laws.

The legislative branch (the rest of the class) is made up of Congress, which is composed of the House of Representatives and the Senate. Its job is to make the laws. Congress also decides who and what to tax and how to use tax money. Each house of Congress meets separately. However, they can come together for joint sessions.

The students must elect a president and a vice president to lead the executive branch. (If this will be too fraught a situation for the students, the teacher may randomly—or deliberately—assign roles.) The president then assigns cabinet positions to the other students in the executive branch. Students in the legislative branch group must be divided into senators and congressmen/congresswomen.

For the remainder of the unit, the teacher will ask the students in each group to think about what role their branch would play in a given situation. This can be a journaling activity as well as an independent research and essay activity.

Activity 6.6.1.3
The Constitution

The students and the teacher should read the preamble together and discuss its role as a thesis and mission statement:

We the People of the United States, in Order to form a more perfect Union, establish Justice, insure domestic Tranquility, provide for the common defense, promote the general Welfare, and secure the Blessings of Liberty to ourselves and our Posterity, do ordain and establish this Constitution for the United States of America.

The students should make a chart with the purposes of the government on one side and the purposes of the school and the classroom on the other side, using the preamble and the school's mission statement as a guide.

The teacher should lead the class in the writing of a similar thesis and a mission statement for the classroom.

The articles of the Constitution describe and list the responsibilities and limit the power of the legislative, executive, and judicial branches of government. The teacher should quickly lead the class in a discussion of the articles of the Constitution.

After the discussion, the class can be assigned reading from *The History of US Book 4: The New Nation 1789–1850*. The reading should focus on the Constitution, Thomas Jefferson, and Alexander Hamilton.

Extension of the Activity
Learning Through Dilemmas

The teacher should split the class into three groups: the legislative branch, the judicial branch, and the executive branch. (See the role-play activity in 6.6.2.) The teacher should then present each group with a dilemma, and the group should review their articles of the Constitution to determine what is constitutional. For example, the dilemma could be that an eighteen-year-old from Illinois would like to run for election in the House of Representatives as a representative of California.

Optional Extension Activity
Jefferson and Hamilton: A Debate about the Role of the New Government

Students should be divided into two groups. One group will read a book about Alexander Hamilton, and the other will read a book about Jefferson. The Hamilton group may read James Lincoln Collier's *The Alexander Hamilton You Never Knew* or Nancy Whitelaw's *More Perfect Union: The Story of Alexander Hamilton*, which discuss his youth and family and the experiences that shaped his perspective on government. The Jefferson group may read Jennifer Armstrong's *Dear Mr. President: Letters from Philadelphia Bookwork* or Russell Shorto's *Thomas Jefferson and the American Ideal*.

After reading the books, the students should prepare, for their use, a brief fact sheet on the historical background and points of view of Hamilton and Jefferson. Then in class, the teacher should lead a formal debate between the two groups. The teacher should remind the students to stick to the facts and to what they learned about these two historical figures.

They should prepare a *short skit* that depicts the debates of the original writers of the Constitution, the controversies, and the differing viewpoints of the original founders of the nation.

Activity 6.6.1.4
A Closer Look at the Three Branches

Each group from the previous exercise should research their branch of government and present to the class what they've learned. They should be able to answer these questions:

- What is the purpose of the branch?
- What are the powers of the branch?
- What are the limits to the power of the branch?
- Who can be elected to this branch, and how are some of its members appointed?

Students create a large classroom diagram of the three branches of government. The diagram should show the interactions among the three branches. It should also show how the system of checks and balances works. Teacher should consider posting these questions so that the students can refer to them in the comparative activities below.

Activity 6.6.1.5
The Amendments

The teacher will lead a general discussion on the amendments to the Constitution, their history, and the first ten (the Bill of Rights).

Each student will be given an amendment to review and to understand through research. Note that not all of the amendments should be included. The suggested amendments are the first, the fourth–the seventh, the thirteenth, the fifteenth, the nineteenth, the twenty-fourth, and the twenty-sixth. The student should keep the amendment they have been assigned secret from the other students. The student should prepare a *dilemma*, much like those in activity 1. The class should be broken into four groups. Each student will present his or her dilemma to the class, and the groups should work together to identify the amendment that addresses the dilemma and to describe a resolution based on the amendment. Consider the following example: A city has decided to allow citizens to vote only if they pay a tax. The groups should identify amendment twenty-for and describe the resolution of this dilemma. The student who prepared this amendment should then explain the history of the amendment, why it was put in place, and what protections it affords.

Activity 6.6.1.6
Current Events and the Three Branches of Government

Students should research current events and how the three branches of government interact with the events. They should do this in groups of two to three. At this point, the teacher should stress that not all new laws become amendments to the Constitution (e.g., the No Child Left Behind Act, the National School Lunch Program, and the Affordable Care Act).

For example, the students can read Sam Dillon's "Education Secretary May Agree to Waivers on 'No Child' Requirements," which appeared on June 12, 2011, in the *New York Times*. The students can discuss the role of the education secretary (who is appointed by the president and a member of the executive branch) and the role of Congress in creating (and overhauling) No Child Left Behind.

Other topics that they may want to pursue include privacy, freedom versus security, immigration, and freedom of expression and speech.

PART 2
The United Kingdom

Goals and Objectives

1. **Learn** to describe the three branches of government in the United Kingdom and their functions, to describe common law and the lack of a written constitution (as compared to the United States), and to describe the purposes of modern monarchies.
2. **Inspire** in students an appreciation for governing systems very much like our own but different in key ways.
3. **Act** by demonstrating an understanding of the three branches of government in the United Kingdom and of the functions of a modern monarchy through an in-depth study of UK governance and history

Skills and Knowledge

1. Students will describe the three branches of government in the United Kingdom and their functions, describe common law and the lack of a written constitution (as compared to the United States), and describe the purposes of modern monarchies.
2. Students will identify key points in British history, particularly those that pertain to the creation of the modern governing structure.
3. Students will describe the system of common law in the United Kingdom and compare it to the US Constitution.
4. Students will compare very similar systems and highlight the key differences in them.
5. Students will evaluate the two systems for their respective opportunities and challenges.
6. Students will extend their knowledge of the United Kingdom's monarchy to other European monarchies.

Overview

In this unit, students will examine the second case in the extended comparison of governments: the United Kingdom and its constitutional monarchy.

[Note that at this point, the students have studied the three branches of government in the United States and should have developed some analytic tools that will help them move on to an analysis of the three branches in the United Kingdom more independently. As a method of engagement, the unit starts with biographical studies of historical and modern monarchs.]

Activity 6.6.2.1
King George III of England

The teacher will review the life of King George III of England. This will be a review for most who have studied the American Revolution (in the fifth-grade World Course), but the teacher should be prepared for students to need more review or for those who have transferred to the school to be unfamiliar with King George III.

Students (in groups) should be given a variety of choices of ways to summarize their knowledge of King George III. They could, for example, write a play, compose a letter from King George to George Washington, or write an editorial for the *Colonial Times* newspaper as King George III.

Individually, students should research historical and modern monarchs. Ideally, the students will be given many choices from which to choose, but try to have as many students researching modern monarchs as historical monarchs. They should "become" this monarch and present themselves with a brief introduction summarizing who they are, what time period they are from, some of the challenges they faced, and their power or the limits to their power (if any). They then can take questions from the other students.

Activity 6.6.2.2 (One Week)
The Three Branches of Government and the Modern Monarchy in the United Kingdom

In small groups, students should complete independent research projects on the subject of the three branches of government and the modern monarchy in the United Kingdom. They should be able to answer these key questions as well as to provide additional details:

1. When was the current system in the United Kingdom formed? For what purposes was it formed? In what historical context was it formed?
2. What are the powers of each branch of government?
3. What are the limits to the power of each branch?
4. What is the role of the monarchy? What is the power of the monarchy, and what are the limits to the power of the monarchy?

Students should research a current event in the United Kingdom and examine how that event is affected by the three branches and the monarchy as part of their analysis.

The teacher should discuss with the students the lack of a constitution in the United Kingdom and how the system of common law is similar to and different from a constitution.

Activity 6.6.2.3
Comparison between the United States and the United Kingdom

The students should create a chart comparing the powers and the limits to the powers of the three branches in the United States and the United Kingdom. They should use this chart to write a one-page essay on the similarities and differences in the branches of government of the two nations. This essay should be considered a draft, as a more formal essay will be written after the next unit is completed.

Part 3
China

Goals and Objectives

1. **Learn** to describe the three branches of government in China and their functions and to compare how the three branches function in a communist regime with how they function in other systems.
2. **Inspire** in students an appreciation for governing systems very much like our own to inspire cooperation with China.
3. **Act** by demonstrating an understanding of the three branches of government and by comparing those of the United States and China.

Skills and Knowledge

1. Students will describe the three branches of government in China and their functions and compare how the three branches function in a communist regime with how they function in other systems.
2. Students will identify key points in Chinese history, particularly those that pertain to the creation of the modern governing structure.
3. Students will evaluate key differences between the three branches as they operate in China.
4. Students will compare dissimilar systems and highlight the key differences.
5. Students will evaluate multiple systems for their respective opportunities and challenges.

Overview

In this unit, students will examine the third case in the extended comparison of governments: China.

Activity 6.6.3.1
The Three Branches of Government in China

The teacher should lead a discussion about the three branches of government in China as a general introduction to the topic. The students then conduct their own research projects on the three branches and how they operate. The students should present these projects to the class.

The teacher should split the class into three parts (the three branches). Current events in China should be presented to the class, and the groups should be given time to develop an idea of how their branch of government is interacting with the events. They should also answer the following questions about their branch:

Who makes decisions?
What powers do each branch have in this case?
What are the limits to the power of the branches?
How do the three branches function together?
What are the limits to civilian action?

Activity 6.6.3.2
A Final Comparison

The teacher should guide the students in adding China to the comparison chart of the United States and the United Kingdom. Once all of the students have a complete chart, they should use their chart to finish the comparative essay begun in the previous unit. This essay should be a formal writing assignment.

As an extension, students could also compare the governing systems in the United Kingdom and Japan.

Resources

- The US Constitution (http://www.archives.gov/exhibits/charters/constitution.html)
- Federal Resources for Educational Excellence (http://free.ed.gov/subjects.cfm?subject_id=19)
- Teaching With Documents (http://www.archives.gov/education/lessons/constitution-workshop/)
- Teaching American History (http://teachingamericanhistory.org/)
- The Constitution of the Republic of China (http://www.taiwan-documents.org/constitution01.htm)
- UK Parliament (http://www.parliament.uk/about/how/role/parliament-government/)
- UK Government (http://www.direct.gov.uk/en/index.htm)

Unit	6.7
Topic	**Complex Identities: Code Talkers**
Theme	**ICC: interpersonal (diverse cultural perspectives, one's own identity and culture, others' identities and cultures, and empathy); ICC: intrapersonal (recognizing prejudice, minimizing the effects of prejudice, and conflict-resolution skills); ethics: showing humility and respect, trust in institutions, breakdown of trust in institutions, commitment to equality, the value human potential, and commitment to supporting human rights; work and mind habits: cross-cultural perspective taking, cultural change, and variation within cultural groups; knowledge: economics, trade, and demography (economic development and poverty); culture: world history; and investigative and analytical skills: evaluate sources of information and use evidence**
Region	**United States and Mexico**
Length	**Four weeks**

Goals and Objectives

1. **Learn** about the role that some indigenous cultures are playing in the fight for the environment.

2. **Inspire** students to reflect upon the power of the disenfranchised, the importance of land, what constitutes a "good" life, and the role of governments and corporations.

3. **Act** by identifying major actors and groups in the indigenous environmental movement and by recognizing that "traditional" lifestyles can also be dynamic, modern, and prosperous.

Skills and Knowledge

1. Students will learn about different indigenous communities that are fighting to preserve the environment. They learn what they call themselves, where they are located, some of their major traditions and philosophies, and the history of their pursuit of environmental rights.
2. Students will become aware of governments' and business' perspectives on land use and their benefits and costs.
3. Students will understand notions of sovereignty, colonialism, exploitation, and segregation.
4. Students will have an understanding of the important roles that indigenous people play today—and not just within a historical context.
5. Students will know the power of the figures who have become symbols in indigenous-rights disputes.

Overview

In this unit, students prepare to learn about Navajo code talkers by examining injustice in their own lives. They further learn about sovereignty and identity by doing research projects on other indigenous groups.

Activity 6.7.1
Unfairness and Me

In this activity, students will tell a three-minute-long personal story of a time when they were treated unjustly or unfairly. Students should make the narrative interesting and answer the following questions:

- Why do you think that you treated unfairly?
- What do the concepts of fairness and justness mean to you?
- How could amends be made?

The story should be a personal one that touched the student in some way.

Activity 6.7.2
Code Talkers

In this activity, students are taken back through history by exploring the web page "Native Words, Native Warriors," . (See http://www.nmai.si.edu/education/codetalkers/.) Students are introduced to the American Indian code talkers in the First World War. Students write an op-ed that answers the following questions:

- What was the role of the American Indian code talkers (From the Navajo community)?
- Was the treatment of the code talkers and the lack of recognition of them after the war fair or unfair?
- What were some of the difficulties they had in finding jobs after returning from the war? How do you think leaving their native communities (which many had to do) affected them?
- Why did it take until 2000 for them to get recognition?
- What are the other ways beyond medals that the code talkers could be honored, respected, and remembered?

Activity 6.7.3
Sovereignty

This particular unit begins with a simulation wherein the teacher divides the students into groups representing nationalities (fictitious ones or real ones based on the nationalities of the students). Each group is asked to come up with a list of things common to its culture. Such a list could include the language used at home, the customs and festivals, and art and other forms of cultural expression.

The teacher then systematically introduces some situations in which certain groups are marginalized and are not allowed to express their freedoms and their culture in specific ways or are denied essential rights. The teacher asks the students to reflect on whether that practice is fair or unjust (and why), on how it makes them feel, and on how amends could be made.

Next the teacher introduces the concepts of sovereignty and indigenous people's right to sovereignty. Students are split into groups, and each group compares its own country case and eventually presents to the class on the case of Indigenours Rights in Mexico and the United States. In their presentations, the groups should answer the following questions in particular:

- Do the constitutions of each of the nations provide for the right to sovereignty?
- When did the right to sovereignty come into place?
- What are some of the provisions of it?
- How many recognized tribal governments exist in each country?
- Are there official reservations recognized by each of the governments?
- Is there a government agency or department that specifically looks into the affairs of indigenous people in each of the countries?
- What are the rights and benefits of tribes? Are there differences in their rights from state to state? (There are in the case of the United States.)

Students will analyze the census of Mexico, which reports not only racial ethnicity but also political ethnicity as way to recognize the indigenous people in the country

Activity 6.7.4
Taking Sides
(Note that this could be an optional activity based on the availability of time and the interest of the class. Alternatively, it could be included in activity 5, which concerns comparisons.)
In this activity, students will be introduced to the background of the Zapatista rebellion in Mexico in 1994. Students will be divided into groups wherein they will get information about the Puebla Panama Plan and the criticism around it in 2001. One group will represent the government of

Mexico and will defend the economic gains from this investment, and the other will represent the indigenous groups.

Activity 6.7.5
Comparisons

In this unit, students conduct in-depth background research, using a number of online resources, the census, and newspaper articles, students compare the status of indigenous people in the United States and Mexico.

- Students should discuss socioeconomic indicators, like access to health services, jobs, and education and graduation rates. (Students could compare New York City to Mexico City if data is available for Mexico City.)
- Students should describe the languages spoken in schools. (In Mexico, the Law of Linguistic Rights of the Indigenous People recognizes sixty-two indigenous languages as "national languages," which have the same validity as Spanish in all territories in which they are spoken. For the United States, study the 1990 Native Americans Language Act and the story of boarding schools in the United States.)
- Students should discuss the amount of recognized indigenous tribes in each of the countries.
- Students should discuss reports of racism in both countries.

Activity 6.7.5
Reporting on the UN Declaration on the Rights of Indigenous Peoples

In this unit, students are introduced to the basis of the UN Declaration on the Rights of Indigenous Peoples. In particular, students will examine the case of the United States and why it signed the declaration only in 2007. The teacher may also present portions of the UDHR to bring the concept back later this year and to encourage debate about the universality of the UDHR, given some of the previous instances of exclusion of indigenous peoples from human rights legislation.

Students are introduced to some of the proceedings of the 2010 White House Tribal Nations Conference and to President Obama's designating November 2010 as National Native American Heritage Month.

Students create and post online a video of an interview with a Native American tribe member brought into the classroom as a guest. They can ask for the guest speaker's perspectives on the challenges that his or her tribe continues to face in dealing with government authorities.

Resources

- http://www.pbs.org/circleofstories/wearehere/culture_gallery.html
- http://www.pbs.org/circleofstories/educators/lesson2.html
- http://www.culturalsurvival.org/ourpublications/csq/article/indigenous-rights-and-self-determination-mexico

Theme

Understanding the power of ordinary citizens to improve society and the world.

Description

This year expands the concept of organizing to include the concept of taking an organization and creating a movement. Individuals who have been instrumental in furthering voting rights, human rights, and environmental movements are studied, and their roles as uniters and collaborators are emphasized, as real change makers inspire and work with others—they don't go it alone. Students will learn about gender equity and equality, people who are trying to create a fundamental shift in global energy policy, and the role of inventors in bringing social change. Throughout the year, they will work on an extended service-learning project to bring their study of movements to life, and the year culminates in a socially conscious business-plan exercise that will be implemented in the eighth grade.

Looking Back

How Do People in Societies Organize Themselves?

Looking Forward
Movement and People: A View from Thirty Thousand Feet

Overview of the Units

1. Organizing a Just Community: Stranded Island
2. Governance
3. The UDHR and the SDGs
4. Introduction to a Yearlong Service-Learning Project
5. The Civil Rights Movement and Change Makers
6. SDG 5: Gender and Equity
7. The Environmental Movement: Energy Change Makers
8. Inventors as Change Makers
9. Social Entrepreneurship Business-Plan Exercise

Capstone
Drawing on the principles of design thinking and of creation of business plans for social enterprises, students develop a project that is aligned with one of the Sustainable Development Goals.

Unit   7.1
Topic   **Introduction and Classroom Organization**
Theme   **ICC: interpersonal (working in intercultural teams); work and mind habits: innovation and creativity; and ethics: common values**
Region   **Any/all**
Length   **One week**

Goals and Objectives

1. **Learn** about membership in society, to organize toward attaining some kind of common goal, and to reflect on their own practices and interactions with one another.
2. **Inspire** students to reflect on their own practices and interactions with one another in order to create a well-functioning classroom and a positive classroom environment.
3. **Act** by collectively working toward sustaining and enabling a positive classroom environment.

Skills and Knowledge

1. Students will discuss what it means to have a functioning, "good" community in the classroom, their own roles in the classroom, and the role of fair procedures and processes in the classroom.
2. Students will learn about the process of voting.
3. Students will experience the process of organizing themselves.
4. Students will learn about themselves and one another, particularly about their leadership qualities.

Overview

In this unit students are given an overview of the year so that they will be aware of the focus of the units as well as of the big picture that emerges when studying these various pieces. Students partake in a voting process to understand the nuances behind it and to understand that voting is a way to elect leaders and to organize themselves toward a common goal. Students specifically organize themselves with little direction from the teacher and in the process are asked to reflect on the team dynamics and the differences that play out.

Activity 7.1.1
Road Map of the Year

The first activity serves as an introduction to and an overview of the year and its key ideas and activities. This is a teacher-led activity, and it provides students with a road map of what to expect during the year so that they can be aware of the big-picture theme of the year.

Activity 7.1.2
Who Am I?

Students will introduce themselves by composing and then reading aloud short "I am" poems based on the resource given below. This link contains a sample of a typical "I am" poem and will help students articulate their own identity and help the class identify common themes in their collective identity.

Resources

The I Am Poem that relates to students' identities (http://score.rims.k12. ca.us/score_lessons/symbols_freedom/pages/i_am_poem.html)

Activity 7.1.3
Organizing Ourselves

(Note that there are three variations of this activity and that the teacher may choose to pick one or a combination of all three. Each option is different in that each approaches the concepts associated with organizing ourselves as individuals and as a larger collective in a different way.)

OPTION A

1) On the second or third day, students will come into the classroom and find the teacher holding a sign that says "I will not be speaking today. All of the instructions for today will be shown on the projector screen." The projector screen will say the following:

   a. We were on a class field trip to Fiji when our plane suddenly crashed onto a deserted island. Unfortunately, none of the teachers or adult chaperones survived. Take thirty minutes to organize yourselves, and decide the following:

      i. how you will make decisions

      ii. how to obtain food, water, and shelter

      iii. what you will do to be rescued and how you plan to be rescued

      iv. any other concerns you might have

   b. The teacher stands or sits in the back and takes notes. Once the group has come to some consensus, he or she will put up the following instructions:

      i. "Divide yourselves into five groups. Using only the items in the classroom/backpack, each group should build a tower. You have five minutes."

   c. After five minutes, the teacher will put up the following instruction:

      i. "Now do one thing to a tower that belongs to another group."

    d. For homework, students reflect on the day's activities and answer the following questions:

        i. What did you learn about yourself and your classmates?

        ii. Was what happened realistic? Why or why not?

        iii. If you were stranded on the island with your classmates for six months, would you be concerned? Why or why not?

        iv. What did you like about the way the group organized itself? Why? What didn't you like about it? Why? How would you have done things differently?

        v. Who assumed leadership? How?

        vi. Do you have other reflections about today's activity? If so, what are they?

2) The following day, the class will debrief the activity and discuss the reflection questions, noting uses of power and authority, decision-making processes, leadership, democratic participation (or lack thereof), destructive tendencies (or lack thereof), and so on. This activity will be referred to during the rest of the year and can be revisited every few weeks, with variations. (For example, before the unit on the women's movement, set up the same scenario, but say that only the girls can vote on decisions or lead. Note, though, that some of these variations can create conflict and will need to be managed tactfully by the teacher.)

OPTION B

Students will reflect on good and bad classroom experiences and brainstorm on what could have led to those experiences (e.g., student and teacher characteristics, procedures, processes, etc.). They will discuss and come to an agreement on the behaviors and norms they want to practice and see practiced in this year's classroom.

1) Students will be given selected quotations about citizenship and will discuss what it means to be a good citizen in a classroom.

Resource

The following web page contains quotes by famous eminent political leaders going back in time regarding the value of citizenship and its importance in a functioning civil society: http://www.sos.wa.gov/elections/mock/lessonplans/2010/Lesson%201-%20 Citizenship.pdf

2) Students will hold elections to elect three people to represent them for the first six to twelve weeks in decisions made about classroom proceedings. Students can nominate each other or themselves, and each nominee will give a short platform speech. The idea is that elections should be held every six to twelve weeks and that the election process should become more elaborate as they learn more about political processes.

  a. This activity will be referred to during the rest of the year and can be revisited with variations in different units.

      i. For example, before the unit on the civil rights movement, the teacher can say that only students wearing a certain type or color of clothing can vote on that day's decisions.

Option C

1) Introduce the concepts of membership, inclusion, exclusion, and responsibility, and pick any applicable Facing History and Ourselves lesson. The teacher can choose from a variety of different lesson plans that focus on membership in society from the Facing History database (https://www.facinghistory.org/educator-resources).

Resources

1) Stranded on an island activity (http://www.fsec.ucf.edu/en/education/k-12/curricula/bpm/lessons/lesson01/L1_act_stranded.htm)

2) Stranded on an island activity with an emphasis on economics and distribution of resources (http://www.lessonplanspage.com/SSSurvivalStranded45.htm)

Unit	7.2
Topic	Governance
Theme	Ethics: trust in institutions, breakdown of trust in institutions, ethical frameworks, commitment to equality, and valuing human potential and ICC: intrapersonal (minimizing the effects of prejudice and conflict-resolution skills)
Region	United States, Brazil, and India
Length	Four weeks

Goals and Objectives

1. **Learn** about the history of voting in the United States, the expansion of the right to vote to include both genders and all races, and the right to vote across different cultures.
2. **Inspire** students to feel compelled to vote when they reach majority, to feel excited about their voting future, and to encourage others both personally and through collective action to vote
3. **Act** by demonstrating an understanding of the voting process through an accurate historical analysis and through the creation of a narrative for the purposes of a campaign.

Skills and Knowledge

1. Students will identify the key elements of movements to expand the right to vote (to women and to minorities), including the change makers in each movement.
2. Students will describe voting movements in other cultures.
3. Students will appreciate the nuances of voting and understand that "free and fair elections" are a fundamental tenet of a functioning democracy.

4. Students will identify and articulate the methods used by change makers to bring to the forefront universal adult suffrage.
5. Students will create a voting campaign and examine its nuances.

Overview

This unit seeks to provide students with an understanding of suffrage. Through the cases of various suffrage movements in the United States, students will examine issues associated with prejudice and inequality and begin to understand why voting is crucial to establishing legitimacy in a functioning democracy. The examples then extend to include different parts of the world where suffrage has been emphasized in both historical as well as more contemporary contexts. Students are familiarized with change makers in the US suffrage movements and the methods that they used. Students also examine the ways that voting is being promoted in different parts of the world. The activities aim to create excitement and ownership around the students' responsibility to vote when they come of age.

(Note that this entire unit on governance is divided into three parts, with suggested activities in each part. Part three can be optional depending on how much time is left.)

Part One
Suffrage in the United States

Activity 7.2.1
Warm-Up and Introduction to Suffrage Movements

The teacher gives each student a card with his or her "identity" on it. These identities should vary by race, age and gender. Almost all of the cards should represent people with the right to vote in a state or federal election. Include around one card whose identity is seventeen years old and around one card whose identity is a non-naturalized immigrant. Make sure that only two or three students have identities that would have allowed them to vote in 1790. Have all of the students stand up.

Then say the following: "The year is [current year]. All citizens of eighteen years of age or older have the right to vote. If you do not have the right to vote, please sit down."

(The seventeen-year-old and the non-naturalized immigrant sit down.)

Then introduce the following scenarios:

"The year is 1919. Women are not allowed to vote. Native Americans are not US citizens and are not allowed to vote." (In 1920 the nineteenth amendment was enacted and guaranteed women the right to vote; both male and female citizens can vote. In 1924 Native Americans were granted citizenship and the right to vote.)

"The year is 1869. African American citizens, though have been free since the Civil War ended, are not allowed to vote." (In 1870 the fifteenth amendment was enacted and gave former slaves the right to vote; adult *male* citizens of any race could then vote.)

"The year is 1849. If you do not own property, you are not allowed to vote."
(In 1850 the requirement that voters own property and pay taxes was lifted.)

"The year is 1790. Only white male property owners can vote."

Activity 7.2.2
Understanding the History of the Right to Vote in the United States

The teacher splits the class into four groups. Each group researches one of the following suffrage movements: women's suffrage, African Americans' suffrage, voting rights based on property (the lifting of property requirements), and Native Americans' suffrage.

Each group should undertake its research based on the following questions:

1. What were the arguments for and against suffrage?
2. Do you believe those arguments were justifiable?
3. Why did the right to vote not extend to these groups in particular?
4. What methods were used by each of the groups to bring their cause to the forefront?
5. How does the granting of the right to vote to each of these groups affect citizens' right to vote today?

   (Note that the students can analyze data on demographics from the US Census Bureau's site to examine the trends in elections in the United States over time:
   http://www.census.gov/hhes/www/socdemo/voting/publications/p20/2008/tables.html)

Based on this information, each group presents its analysis to the class, and the class creates a time line of the history of suffrage in the United States.

Resources

1. A sample lesson plan on understanding voting rights in a historical context and on the ways in which a historical time line of suffrage in the United States can be created (http://www.history.org/history/teaching/enewsletter/volume4/september05/teachstrategy.cfm)
2. The American Memory Time Line, which represents historical facts about each of these suffrage movements and includes primary documents that students can use in their research (http://www.loc.gov/teachers/classroommaterials/presentationsandactivities/presentations/timeline/)
3. A high-quality lesson plan on women's suffrage and a background on their voting rights (http://edsitement.neh.gov/lesson-plan/voting-rights-women-pro-and-anti-suffrage#sect-introduction)

Activity 7.2.3
Change Makers in the Suffrage Movement

Each group should identify change makers in each suffrage movement. Each member of the group should research one change maker and create a short biography on his or her life based on some of the following questions:

1. Who is the change maker and what is his or her background?
2. Why did the change maker take responsibility in the suffrage movement?
3. What were some of the challenges that he or she faced, and how did he or she overcome them?
4. Were the methods used by the change maker justified? Did the means justify the ends?
5. Are these same methods relevant today?

An alternative to this is for each student to take on the persona of the change maker he or she chose to study. There should be one change maker from each suffrage movement in a new group. This group will have a round-table discussion, and each will present the story of his or her life. Other group members should ask him or her questions (meaning that this shouldn't be a round-robin presentation but a conversation).

Resources

1. A multimedia- and story-based introduction to the works of Elizabeth Cady Stanton and Susan B. Anthony that explains their roles in the suffrage movement
(http://www.pbs.org/stantonanthony/)
2. The last two books in this list (http://www.the-best-childrens-books.org/suffragette-movement.html)

Part Two
The Expansion of the Right to Vote in Other Countries and the use of the United Nations' Universal Declaration of Human Rights to advance human rights

Activity 7.2.4
Universal Adult Suffrage in the World

In this activity, students are divided into various groups in which they examine the differences in universal adult suffrage across the world at different points in time. Students may be divided by time periods or by regions of the world, and they will create a brief profile explaining who was excluded in their time period or country prior to adult suffrage and then present the profile to the class.

Examples may include the case of Brazil, where priests were excluded from the right to vote, and the events that led to formal universal suffrage in India (e.g., the creation of the Indian constitution after independence).

Resources

1. This table of universal suffrage by country, which the students can use to examine the discrepancies between male and female suffrage across the world
   http://en.wikipedia.org/wiki/Universal_suffrage
2. Recent news items associated with granting women the right to vote in the UAE and Kuwait as recently as 2005
3. An excellent site that includes lots of child-friendly information about women's role in political participation across the world through different case studies and a time line of different suffragist movements across the world to ensure that suffrage is inclusive of women
   http://womenshistory.about.com

Activity 7.2.5
Universal suffrage through the UDHR

The students are introduced to article 21 of the UDHR and particularly to section 3: "The will of the people shall be the basis of the authority of government; this will shall be expressed in periodic and genuine elections which shall be by universal and equal suffrage and shall be held by secret vote or by equivalent free voting procedures."

The following key ideas (among others) should be highlighted in this discussion:

- the will of the people and the authority of government
- genuine and free and fair elections
- universal and equal suffrage
- secret vote

Resources

1. Subarticle 3 of article 21 in the UDHR (http://www.un.org/en/documents/udhr/index.shtml#a23)

Part 3
Voting Campaigns

Activity 7.2.6
Voting Trends

(Note that this activity can be optional depending on how much time is left.)

In the computer lab, students compile voter-turnout data over time.

Students create a spreadsheet with voter-turnout rates for presidential elections in Brazil, India, and the United States. It will immediately become obvious that the voter-turnout rate in the United States is far lower than those of Brazil and India.

The teacher should lead a discussion around the students' reactions to this information. (In the seventh grade, some of the theories around why voting has decreased may be too complicated, but some of the primary theories concerning social capital, apathy, and levels of trust among different populations can be discussed.)

Resource

1. Source of data for examining voting trends (http://www.idea.int/vt/ country_view.cfm?CountryCode=IN)

Activity 7.2.7
Promoting Voting

Students research different organizations that aim to increase voter turnout. Suggested resources are listed below.

1. Rock the Vote, a campaign started to promote greater youth engagement in elections and to create an ownership in. the political processes in the United States (http://www.rockthevote.org/)
2. Project Vote (http://projectvote.org/?gclid=CM-v2cWc9aYCFQF M5QoddRJVBg)
3. Native Vote, a voting campaign run by the National Congress of American Indians (http://www.nativevote.org/)
4. You Don't Need a Home to Vote, a campaign to increase voting in the homeless population (http://www.nationalhomeless.org/projects/vote/index.html)

Students should spend time perusing these and other websites. They should then decide on one in particular to research in depth. Students will create a media documentary or write a paper that uses information from their research to encourage voter turnout.

Unit	7.3
Topic	**Universal Declaration of Human Rights, Change Makers Who Have Expanded Rights, and an Overview of the SDGs**
Theme	**Work and mind habits: variation within cultural groups; ethics: trust in institutions, humility and respect, ethical frameworks, the value of human potential, and the importance of global compacts; ICC: intrapersonal (recognizing prejudice and minimizing the effects of prejudice); and globalization**
Region	**Developing world**
Length	**Three weeks**

Goals and Objectives

1. **Learn** about the universality and centrality of needs and rights as an expression of ensuring that universal human needs are met. Students also learn about the SDGs and their role in ensuring that rights are guaranteed.
2. **Inspire** students to take action to preserve human dignity for other children in the world and to reflect on how their own actions can make a difference in the arena.
3. **Act by** demonstrating an understanding of and an appreciation for rights and by behaving in ways that are mutually respectful and preserve human dignity.

Skills and Knowledge

1. Students will identify the differences and commonalities in needs across the world and understand the importance of rights.
2. Students will understand and appreciate the concepts of dignity, equality, nondiscrimination, and justice.

3. Students will develop trust, see value in the UDHR as a normative framework, and become familiar with its history.
4. Students will personalize the principles enshrined in the UDHR and the importance of responsibilities in upholding these rights.
5. Students will draw linkages between the UDHR and the SDGs.
6. Students will become inspired to develop an action orientation and to infuse HR principles and themes within their service-learning projects as well as within their day-to-day actions in class

Overview

Students begin with an understanding of needs and wants, and through exchanges with peers, they seek the centrality of human needs. They are familiarized with a brief history of the UDHR and with its value as a normative framework in protecting the rights of all people. It also stresses the responsibility of individuals to embody these HR principles in their day-to-day lives and actions. Links and associations are also drawn with the SDGs so that students can see the SDGs as an expression of the rights themselves.

Activity 7.3.1
Needs, Wants, and Scarcity of Resources

Students connect with their pen pals or existing sister schools and exchange information regarding what they currently need to lead full lives. Students then draw a laundry list of needs and wants in different parts of the world. The teacher facilitates a discussion with the class concerning the following questions:

1. What are needs?
2. What are wants?
3. Are there similarities and differences between the two?
4. What are some differences and similarities in needs and wants across the world?

The teacher then asks the students to consolidate all of the lists together to form one list and to identify the most important needs.

(Note that the teacher should also play the role of the devil's advocate and get the students to defend their stances about their needs. The aim of this exercise is for the students to learn to work collaboratively through their differences and conflicts. Through this, the teacher should also be able to facilitate an understanding that resources on the earth are limited, that sometimes, there can be a scramble for resources, and that countries may want to prioritize certain needs over others.)

Resource

A list of needs identified by children in Ethiopia, South Africa, Lebanon, and the United Kingdom that has been created for schools in the United Kingdom but can be easily adapted for the purposes of this activity (http://www.oxfam.org.uk/education/resources/developing_rights/files/lesson2_the_next_generation.pdf)

Activity 7.3.2
Introduction to the UDHR

The teacher introduces the students to the UDHR and provides the class with a brief history of it using the resources listed below

(Note that since the Second World War has not been covered yet, the teacher should avoid going into in-depth detail about the war as a critical point for necessitating the UDHR. Instead the focus should be on the UDHR as an articulation and expression of humanity that works toward respecting and preserving the rights and dignity of one another.)

Students then undertake a text analysis of the preamble of the UDHR as well as of article 1 of the UDHR using a child-friendly version of it (listed under resources).

Resources

1. Excerpts from these two animated films about the story of the UDHR and what it embodies:
   (http://www.youtube.com/watch?v=hTlrSYbCbHE&feature=player_embedded
   http://www.youtube.com/watch?v=oh3BbLk5UIQ&feature=related)
2. Child-friendly text of the UDHR (the first two pages) (http://www.eycb.coe.int/compasito/chapter_6/pdf/1.pdf)

Activity 7.3.3
The UDHR and the SDGs

(There are two options for this, and the teacher may use both or either one based on the existing levels of knowledge about the SDGs in the class.)

OPTION A

Students are asked to undertake a background study about the SDGs and to write a biographical sketch of the SDGs that answers the following questions about it:

1. When were the SDGs introduced? Why?
2. What are the goals of the SDGs? What do the SDGs represent collectively?
3. When are the SDGs to be achieved by?
4. Are all of the SDGs equally important, or do you believe that one may be more important than the others?

Students examine the SDGs and the UDHR side by side and draw out any overlaps between the two documents. Students are asked to articulate any direct or indirect linkages that they find between the two.

Students read the following comic book on the SDGs: https://www.tes.com/worldslargestlesson/read-comic-book/

The teacher reviews the SDGs using the lesson "A Global Goals Assembly" (https://www.tes.com/worldslargestlesson/).

(Note that the teacher should facilitate the discussion so that students understand the SDGs as an expression of rights and the achievement of the SDGs as a fulfillment of the most basic HRs enshrined in the UDHR to ensure that the dignity of all individuals is upheld.)

OPTION B

The teacher may choose to pick excerpts from reports that draw linkages between the UDHR and the SDGs.

The students can also map out countries where HR violations are common, identify the progress of the SDGs in those countries, and examine whether there are any associations between the progress of the SDGs and those violations.

Resources

- Excerpts from the 2000 *UN Human Development Report* (http://hdr.undp.org/en/reports/global/hdr2000/)
- Excerpts from the UN *Human Development Report* on the SDGs http://hdr.undp.org/en/reports/global/hdr2003/
- *The State of the World's Human Rights*, Amnesty's annual report http://www.amnesty.org/en/annual-report/2011
- Sustainable development goals (http://www.un.org/sustainabledevelopment/sustainable-development-goals/)
- Sustainable Development Goals progress tracker and relevant statistics (http://unstats.un.org/unsd/mdg/Host.aspx?Content=Products/ProgressReports.htm)

Teacher Resources

- Sample lesson plans on the UDHR
  (http://hrwstf.org/education/Ten_UDHR_Lesson_Plans.pdf)
- Sample lesson plans from UNICEF about the SDGs
  (https://teachunicef.org/teaching-materials/topic/sustainable-development-goals)
- The World's Largest Lesson
  (https://www.tes.com/worldslargestlesson/the-goals/
- Teaching the SDGs
  (https://www.populationeducation.org/content/teaching-sdgs-easy-1-2-3-sustainable-development-goals-your-classroom)
- A good resource from Oxfam with lesson plans (recommended)
  (http://www.oxfam.org.uk/education/resources/change_the_world_in_eight_steps/
  http://www.oxfam.org.uk/education/resources/sustainable-development-goals)

Unit	7.4
Topic	Democratic Life and Participation
Theme	Work and mind habits: innovation and creativity; ICC: intrapersonal (curiosity about global affairs and conflict-resolution skills); and ICC: interpersonal (working in intercultural teams)
Region	Developing world (since the project relates to the SDGs)
Length	Two weeks and then subsequently two hours per week since this relates to the capstone project

Goals and Objectives

1. **Learn** about the following strategies for successful project planning: identification of an issue, research, action planning, implementation, reflection, and evaluation. Students also learn about the process of civic participation by experiencing it themselves.
2. **Inspire** students to take on projects related to issues that are important to them and to see themselves as change makers with agency and efficacy.
3. **Act** by demonstrating an understanding of civic participation through the completion of an experiential civic project.

Skills and Knowledge

1. Students will use various strategies to identify an issue and to create a project to help solve it. They will research the causes of and key levers of influence on the issue, identify potential partners and build relationships with them, plan and execute a project to address the chosen issue, and continuously monitor and reflect on their progress and process.
2. Students will connect the experience of the project with that of civic life and specifically with organizing, campaigning, and acting in the public sphere.

3. Students will connect the project to the SDGs that were the subject of unit 3.

Overview

The teacher introduces the topics of working together to achieve the SDGs and Design for Change. Collectively, students pick an issue and an SDG that they are passionate about and want to influence. Students identify possible ways in which they can best impact the issue. While deciding on an issue as well as on a project strategy, students use some of the skills and tools they learned previously, such as organizing themselves so as to arrive at a consensus and apply the principles of Design for Change. This experiential learning is based on the principles of civic engagement and is completely student driven with minimal interference from the teacher.

Activity 7.4.1
Learning Design for Change

The teacher leads a session on Design for Change using the following resources:

https://www.tes.com/worldslargestlesson/taking-action/
http://www.designthinkingforeducators.com/
http://www.designthinkingforeducators.com/toolkit/
https://www.ideo.com/work/toolkit-for-educators

Activity 7.4.2
Picking an Issue

Students review the SDGs with the goal of creating a project in mind. (Note that examples of sample projects are given at the end of the activities in this unit.)

Students conduct research on issues around the SDGs that interest them. Students brainstorm projects and issues; the teacher assists the students in settling on one issue. They could use an affinity diagram and create a "campaign" for their issue.

(Note that in this lesson, to create an affinity diagram, the students write ideas for issues or projects on sticky notes and put them on the board randomly. The students then organize the ideas into categories or broader themes and vote for a category or theme. After voting for a category or theme, they generate a new list of issues or project ideas that fall under that category or theme. Students then vote to choose one issue under the theme. This final vote decides the issue around which the students will build a project.)

Activity 7.4.3
Background Information on the Issue
Once the issue is decided upon, students conduct specialized research into that one issue. In groups, students seek to find out about the issue and its

1. causes;
2. history;
3. measurement tools and metrics; and
4. people, groups, and organizations and their mission and actions.

Groups present their findings to the class. If the issue is complex, the class will vote on a particular subissue.

Activity 7.4.4
Brainstorming about a Project to Address the Issue
The class brainstorms possible projects to address the issue. The project should involve multiple entry points into the problem. Ultimately, part of the project should involve *education and awareness building*, part of the

project should involve *direct action*, and part of the project should involve *political interaction*.

Activity 7.4.5 (Twenty-Four Weeks)
Project Continuation
At this point, the students work on the project for two hours per week for about twenty-four weeks.

The teacher should guide the students through the phases of the project:

1. In phase 1, the classroom organizes around one issue or subissue.
2. In phase 2, students research the topic broadly, identify potential partners, reach out to them to form relationships, and conduct interviews.
3. In phase 3, they narrow down the issue into a manageable potential project and identify how the project's "baseline" can be measured.
4. In phase 4, they brainstorm the project's action plan and come to a consensus on elements of the project that involve education and awareness building, direct action, and political interaction
5. In phase 5, they create a time line and a calendar.
6. In phase 6, they implement the action plan, formatively evaluate the project's progress and impact, and make changes.
7. In phase 7, they perform a summative evaluation of the project and redesign it.
8. In phase eight, they continue with the redesigned action plan and evaluate progress.
9. In phase nine, they celebrate the project and hold a showcase.

Note that the following elements of a good experiential learning design should be present throughout the project. They have been adapted from the National Youth Leadership Council's guidelines for service learning, by Shelley Billig:

1. Curriculum integration—that is, opportunities to integrate the project into civic education, language-arts instruction, mathematics, history, and other subject areas depending on the issue—should be continually capitalized upon. The students should also recognize the integration into and connections with other areas of learning.

2. Reflection on the project is necessary. Students should reflect on both their progress and process continually throughout the project. Students should always be encouraged to suggest project changes based on their reflection. Reflection should be cognitively challenging (not simply journal writing).

3. The youth voice should be emphasized. This should be the students' project. The skilled teacher will guide the students in the appropriate directions and help them build the necessary partnerships and relationships, but the students should have choices regarding the issue and project. Often students are asked to engage in projects that the teacher creates, which may have negative effects on the desired civic outcomes.

4. The duration of this project is important. This project must be given ample time. The duration of the experience is directly related to the desired civic outcomes. A common pitfall is to not give students enough time, in which case the project will have less of an impact or the teacher will take on work that the students should be doing to save time. Students should also be given the opportunity to build relationships that could continue past the project duration. Also, there should be an opportunity to redesign the project or to make further plans based on its initial impact and on the students' evaluation of it.

Resources

- Joel Westheimer and Joseph Kahne's "What Kind of Citizen?," which is essential reading
  - http://engagestudiothinking.files.wordpress.com/2010/03/threekindsofcitizenship_excerpt.pdf

- Note that even though this unit is not a service-learning unit, this service-learning literature offers a great deal of information on best practices and teacher resources:
  - CIRCLE (http://www.civicyouth.org/ResearchTopics/research-topics/service-learning/)
  - National Service Learning Clearinghouse:(https://gsn.nylc.org/clearinghouse)
  - National Society for Experiential Education (http://www.nsee.org/eea.htm)
  - Association for Experiential Education (http://www.aee.org/)

Some example projects

1. COMIC BOOKS AGAINST HIV/AIDS PREJUDICE

After an analysis of the prejudice faced by people with AIDS, fifth graders decided to teach younger students about acceptance and respect. As their project, these students researched local health organizations with help from these agencies; they created a comic book character and a story line to teach young people to treat people living with HIV/AIDS with respect. Copies were distributed to classrooms and at a community fair. Prevention messages were a key component of the comic books and provided students with the opportunity to express their own thoughts, opinions, and creativity.

(Note that this is adapted from "The Complete Guide to Service-Learning," Copyright © 2004 Cathryn Berger Kaye. All rights reserved. Used with permission of Free Spirit Publishing Inc., Minneapolis, MN. (866) 703-7322. www.freespirit.com.)

2. DECLARATION ON THE RIGHTS OF THE CHILD

Based on their study of the Declaration on the Rights of the Child and the UDHR, students initiated a wide range of projects. For example, they presented at the city hall on the rights of the child, organized a peace-site rededication and a peace-prize festival, and directed and performed a play about child labor that inspired the school board of the district to agree to not buy soccer balls made by child labor.

The projects built on the students' public speaking, interviewing, and photography skills and were based on discussions, reflection, and analyses.

3. **BUS IDLING AND AIR-QUALITY IMPACTS**
High school students in Vermont monitored the air quality outside of their school, and after finding high levels of pollutants, they identified idling vehicles (e.g., buses) as a source. To take action, they presented their findings and policy recommendations to the school board as well as to the state legislative transportation committee.

(http://www.kidsconsortium.org/minigrantprojectexamples.php)

Unit	7.5
Topic	**Civil Rights Movement and Change Makers**
Theme	**ICC: interpersonal (empathy); ICC: intrapersonal (recognizing prejudice and minimizing the effects of prejudice); ethics: ethical frameworks, common values, commitment to equality, the value of human potential, and commitment to supporting human rights; work and mind habits: innovation and creativity; and arts: visual and literature**
Region	**United States, India, Myanmar, South Africa, and the world (based on HR violations)**
Length:	**Four weeks**

Goals and Objectives

1. **Learn** about the civil rights movement and the rights it addressed as well as the ways in which different change makers across the globe have advocated for human rights and the SDGs using different approaches.
2. **Inspire** students to effect change in an issue that is important to them based on the different approaches used by various change makers.
3. **Act by** demonstrating an understanding of the different ways through which change may be created and by reflecting on the direction that they want their own projects to take.

Skills and Knowledge

1. Students will identify important phases in the US civil rights movement as well as the importance of the movement's work in advocating for the right to equality.
2. Students will identify the change makers in each of these phases and the different approaches they took to ensure that the civil rights movement would become a mass movement.

3. Students will understand the nature of different HR violations and demonstrate an understanding of the existing state of HR in the world today.
4. Students will interact with real-life change makers and contrast and compare the relevance of different methods used by change makers across time.

Overview

Through the lens of the civil rights movement in the United States, students learn about the violations of the fundamental right to equality. Students examine the various turning points in the movement and explore why those points continue to be a series of relevant landmark events. Students are introduced to the various forms of HR violations in the world, to change makers in historical and contemporary times who have made a difference in upholding HR, and to those who have worked toward the SDGs. Through interactive sessions with real-life change makers, this unit aims to introduce students to the plethora of approaches to advocating for HR and the SDGs.

(Note that activity 7.5.1 should be given due time, and thus, the teacher may choose to make activity 7.5.2 optional and to add portions of it to activity 7.5.3.)

Activity 7.5.1
The Civil Rights Movement: History and Change Makers

Students will learn about the civil rights movement and the key turning points in the history of civil rights. They also undertake background research on the different change makers in each of these key events.

Note that there are already many existing lesson plans and units available online. Some good resources have been outlined in the resources below.

The main thrust of the unit should be on the civil rights movements as a response to the fundamental violation of the right to equality. By the end of the unit, students should understand that despite the expression of rights in the UDHR, a universal declaration doesn't always translate into the preservation and practice of these rights; they should also understand that it is necessary for ordinary individuals to take action and to make an effort to embody these principles and to ensure that all people are treated with equality, respect, and dignity. The activities should draw on literature and music from the times, and the students should closely examine that literature and music. The activity should end with the women's suffrage movement, as that relates directly to the next unit, on SDG 5 and gender equality.

Note also that an optional activity may be included. In the activity, the teacher will select songs from any of the following resources (or from other resources), teach them to the students, and sing them together with the students. Each song's lyrics can be printed and studied within historical and cultural contexts. Students will be asked to express in their own words how the concept of freedom is expressed in each of the songs. Resources for this optional activity are listed below.

Resources

- Facing History and Ourselves is an excellent resource that has links to several lesson plans as well as to the Boston Public Schools' curriculum on civil rights (a 268-page curriculum for tenth graders that can be adapted based on the needs of the class). Links are also drawn to a series of PBS documentaries about civil rights. This resource is rich with reading material for children as well as with audiovisual aids that can be used in the class.
- Unit on the civil rights movement and PBS's *Eye on the Prize* series, which was developed by the Yale-New Haven Teachers Institute. This goes into great detail that is not warranted at this stage, but it has some interesting discussion questions:

http://www.cis.yale.edu/ynhti/curriculum/units/1992/1/92.01.03.
x.html.

Database of lesson plans on civil rights (http://www.multcolib.org/
homework/civilrights/lessons.html#civilrights)

- PBS's *Eyes on the Prize* "Freedom Songs of Civil Rights", a resource
that outlines how educators may use freedoms songs of the civil
rights to teach about the historical, political, and social contexts of
the civil rights movement (http://www.pbs.org/wgbh/amex/eyeson-
theprize/reflect/r03_music.html)

Optional Activity 7.5.2
Human Rights Violations

In groups, students research the various kinds of human-rights violations
across the world and the current state of HR.

Resources

- Video resources (http://www.pbs.org/wnet/wideangle/category/
episodes/by-topic/human-rights/page/2/)
- *The State of the World's Human Rights*, Amnesty's annual report
- https://www.amnesty.org/en/latest/research/2016/02/annual-
report-201516/

Activity 7.5.3
Change Makers

The students are then introduced to change makers and individuals who have
taken action over time to protect and safeguard human rights. Individuals
who can be discussed include

1. Nelson Mandela
2. Mahatma Gandhi
3. Eleanor Roosevelt
4. Aung San Suu Kyi
5. citizens in India addressing untouchability and breaking down caste barriers (http://www.viewchange.org/videos/the-untouchables-breaking-down-caste-barriers-in-india)
6. young people making change (http://www.youthforhumanrights.org/)
7. Craig Kielburger of Free the Children (http://www.freethechildren.com/getinvolved/youth/craig/)

Students may study these change makers by using a rubric to answer some of the following questions:

1. Who are these people? What is special about them?
2. Which HR were they trying to protect?
3. What methods did they use?
4. Are the methods they used applicable and relevant in modern times?

Students undertake biographical research on these individuals, and certain students impersonate these individuals in class while the others interview them (using the guiding questions above). This will help the students practice their interview skills and prepare to interview the real change makers who will be invited into the class.

Subsequently, real-life change makers in the New York City (or relevant) area who have made a difference in the field of HR or the SDGs are invited into the classroom. (Note that a partnership with an organization such as Amnesty International or Human Rights Watch, both of which have large offices in New York City, can be fostered and will enable the teacher to bring real-life HR change makers into the classroom.)

The students can have a classroom discussion or complete a journaling activity to reflect on the differences between these real-life change makers and the ones they studied. The students should address the following questions:

1. What are the similarities and differences in the change makers?
2. What are the approaches they adopted to safeguard human rights?
3. Why do you think they decided to take action and responsibility?
4. What does taking responsibility mean to you?
5. What kind of responsibility would you like to take in the global HR movement?

(Note that these reflections should be documented and used to guide the children in their service projects. This can be a very powerful and moving unit for the children if done appropriately and if they are guided through the reflection exercises. Every attempt should be made to ensure that the children feel optimistic and are inspired to take action. Students may also read about actions that other children around the world are taking to effect change. See the book *Real Kids, Real Stories, Real Change: Courageous Actions Around the World:* http://www.amazon. com/exec/obidos/ISBN=1575423502/bravegirlsandstrA.)

Unit	7.6
Topic	SDG 5, Gender Equality and Women's Empowerment
Theme	ICC: interpersonal (one's own identity and culture and others' identities and cultures); ICC: intrapersonal (curiosity about global affairs, recognizing prejudice, and minimizing the effects of prejudice); ethics: commitment to equality and common values; work and mind habits: cross-cultural perspective taking); economic development; and globalization
Region	Developing world (as this unit focus on SDG 5)
Length	Two weeks

Goals and Objectives

1. **Learn** about the importance of gender parity and its links with the other SDGs.
2. **Inspire** students to treat everyone equally and with respect and to reflect upon how small actions and behaviors can make a difference in combatting gender stereotypes.
3. **Act in** ways that are gender sensitive and demonstrate an understanding of the importance of treating men and women equally.

Skills and Knowledge

1. Students will become familiar with the importance of SDG 5, its targets, and its indicators.
2. Students will draw links between gender inequality and social, political, and economic inequality.
3. Students will understand the relevance of and need for women's empowerment and its role in national, international and global development.

4. Students will interact in gender-sensitive ways with one another.
5. Students will examine the nature of gender challenges and gaps across different parts of the world.
6. Students will develop the reflective capacity to understand gendered roles in society and identify the role they want to play in bridging the gender divide.

Overview

In this unit students are introduced to the various dimensions of gender inequality across the world. Students closely examine SDG 5 and its associated targets and measures. Links are drawn to other units in which students were introduced to women change makers who made a difference in the different spheres of human development. Through the use of interactive maps and audiovisual materials, students examine trends in the gender gaps across the world. Through the use of literature, students challenge some of their own existing assumptions about the roles of men and women in society and become more reflective and aware of the difference they can make in challenging some of the existing preconceived roles and notions.

Activity 7.6.1
Introducing Gender Inequality and SDG 5

Students interact with peers in different parts of the world to closely examine

1. the chores children in their respective countries do at home
2. the jobs that only men or only women perform and the jobs that both genders perform
3. whether the country has a history of women political leaders
4. the ratio of the genders in the country.

Using this background information, the students create country profiles and present them to the class.

Using an interactive map, the teacher introduces the concept of a global gender gap and asks the students to do a close text study of what the UDHR and the SDGs say about the role of gender and equality.

Students may begin by reading literature that shatters gender stereotypes (listed under resources) and by reflecting on why the characters can/can't perform certain roles.

Resources

- The lesson plan "Mission Gender Equality" (https://www.tes.com/worldslargestlesson/)
- Jimmy Carter book and Ted talk on Violence against women
  - A Call to Action. Women, religion, violence and power.
  - https://www.ted.com/talks/jimmy_carter_why_i_believe_the_mistreatment_of_women_is_the_number_one_human_rights_abuse?language=en
- Sample lesson plans and ideas for introducing concepts associated with gender inequality(http://www.thirteen.org/edonline/wideangle/lessonplans/girlsspeak/procedures.html)
- Databases of relevant gender-neutral literature
  - (http://journal.naeyc.org/btj/200303/Books4Children.pdf)
  - http://genderequalbooks.com/Brave_Girls_book_list.html)

Activity 7.6.2
Examining the Dimensions of Gender Equality

The class can be split into three groups, each of which will examine a different aspect of gender equality, as explained below.

GROUP A. GENDER AND EDUCATION

1. Students in this group read about a day in the lives of girls across the world. Pick any one of the following readings:
   a. Nicaragua (http://www.unicef.org/dil/haitza/haitza5_content.html
   b. India and night school (http://www.teachersdomain.org/resource/wa08.socst.world.glob.nightsch/)
   c. Benin (http://www.teachersdomain.org/resource/wa08.socst.world.glob.benin/)
   The students note the similarities and differences in the lives of each of these girls and the reason for their educational circumstances.
2. Students in this group role-play, making hard decisions to answer the question of whether Jaya can go to school. This role-play exercise examines the decision to send Jaya to school from the perspectives of different people in her family and brings to light the opportunity costs associated with schooling and some of the reasons that children may drop out or not enroll in school in the developing world (http://www.oxfam.org.uk/education/resources/change_the_world_in_eight_steps/files/goal_3.pdf).
3. Students also collect compelling statistics regarding enrollment rates for girls in primary education across the world. (See UNICEF's *State of the World's Children* annual reports for statistics: http://www.unicef.org/sowc2011/.)

GROUP B. GENDER AND HEALTH

1. The students in this group superimpose over one another maps that indicate access to primary health care as well as maps that display skewed sex ratios in the world.
2. Students are asked to be observant of any interlinkages between health care and sex rations.
3. Students also undertake background research about malnutrition among girls and women, female infanticide, and HIV/AIDS.

GROUP C. ECONOMIC INEQUALITY AND GENDER

1. Students engage in a discussion about what economic inequality means and learn to plot gender maps of the world that indicate the percentage of women who can, for example, own land, get paid as much as men, and hold jobs.

2. The students undertake background research on the concept of microfinance and on how it's beneficial to women across the developing world. In class students discuss the following videos and why they think economic empowerment of women is important:

   a. Liberia (http://www.viewchange.org/videos/liberia-microfinance_)

   b. Afghanistan (http://www.viewchange.org/videos/kandahar-treasure)

Activity 7.6.3
Gender and Development

1. The students in the class form a web explicitly laying out the linkages between poverty, education, health, gender equality, and overall development. The teacher walks the students through these linkages and helps them draw the connections between them in a chain-effect game.

2. The students can also work on projects with peers across the world to examine the status of girls and young women in different parts of the world and to draw similar linkages. The following videos can be shown to steer their thinking:

   a. "The Girl Effect" http://www.youtube.com/watch?v=1e8xgF0JtVg; http://www.youtube.com/watch?v=WIvmE4_KMNw&feature=relmfu

   b. "Women's Empowerment in Nigeria" (http://www.youtube.com/watch?v=O9M9seZ497U&feature=player_embedded)

   c. Videos from other countries (http://www.viewchange.org/videos?t=gender)

3. Students may also read parts of UNDPs reports and study the newly created Gender Development Index http://hdr.undp.org/en/statistics/indices/gdi_gem/.

Activity 7.6.4
Reflecting on My Role

Students write a reflection paper that answers the following questions:

1. What are your strengths and weaknesses?
2. Has your gender played a role in your strengths and weaknesses?
3. Are strengths and weaknesses linked to gender?
4. What is the role of boys and male teenagers in promoting gender equality?
5. What is the role of girls and female teenagers in promoting gender equality?

Unit	7.7
Topic	**Energy and Environmental Movements**
Theme	**Global risk: environment; globalization; and ICC: intrapersonal (curiosity about global affairs)**
Region	**United States, India, Kenya, and Malawi**
Length	**Three weeks**

Goals and Objectives

1. **Learn** about environmental movements and their champions as well as about energy sources.
2. **Inspire** students to think about what role they can play in preserving the environment, particularly when it comes to energy choices.
3. **Act by** critically evaluating the often-politicized information presented as energy facts.

Skills and Knowledge

1. Students will become familiar with the important aspects of an environmental movement and also know the time line of the modern American environmental movement. They will also become familiar with the similarities and differences in the environmental movements in India, Kenya, and the United States.
2. Students will become aware of the Pickens Plan.
3. Students will identify energy trends since 1945.
4. Students will verify the credibility of information from different sources.
5. Students will demonstrate an understanding of the link between energy, war, and politics as well as of the relationship between one's energy use and lifestyle.
6. Students will evaluate the costs and benefits of various different energy types.

Overview

Students are introduced to different environmental movements across the world and to their defining characteristics. Students will also be able to identify the change makers in each of these movements and their approaches to drawing attention to and support for the issue. Through an analysis of some of the various sociopolitical, economic, and personal choices that individuals and societies make collectively, students will be able to articulate these interrelationships and how they affect communities' and societies' choices of an energy source. Using country and region profiles, students will analyze trends and data to examine the energy sources in different parts of the world and will form hypotheses about those different trends. Students will also work toward creating an energy plan for wind energy specifically through the study of T. Boone Pickens and William Kamkwamba. Other change makers introduced in this unit include Nobel Prize winner Wangari Mathai and the activists of the Chipko movement in India

Activity 7.7.1
The Chipko Movement, the Green Belt Movement, and the Role of Women in These Movements

Through this activity students will

1. learn about the important role that women have played in environmental movements in three countries
2. learn to identify how women and particularly disadvantaged women have become change makers
3. learn to determine the different circumstances that can motivate change makers.

Students research the lives of women change makers in environmental movements (e.g., Rachel Carson and Wangari Mathai) and compare the differences in their circumstances and opportunities. Next, students look at the founders of the Chipko movement in India and at what is known of their lives, circumstances, and opportunities. The class then discusses whether movements must be born out of necessity, interest, or some other factor.

Activity 7.7.2
Learning about the Modern American Environmental Movement

Through this activity in particular, students will

1. learn about the major figures and events of the movement
2. critically evaluate sources for reliability, completeness, and biases
3. analyze what constitutes a movement and how movements gain power.

First students learn about the modern American environmental movement. They can compare time lines of the movement as presented by different sources, including PBS, World Watch, *Wikipedia*, and other sources (listed below). Students compare and contrast the time lines. They look for common figures and events as well as for differences between the time lines. In groups, they use the Internet to find credible sources to use to research different events and figures in the story of the modern environmental movement. They then evaluate the different time lines they looked at to determine whether any of them have an agenda or whether one tells a more complete story than the others.

Resource

- Different time lines of the modern environmental movement (www. pbs.org/wgbh/americanexperience/features/timeline/earthdays/ http://www.worldwatch.org/brain/features/timeline/timeline.htm http://en.wikipedia.org/wiki/Environmental_movement)

Activity 7.7.3
Energy Options

Through this activity students will learn about the different sources of energy, learn about cost-benefit analyses, and learn about consumption patterns around the world.

Students visit energy.gov, and in small groups, they use that resource and others to research energy sources including bioenergy, coal, fusion, geothermal, hydrogen, hydropower, natural gas, oil, and renewables (e.g., solar and wind). The teacher then explains the basic concept of benefits and costs: that one way people make choices is by weighing how much a given choice will cost against what its benefits will be. They should include the production, world security, human, health, economic, and environmental benefits and costs, among others. Students are then asked to try to determine some way to evaluate what the long- and short-term benefits and costs of each energy choice could be. Next, the teacher leads the class in a look at energy consumption patterns throughout the world, using a tool such as the UN's *2007 Energy Balances and Electricity Profiles* (http://unstats.un.org/unsd/energy/balance/default.htm).

The teacher then facilitates a discussion by asking the following questions:

1. Why do some countries use more energy than others?
2. Why do some countries use different types of energy than others?
3. How do these trends compare by region?
4. Which regions or countries tend to be better for the environment in terms of energy consumption?
5. Are there any associations between energy types and zones of conflict?

Note that one of the opportunities of this lesson is to show how energy choices can have a profound effect on human life far and wide. In as many ways as possible, bring to light the advantages and disadvantages of energy choices in terms of global security (e.g., war-torn countries and oil), working conditions (e.g., historic coal miners in Appalachia), and the environment (e.g., desertification and drought due to climate change).

Activity 7.7.4
The Pickens Plan and the Boy Who Harnessed the Wind

Through this activity, students will learn to critically evaluate the persuasiveness of an argument.

Students will learn about the lives of T. Boone Pickens and William Kamkwamba and their trajectories to becoming activists for wind energy. First, using what they learned in the previous activity, they will brainstorm as a group on what information they would want and need in order to make a decision regarding an energy plan. Next they will visit pickensplan.com and williamkamkwamba.typepad.com and evaluate the websites for their persuasiveness. They will see whether those websites provide all of the information that they think they need to make a decision, and they will discuss what additional information those websites provide.

Resources

- Advanced Placement Environmental Science, Topic V: Energy Resources and Consumption (https://apstudent.collegeboard.org/apcourse/ap-environmental-science/course-details)
- *Frontline's* "The Spill" (a sixty-minute-long episode)
- *World Development Report 2010: Development and Climate Change*
- PBS's *Earth Days* (a two-hour-long film)

Unit   7.8
Topic   Collective Buying Power and Corporate Social Responsibility
Theme   ICC: intrapersonal (curiosity about global affairs); work
            and mind habits: innovation and creativity; economic devel-
            opment; globalization; and politics
Region   Organization of the Petroleum Exporting Countries
Length   Three weeks

Goals and Objectives

1. **Learn** about collective buying as a way to participate in society
   and how it has given rise to corporate social responsibility (CSR)
   programs.
2. **Inspire students to** think about the consumption choices they
   make and the invisible power of those choices.
3. **Act by being** savvy and critical consumers.

Skills and Knowledge

1. Students will understand and appreciate the power of consumers.
2. Students will be introduced to and become familiar with the history, power, objectives, and members of OPEC.
3. Students will examine the concepts of supply and demand.
4. Students will analyze the nuances of corporate social responsibility,
   including how it is used as a signal tool for effective marketing, and
   evaluate CSR programs.

Overview

Through an interactive game, students learn about the concept of buying
power as well as about the role of CSR in signaling to customers. Students

learn about the power of consumers, about how consumers are an important constituency for organizations that sell consumer goods, and about the ways in which consumers may significantly influence organizations to use ethical means of production. Through an examination of OPEC, students are familiarized with the basics of the demand and supply of petroleum and with how countries collectively work toward ensuring the stability of petroleum prices in the global economy.

Activity 7.8.1
Buying Power

The teacher gives each student a certain amount of "money." Each student is able to buy products from a classroom store. Each product is produced by a different company, and each company has a profile card that the students are not allowed to see. The teacher explains to the students that every time they spend a dollar on goods from a certain company, that company will be able to use a portion of that dollar to expand and will thus become bigger and more powerful. In the first round, there is an equal amount of each product. Before the second round, the teacher adds one more product for every two dollars that was spent on that product in the first round. Therefore, the most popular company will take a larger share of the shelf space. Students are then given more money to spend in the second round, and the teacher again increases the number of the popular products. For the third round, the teacher places a card with a company profile in front of each product and gives the students more money to spend. Some companies' profiles talk about the fair wages they pay their workers and the sustainable manufacturing technologies they use. Other companies' profiles talk about how they keep costs low by using cheap labor overseas. In the third round, the students use the company profiles to make buying decisions, and then the teacher replenishes the supply of products as before. In the fourth round, however, the teacher places news articles praising companies for social responsibility or denouncing them for nefarious practices like child labor and sweatshop conditions. After the students spend their money, the teacher debriefs the class by asking which companies were successful when little information was shared versus when more information was shared.

Note that an alternative activity that will meet many of the learning goals and can be used in place of this one is the Stock Market Game (www.stock-marketgame.org). Based on the time available, as a follow-up activity, students may also undertake background research on the CSR initiatives of their favorite candy or clothes manufacturer in the market.

Activity 7.8.2
The Price of Gasoline—What's behind It?

Through this activity students will learn about OPEC, the basics of supply and demand, and the ways that several countries have organized themselves around this particular issue.

Use this lesson plan to learn about the Organization of the Petroleum Exporting Countries and the many factors including demand (which is another way of looking at collective buying power) that influence gas prices: http://www.econedlink.org/lessons/index.php?lid=664&type=afterschool

Unit	7.9
Topic	**Inventors as Change Makers and Sustainable Technology**
Theme	**Work and mind habits: innovation and creativity; ethics: common values; and global risk: environment**
Region	**Any/all**
Length	**Four weeks**

Goals and Objectives

1. **Learn** about how inventions can lead to rapid social and environmental change.
2. **Inspire** students to plan a future in which new technology helps preserve the environment.
3. **Act by** becoming more mindful of the technology they use and of its impact on the environment.

Skills and Knowledge

1. Students will learn about key inventors who have been environmental activists.
2. Students will understand that change comes through members of very different fields and through different approaches.
3. Students will examine how some everyday technologies became more environmentally friendly because of supply and demand.
4. Students will be inspirited to work together in teams to execute a plan and to create their own inventions.

Overview

In this unit students examine an everyday technology in great depth. They analyze its inventor, the situations that led to its creation, the different variations of it, and how it became popular. Students will chart the progress of the invention over time and examine its impact at each of these different points. In addition to performing this analysis and studying existing environmental problems, students will also engage in imagining what this technology could look like fifty years hence.

Activity 7.9.1
Designing a Friendly Future

Students work in teams to research an everyday technology. Students could research lightbulbs, cameras, or some other technology. Their research will need to cover the following areas:

1. The inventor(s)
   a. Biographical information
      Training
   b. Collaborators
   c. Inspirations and/or trailblazers who helped pave the way for the inventor
2. The idea
   a. The first iteration of the idea
   b. The idea's genesis/conception
   c. Early champions of the idea
3. The invention
   a. The first incarnation of the invention
   b. The resources needed for the invention (including manpower, expertise, raw materials, and funding)
   c. The drawbacks of the initial invention
4. The spread
   a. How the invention caught on
   b. Who marketed it and to whom
   c. How quickly it became popular

5. The evolution of the invention
   a. How the invention has changed over time
   b. How it has gotten better and worse
   c. What it will look like in the future
6. The impact of the invention:
   a. How it has impacted society
   b. How it has impacted culture
   c. New inventions that it made possible

They should show the technology and its aspects at different stages, and then they should try to envision what the technology could look like in fifty years. They will present the evolution of the technology to the rest of the class.

Resources

- Buckminster Fuller Institute (http://www.bfi.org/)
- PBS's *American Masters* "Bucky Fuller" (http://www.pbs.org/wnet/ americanmasters/episodes/r-buckminster-fuller/about-r-buckmin- ster-fuller/599/)

The World Course
Eighth Grade: Migration

Theme
Migratory Movement and People

Description

Students begin the year with the end in mind, as they are introduced to the concept of social entrepreneurship and told that they will be building a social enterprise during the year in the first unit. They then learn about the opportunities and challenges in current global trends for their project. During the rest of the year, they tackle the issue of demographic changes and tools, exploring causes such as migration and consequences such as the interaction between increased human population and effects on the environment. As they go on a cultural scavenger hunt of New York City and engage in other activities, the students recognize that fluctuations in populations are not recent phenomena but a part of a historical pattern of movement that already exists. They spend twelve weeks studying the impact of one particular migration pattern—the Silk Road—and how the cultural exchanges that took place on that road affected art, music, trade, and belief systems. They then apply what they have learned about historical patterns and modern tools of demography to a case study of modern China and India by participating in a mock summit (unit 7). As their culminating activity, they give a presentation to the school community on their yearlong social-enterprise project.

Looking Backwards
Driving Change in Society

Looking Forward
Students develop a high school capstone project and select three semester long courses that help them gain depth in understanding of economic development, public health, global conflicts, environmental sustainability and emerging technologies.

Overview of Units

1) Introduction to Social Entrepreneurship
2) The Population Paradox: Opportunities and Challenges in Current Global Trends
3) Population Pyramids and Introduction to Basic Demography
4) Human-Environmental Interactions and Comparisons Across Species
5) New York City Scavenger Hunt: Introduction to Immigration and Migration
6) Migration and International Development: Reasons for and Effects of Migration
7) Along the Silk Road: An In-Depth Look at the Cultural Exchange and the Effects of Migration on Art, Music, Trade, and Belief Systems
8) Modern Populations: Case Study of China and India
9) Presentation of Social Enterprise

Capstone Project
Students will create a social enterprise around one of the SDGs and present their work at the end of the year.

Unit	8.1
Topic	**Social Entrepreneurship**
Theme	**Ethics: value of human potential and work and mind habits: innovation and creativity**
Region	**Various**
Length	**Two weeks**

Goals and Objectives

1. **Learn** what social entrepreneurship is and how social entrepreneurs are addressing some of the major global challenges.
2. **Inspire** students to initiate a social-entrepreneurial venture to address one of the SDGs.
3. **Act by** establishing a social enterprise.

Skills and Knowledge

1. Students will study the work of various social entrepreneurs.
2. Students will recognize the value of social innovation in addressing development challenges.
3. Students will identify the steps involved in establishing a social enterprise.
4. Students will plan a social enterprise and develop an implementation plan.

Overview

This unit builds on the last unit of the seventh grade, when the concept of social enterprise was studied. The students begin eighth grade with an introduction to—or a review of—social enterprises and create a social enterprise around one of the SDGs for their end-of-the-year project. This enterprise is developed and put into practice during the year, and students periodically reflect on the results of their enterprise. They use those reflections to review the theory of action of the enterprise and to make adjustments to their business plan. The year ends with a presentation of the enterprises created by the students and a discussion of their results.

Activity 8.1.1
What Is Social Entrepreneurship?

The teacher will introduce this activity with a presentation that explains the concept of social entrepreneurship. The students will describe the growing role played by the citizen sector in generating innovation to address global challenges and will provide a range of examples of social entrepreneurs. The introduction will highlight the various approaches to financing social enterprises (e.g., for profit, hybrid, and not for profit). If possible, invite actual social entrepreneurs to visit the class and to make short presentations describing their work and sharing their passion.

Resources

- A resource featuring examples of youth who are social entrepreneurs (https://www.changemakers.com/blog?page=17)
- Videos on innovations in addressing social challenges (http://www.pbs.org/frontlineworld/educators/social_entrepreneurs.html)
- *Social Entrepreneurship: What Everyone Needs to Know*, by David Bornstein and Susan Davis
- *Tactics of Hope: How Social Entrepreneurs Are Changing Our World*, by Wilford Welch
- *The Five Most Important Questions You Will Ever Ask about Your Organization*, by Peter Drucker and Jim Collins
- *Start Something that Matters*, by M. Mycoskie.
- *The Lean Startup*, by Eric Ries.
- *The Innovators*, by Walter Isaacson

Activity 8.1.2
What Are the Sustainable Development Goals?

In a class discussion, students will review the SDGs and discuss examples of how social entrepreneurs are addressing them. Students can work in small groups, and each group can have a discussion about a different SDG. The groups will then summarize their work for the entire class.

Resources

The following are good resources for teaching the SDGs and can be used to provide students with context when they choose topics to focus their social enterprise on:

- Comic book on the Sustainable Development Goals (https://www.tes.com/worldslargestlesson/read-comic-book/)
- The lesson plan "A Global Goals Assembly" (https://www.tes.com/worldslargestlesson/)
- https://sustainabledevelopment.un.org/?menu=1300
- https://www.tes.com/worldslargestlesson/the-goals/
- https://www.ted.com/talks/michael_green_how_we_can_make_the_world_a_better_place_by_2030?language=en
- https://www.ted.com/talks/jamie_drummond_how_to_set_goals_for_the_world?language=en

Activity 8.1.3
Designing a Social Enterprise

In small groups of between five and six, students will design a social enterprise. They will draw on the SDGs to define a problem area. They will then define a mission for their organization, identify their business model, and develop a business plan. Teachers will review the concepts of Design for Change and Design Thinking, which were taught in the previous year.

Once the social enterprise is designed, students will implement it throughout the year, checking in periodically in class to review how the concepts learned in activities 8.1.1. and 8.1.2. apply to what they are experiencing. Ideally, students will be paired up with mentors who are actual social entrepreneurs or with volunteers who work with social enterprises in their city, and the mentors will provide coaching. Parent volunteers may also be able to contribute in this way.

At the end of the academic year, in weeks thirty-five and thirty-six, there will be a capstone exhibition for which the students will prepare a written report and a PowerPoint presentation (or another media presentation of their choice) summarizing their enterprise and what it accomplished. Students will also make a short presentation to peers, parents, and local entrepreneurs describing what SDG they set out to address, the value proposition of their enterprise, their business model, how they assessed their plan's impact, and what they learned along the way. It would be helpful if people with experience in philanthropy, corporate social responsibility, or social enterprise could be invited to serve as a panel of jurors and to offer feedback to each team of students.

Resources

- Consider the following resources on Design for Change:
    o https://www.tes.com/worldslargestlesson/explore-global-goals/, https://www.ideo.com/work/toolkit-for-educators, and http://www.designthinkingforeducators.com/
- The following organizations provide curriculum to teach business skills to middle school students: http://www.teachingkidsbusiness.com/Home.htm and http://www.jany.org/
- https://www.nfte.com/
- Wolk, A. and K. Kreitz. 2008. *Business Planning for Enduring Social Impact: A How-To Guide*. Students should read pages 1–26 of this book from Root Cause. This book covers business planning for

enduring social impact, planning to plan, and articulating a social-impact model. It will become a reference guide that the students will refer to during the year as they implement their business plan.

Unit	8.2
Topic	**The Population Paradox: Opportunities and Challenges in Current Global Trends**
Theme	**Environment, geography, and demography**
Region	**Global, the United States, India, Kenya, and Japan**
Length	**Two weeks**

Goals and Objectives

1. **Learn** about the opportunities and challenges of current demographic trends.
2. **Inspire students to** ask questions about global action or inaction in light of foreseeable demographic trends.
3. **Act by** using tools such as demography when making decisions about the future.

Skills and Knowledge

1. Students will increase their depth of understanding of demographic issues.
2. Students will be introduced to the population paradox.
3. Students will use mathematics concepts including exponential functions, best-fit lines, and more to answer a real-world question.

Activity 8.2.1
Exploring the Population Paradox on NOVA

(This lesson in adapted from NOVA's teacher guide on *World in the Balance*: http://www.pbs.org/wgbh/nova/teachers/activities/pdf/3108_worldbal. pdf.)

The purposes of this activity are to increase the depth of the students' understanding of demographic issues and to introduce the students to the population paradox.

Prior knowledge needed for this activity includes basic math skills and a basic understanding of demography.

The teacher uses this guide (http://www.pbs.org/wgbh/nova/teachers/activities/pdf/3108_worldbal.pdf) to support the viewing of NOVA's film *World in the Balance*.

(Note that this activity will allow students to use their math skills. In fact, it may be useful to have students complete all or part of this activity in their math class after watching the film in the World Course.)

Resources

- *NOVA's World in the Balance* (http://www.pbs.org/wgbh/nova/worldbalance/)
- Population Reference Bureau (www.prb.org)

Unit   8.3
Topic   Population Pyramids and Introduction to Basic Demography
Theme   Global risk: economic; demography; and poverty
Region   Various
Length   Two weeks

Overview

This unit builds on an introduction to the study of demography and population studies and introduces the concepts of mortality, fertility, marriage, and migration levels and patterns. Students will be introduced to the main sources of demographic information. The teacher will introduce the concept of distribution of populations by categories (age, sex, race, and ethnicity) and the concepts of density, distribution, and scale. Concepts of birthrates, mortality rates, fertility rates, age-dependency ratios, and age-sex graphs are explained. The teacher also introduces several sources of demographic data and displays and explains several population charts.

Goals and Objectives

1. **Learn** the basic concepts of demographic analyses and population studies.
2. **Inspire** students to pursue independent studies of populations using the sources provided in this unit, and ask questions such as the following: How does the study of past demographic trends help to predict future demographic structures? How do changes in demographic structures affect social, political, and economic events?
3. **Act by** examining the relationship of populations to sociological and cultural changes and to political and economic development.

Skills and Knowledge

1. Students will learn the categories for demographic analysis (age, gender, and race).
2. Students will learn to describe the concepts of birthrates, mortality rates, fertility rates, and dependency ratios.
3. Students will learn the major sources of demographic information.

Activity 8.3.1

Introduce this activity with the Gapminder video "200 countries, 200 Years, 4 minutes." A discussion of the following video would be a good warm-up to this unit:

http://www.gapminder.org/videos/200-years-that-changed-the-world-bbc/

Activity 8.3.2
Foundations of Demography

The teacher will introduce the concept of distribution of population by categories (age, sex, race, and ethnicity) and the concepts of density, distribution, and scale. The concepts of birthrates, mortality rates, fertility rates, age-dependency ratios, and age-sex graphs will also be explained. The teacher also introduces several sources of demographic data and displays and explains several population charts.

http://www.prb.org/Educators/LessonPlans/2005/
PopulationBuildingaFoundation.aspx

Activity 8.3.3
Population Pyramids

The teacher will introduce the field of demography, explaining population pyramids and the concept of population levels and trends. In class students will examine how population pyramids change over time in the same country and compare population pyramids across countries. charts. These data can be found here: (http://www.prb.org/Educators/LessonPlans/2000/PyramidBuilding.aspx}

Data on population pyramids across different countries (http://www.un.org/esa/population/)

The teacher will organize the students into small study groups, and the groups will examine how the youth bulge in some regions of the world relates to political developments—for example, to unrest in the Middle East.

Activity 8.3.4
The Relationship of Population Composition and Change to Political and Economic Development

The teacher will introduce the field of population studies, examining how population change influences political and economic processes.

For example, this video explains the relationship between poverty and population growth:

http://www.gapminder.org/videos/population-growth-explained-with-ikea-boxes/.

Resource

- The following are lesson plans for population studies:
  - http://www.prb.org/Publications/Lesson-Plans/MakingPopulationRealNewLessonPlansandClassroomActivities.aspx

Teacher Resources

- Shyrock S, Siegel JS, Stockwell EG. *The Methods and Materials of Demography*. Academic Press. 1976.
- For teachers and students who can read French, the website of the INED (Institut national d'études démographiques) of France has a section aimed at children and teachers with a number of nice animations (http://www.ined.fr/fr/tout_savoir_population/)

Unit   8.4
Topic   **Human-Environmental Interactions and Comparisons across Species**
Theme   **Global risk: environment; geography; and demography**
Region   **The Arctic**
Length   **One week**

Goals and Objectives

1. **Learn** about how two species—humans and polar bears—interact with their environment.
2. **Inspire students to** reflect on the impacts that human migration, reproduction, and consumption are having on the environment.
3. **Act by becoming** well-informed stewards of the environment.

Skills and Knowledge

1. Students will apply demographic concepts to humans as a species and to polar bears as a species.
2. Students will learn about polar bears and threats to their existence.
3. Students will learn to evaluate humans as a species relatively dispassionately.
4. Students will practice their comparative skills.

Overview

The students are introduced to the basic ideas behind human-environmental interaction by watching the film *Ice Age 2: The Meltdown.*

Activity 8.4.1
Comparing Species with Demography

(Note that if the teacher wants, this activity can extend throughout all of the units on demography rather than just spanning one week. If it is extended, students can add information to their comparisons as they learn new concepts.)

This unit can begin, if the teacher chooses, with a fun film that brings up issues of global warming and the threat to arctic life, such as *Ice Age 2: The Meltdown*. After watching the film, the teacher explains to the class that they will be completing a structured comparison between humans as a species and polar bears. They should be scientific in their approach and evaluate humans as though they have little prior knowledge of their habits, characteristics, and motivations. The teacher can use his or her discretion in determining the criteria for comparison, but some ideas may include

1. major food sources
2. population threats
3. migration patterns
4. reproduction rates
5. life-spans
6. relationships to the environment.

Students should present their reports to one another and to the class as a whole.

Resources 8.4.1

*   *Ice Age 2: The Meltdown* (film)
*   Population Reference Bureau (www.prb.org)

Unit	8.5
Topic	NYC Scavenger Hunt: Introduction to Immigration and Migration
Theme	ICC: interpersonal (all subcategories); ethics: religious diversity; work and mind habits: cross-cultural perspective taking and cultural change; culture: world religions; demography politics: globalization; and the local-global link
Region	New York City
Length	Eight weeks

(Note that this topic is illustrative. If your school is in a different city, change the topic as is appropriate.)

Overview

This unit is an introductory exploration of the concepts of migration and immigration in New York City. It leads the students on a scavenger-hunt research study of New York City via searches on the web and walks along city streets. Students will research different boroughs and neighborhoods and their changing demographics over time.

Optional Preparatory Activity 8.5.1

Students would be asked to describe the neighborhood of the school and would be guided through the activity by the teacher. (See below for a list of possible aspects of the neighborhood to describe.) This activity would prepare the students for their own scavenger hunt in the subsequent activity. Either in this activity or, if this activity is not completed, in the next, there should be a review of and lessons about basic research skills (e.g., how to identify good sources for information and how to determine whether a source/website is reliable).

Activity 8.5.2

Students are divided into different groups and gather research and firsthand information about their assigned/chosen neighborhoods (defined by the teacher for safety reasons, among others). Once they collect the information, they will make a presentation about their neighborhood using posters, video, pictures, and other visual aids.

1) Students should be encouraged to use, practice, and develop teamwork skills and strategies; to learn about one another as classmates; and to explore their own strengths and individual interests during this activity. For example, the students should do the following:

    a. Make a list of roles for the team based on the requirements of the assignment and take turns in the roles or assign each team member a role (e.g., logistics coordinator, timekeeper, recorder, editor, etc.)

    b. Make a list of target dates for parts of the assignments before the delivery of the final product, with assignments for each member of the team

    c. Discuss and agree on how they will resolve conflicts and differences and how they will run their team meetings

    d. Discuss and learn about the experiences, skills, and interests that each team member brings to the work and discuss how they can best use those experiences, skills, and interests to produce the final presentation (these can be discussed as a class before the teams are constructed, or the teacher can administer a survey, make the teams based on interest and skills, and have the students talk about them with one another)

2) Students will be asked to use online searches and other resources in the library to answer questions about their assigned neighborhoods/boroughs. The teacher can write these questions, or the class can do a guided brainstorming session with the teacher about the questions they have. An example of a rubric is included.

	1710	1810	1910	2010
Size of the population				
Number of square miles				
List of ethnicities represented, in order of the most common to the least				
List of languages spoken				
List of religions practiced and/or types of religious institutions in the neighborhood				
Contemporary map of the neighborhood				
List of major businesses in the area				
Other(s)				

3) The students or the teacher will also make a list of pictures to be taken (or menus or other artifacts to be collected) as students travel the neighborhoods. Students should be encouraged to think about and plan ahead for the kinds of pictures they will take and the people they will talk to based on their initial Internet-based research on the neighborhood. They should be ready to explain and justify their decisions to the rest of the class after discussion within their groups. For example, students could take pictures of the following:

a. Five different types of restaurants

b. Five different types of businesses (small, medium, and large in size)

c. Five different landmarks, including memorials, museums, and statues

d. Five different street corners

e. Five different apartments or living spaces

f. Five different places of worship representing different faith traditions

g. Five different parks or recreational places.

4) The students or the teacher should make a list of people to interview/speak with and questions to ask them. They can videotape these short (no more than five minutes), informal interviews. The following is a sample list of people to interview:

a. A small-business owner

b. Someone walking on the street

c. People of various ages

    i. Someone in his or her twenties

    ii. Someone in his or her thirties

    iii. Someone in his or her forties

    iv. Someone in his or her fifties

    v. Someone in his or her fifties

    vi. Someone in his or her sixties

The following is a sample list of questions to ask:

a. How long have you lived in New York City?

b. Why did you come to/decide to live in New York City?

c. Where do your/where did your parents live?

d. Where do your/where did you grandparents live?

e. Where did your great-grandparents live?

f. What are your favorite places in the neighborhood and why?

g. What places should be avoided?

h. What places do you go to daily?

i. Can you describe the place where you live?

j. Where do you work?

6) Students should walk together around their neighborhood (defined by the teacher) under adult supervision (for safety reasons) and gather artifacts, take pictures and videos, and interview people.

7) The students should identify someone who has lived in their assigned neighborhood for thirty years (or the teacher could invite a guest speaker) and interview him/or her more extensively about how he or she perceives the changes in the neighborhood over the years (e.g., the changing demographics, the challenges and benefits of movement and migration, etc.).

8) Once they have collected the data, they will present it to the rest of the class. Using posters, videos, pictures, and other visual aids, they will summarize what they've learned.

Activity 8.5.3 (Optional Preactivity)
My Family History

Note that many students do this type of activity in the younger grades, but not at a very deep level. This activity should go in depth into the history of families in order to connect to the topic. Please substitute historical families (for all students) if there are students present in the classroom for whom examining family histories would be problematic (due to abuse or trauma, for example).

Each student completes an independent study project on his or her family history. Throughout the course of the project, students should complete at a minimum a family tree, a map that shows the movement of the family members over time, and an analysis of the experiences of moving, cultural sharing, and identity formation among the family members. This analysis could be presented in many formats, including, for example, in written family stories, interviews, or a scrapbook. The students should be allowed to be creative and expected to go in depth.

This website is a good resource for examples of family stories: http://www. nyc.gov/html/nyc100/html/imm_stories/index.html.

Optional Activity 8.5.4
Students Study the Different Cultural Influences in New York City Caused by People Moving into the City

(Note that this can be a different way to organize the scavenger hunt—that is, by ethnicities rather than by neighborhoods.)

Students explore the history of the groups that have migrated to New York City (e.g., Irish, German, Italian, Chinese, etc.) and explore the reasons for their migrations and the cultural influences that the groups brought. Students can conduct this study through an examination of the arts of each culture in the cultures' respective neighborhoods and also throughout the city.

Students create "walking tours" of New York City, highlighting major landmarks and cultural buildings.

They may take field trips to a variety of neighborhoods. Each group can prepare a presentation that will be given in an appropriate neighborhood. The students themselves act as tour guides.

Resources

- Berger, Joseph. (2007). *The World in a City: Traveling the Globe through the Neighborhoods of the New New York*. Ballantine Books. (The book is 264 pages.)
- Interactive *New York Times* map on immigration patterns since 1880 (http://www.nytimes.com/interactive/2009/03/10/us/20090310-immigration-explorer.html)

- Maps that show how New York's racial makeup has changed since 2000 (http://www.nytimes.com/interactive/2010/12/14/nyregion/census-graphic-ny.html)
- "Mapping America: Every City, Every Block," a map showing the ethnic distribution of neighborhoods (data is based on 2005–2009) (http://projects.nytimes.com/census/2010/explorer?hp?hp)
- http://en.wikipedia.org/wiki/Neighborhoods_of_New_York_City

The following list of data about demographics is from this article from the *New York Times*: http://cityroom.blogs.nytimes.com/2007/11/14/immigration-in-new-york-city-taking-the-long-view/.

1) Sixty percent of New York City residents are immigrants or children of immigrants. The following is a list of some of their communities and those communities' locations:
   a. The Chinese and Koreans in Flushing
   b. The Dominicans in Washington Heights and the West Bronx
   c. The Guyanese in Richmond Hill
   d. The Carib in East Flatbush
   e. The South Asians in Jackson Heights
   f. The growing Chinese population in Bensonhurst
   g. The polyglot mix of Arabs, Brazilians, and Bangladeshis in Astoria
2) New York was a heterogeneous city from its founding; seventeen languages could be heard in the streets of New Amsterdam in the 1640s.
3) By 1855, New York had become "the most Irish city in America" and was a hub of nationalist politics and even of the Gaelic revival. Irish women were maids and household servants to the wealthy and provided the backbone of the teaching force. The Irish challenged the Protestant-dominated social elite with a rival network of social and political institutions centered on the Roman Catholic Church.
4) Immigration of Italians peaked in the late nineteenth century and the early twentieth century. Early Italian migration consisted mostly of males, and some one-third of Italians returned to Italy. Italians

largely came from agricultural backgrounds; they tended to work for their ethnic kinsmen.

5) The "profound shift" in immigrant population patterns after the 1965 immigration law ended the quota system that had barred most immigrants since the 1920s. In 1970, 18.2 percent of the city's population was foreign born; by 2005, 36.6 percent of it was.

6) In 1970, the leading countries of origin for the city's foreign born were Italy, Poland, the Soviet Union, Germany, Ireland, Cuba, the Dominican Republic, the United Kingdom, Australia, and Jamaica. By 2000, those leading countries were the Dominican Republic, China, Jamaica, Mexico, Guyana, Ecuador, Haiti, Trinidad and Tobago, India, and Colombia.

7) The composition within racial groups has also changed significantly. In 1970, two-thirds of the city's Hispanic population was Puerto Rican; in 2005, Puerto Ricans represented about 35 percent of the Hispanic population, and Dominicans, about 24 percent.

8) The foreign-born population in New York City is most concentrated in its two most populous boroughs: 36.2 percent of the city's foreign born live in Queens, and 31.4 percent live in Brooklyn, compared with 14.7 percent in Manhattan, 14.4 percent in the Bronx, and 3.3 percent on Staten Island.

9) In Manhattan, the only concentrations of immigrants are in Lower Manhattan (Chinatown area) and in Washington Heights, where an estimated ninety thousand to one hundred thousand Hispanics—mostly Dominicans—are clustered.

10) Even on Staten Island, where there is hardly a concentration of immigrations, neighborhoods have been transformed over short periods of time. In the 1990s, the North Shore of the island lost about twelve thousand non-Hispanic whites and gained about ten thousand black and Latino residents.

11) Today, native-born whites with native-born parents represent less than one in five residents of New York City, but only 30 percent of voters are immigrants.

Unit   **8.6**
Topic   **Migration and International Development: Reasons for and Effects of Migration**
Theme   **ICC: diverse cultural perspectives and empathy; ICC: intrapersonal; Interpersonal; ethics: religious diversity and commitment to equality; work and mind habits: innovation and creativity and cross-cultural perspective taking; culture: world history; and politics: globalization and demography**
Region   **Various**
Length   **Three weeks**

Goals and Objectives

1. **Learn** the role immigration plays in the development of host and receiving countries as a whole, learn the diversity of reasons that contribute to the decision to migrate, and learn to view immigration as one of the most important and complex current trends in the world today.
2. **Inspire a curiosity of** understandinghow immigration plays an important role in the allocation of resources across different countries and societies.
3. **Act by** treating immigrants as equals and with respect and by demonstrating multicultural competencies.

Skills and Knowledge

1. Students will analyze global patterns of refugee migration and study maps and other geographic tools to examine migration flows.
2. Students will understand the different push-and-pull factors associated with migration and that there can be multiple factors playing out at once that influence one's decision to immigrate.

3. Students will understand the trade-offs between the costs and benefits associated with migration for the host country and countries of origin.

4. Students will articulate the diversity of experiences that immigrants have and reflect on how those experiences can be positive and enriching ones.

5. Students will explore refugee rights and immigrant rights and be aware of the pros and cons associated with immigration policy.

Activity 8.6.1

The students are asked to interview an adult in their family as well as one other person (with adult supervision) who isn't a family member but is someone the students know (e.g., the owner of a favorite shop, a salesman in a shop, a family friend, etc.)[14] In class each student will present a profile of those people based on the interviews. The students present on where these people were originally from, when they moved to the United States, and why they moved to the United States.

The teacher draws on the discussion and helps introduce the class to the various reasons migration occurs and the fact that it's an ongoing process. The aim is also to show that migration can occur internationally and domestically.

Activity 8.6.2

The teacher provides students with some daunting figures on migration and possibly with a map of global migrant flows in the world—that is, a map that shows where people are moving to. (See http://www.nytimes.com/ref/world/20070622_CAPEVERDE_GRAPHIC.html#.) The students are asked to speculate about the reasons for these movements. Based

---

14 The aim of this activity is also for students to understand how to collect data and undertake research and for them to gain confidence in speaking with people other than those whom they know within their immediate familial context.

on this discussion, the teacher lists three themes/reasons. For each theme, the class is divided into different groups, and the teacher addresses *push* (reasons people leave) and *pull* (reasons people are attracted to other countries) factors.

Group 1: Case of Environmental and Political Factors		
Resources to Draw From	*Activity*	*Discussion and Research*
• http://www.unhcr.org/48ce32c54.html • http://www.youtube.com/watch?v=LpwqK3B2ac8 (This tells the story of a twelve-year-old refugee from Kenya.) • http://www.lostboysfilm.com/learn.html (This concerns the film *Lost Boys of Sudan*—see the educational study guide and classroom lessons.)	• Students can watch a clip from the list given. • Students also read a narrative of a young refugee to understand some of the hardships that young refugees face and the reasons that they became refugees. (See UNHCR Education Materials Catalogue.)	• Who is a refugee/climate refugee?[15] • What are the factors that caused them to leave? • What happened after the earthquake in Haiti? Did people move? Where to? What were the challenges associated with this?

---

15 The teacher should be careful to avoid creating confusion between being a refugee and being a climate/environmental refugee.

Group 2: Case of Economic Factors		
Resources to Draw From	*Activity*	*Discussion and Research*
• http://news.bbc.co.uk/2/hi/7118941.stm • http://www.globalpost.com/dispatch/china-and-its-neighbors/090219/chinas-little-africa-under-pressure	• Students discuss the growing presence of China in Africa and read articles and watch news clips from different media sources. • Students can also see the economics-related information in the following link from the New York Times: http://www.nytimes.com/ref/world/20070622_CAPEVERDE_GRAPHIC.html#.	• What are the economic prospects of migration? • What is labor supply? Labor demand? How does a mismatch between the two influence the prospect of migration[16]?

---

16 This can be a precursor to economics, and a very light introduction is needed.

Group 3: Case of Cultural Factors		
Resources to Draw From	***Activity***	***Discussion***
http://www.pbs.org/ independentlens/ newamericans/ newamericans/mexican_ intro.html Our Selves with Francis Stoner Saunders – a story on Christopher Lydon's Open Source (Public Radio) http://radioopensource. org/borders/	• Students are introduced to the concepts of network effects and diasporas, which may affect the decision to migrate. • This also introduces the social factors behind migration, including factors such as social security, social harmony, and greater social benefits • Also, they might look into how persecution (religious and otherwise) can lead to migration.	• Which countries have good public-service systems and have received high numbers of migrants? (Consider Scandinavian countries.) • Why might cultures and network effects be important considerations in the decision to migrate?

Using the case they have been assigned, the groups will also undertake their own research on each of these factors by reading books and watching clips. The students will present their research on their specific case in class. Students will also be presented with newspaper articles about countries with large receiving and sending migrant populations. Students will be asked to think about which of the three factors above could be part of the reason for these exoduses.

Activity 8.6.3

In this activity, students are divided into two groups. Each group represents a host country (e.g., the United States) and a sending country (e.g., Mexico). In each of the two groups, the students undertake research on the possible impacts of immigration on the two countries. The aim is for students to understand that immigration may impact each of the countries very differently. Students will then be asked to write an op-ed regarding what they believe the costs and benefits of migration are for each of the groups they represent. Some possible discussion points could revolve around the following:

- The concept of Brain Drain (the depletion of the human-resource pool) in Mexico
- Examining who within a household or family bears the brunt of immigration? (Consider those who use household resources to migrate and thus drain the resources of those left behind, and remember that men are more likely to immigrate than women, and thus, families have to fend for themselves.)
- The consequence of immigration for the country of origin: An increase in remittances for Mexico, which contributes to the growth of the economy and to the availability of and access to increased disposable income for households (human capital investments).

Activity 8.6.4

Students are introduced to the PBS documentary *Taxi Dreams*, and they view clips and interviews with thirteen New York City taxi drivers. The interviews include their reasons and motivations for moving to New York City and a summary of the experiences they've had (ranging from positive to negative). (See http://www.amazon.com/Taxi-Dreams/product-reviews/B000K15W7U.)

Using this as a backdrop, students will use online mediums to connect with young people in different schools. They will examine the ways immigrants are treated in their societies, the stereotypes and generalizations made about immigrants, and the degree to which they have assimilated into their societies.

Based on this activity, the students will write a "State of Migrants" blog post and create an online collage of pictures representing the immigrant experience in different countries in the world.

Alternatively, students could also work on exploring some famous immigrants in the United States and examining their unique contributions to the development of society in the United States over the years.

Activity 8.6.5

In this unit, the students revisit the UDHR and are introduced to the role of the United Nations High Commissioner for Refugees and to the concept of refugee rights. In addition, students are split into two groups that will debate the pros and cons of immigration and the need for an immigration policy in particular. Students examine each side of the debate and the issues associated with illegal immigration, resource drains, and so on. They may be presented with an immigration-related dilemma (e.g., given existing push factors in instances of forced migration, what might the pull factors be, and what can governments do?).

The focus is not on going into great depth, as that involves a higher order of understanding. Instead, the focus is on helping students understand that there are pros and cons to every policy. The teacher should be sensitive and extremely careful to ensure that no one particular group is targeted or stigmatized in any manner.

Resources 8.6

- http://www.pbs.org/independentlens/newamericans/newamericans.html
- http://www.nationalgeographic.com/xpeditions/lessons/09/g68/tgmigration.html

Unit	8.7
Topic	**Along the Silk Road: An In-Depth Look at the Cultural Exchange and the Effects of Migration on Art, Music, Trade, and Belief Systems**
Theme	**Arts: literature, visual, music, and dance; economic development; culture: world history and world religions; work and mind habits: innovation and creativity; ethics: religious diversity and ethical frameworks; and ICC: interpersonal (diverse cultural perspectives)**
Region	**China**
Length	**Six weeks**

Goals and Objectives

1. **Learn** how relationships across civilizations translate in artistic influence.
2. **Inspire** students to identify art and spirituality as common elements across diverse cultural groups, as common aspects of the human experience. humanity
3. **Act** by further investigate how various artistic creations reflect cross-cultural influence, and to examine how cultural, economic and technological exchanges are mutually reinforcing.

Skills and Knowledge

1. Students will learn about the points of contact across civilizations that were the result of migration, including those of cultural, economic, and technological exchanges.
2. Students will learn about the influence of Spain and Muslims through Spain to Latin America (this can be an independent research project for students).

Activities

Lesson plans are based on the curriculum unit "Along the Silk Road." There are many resources online about this topic, such as the following:

- http://msh.councilforeconed.org/lessons.php?lid=68366
- http://www.indiana.edu/~iaunrc/content/journeys-along-silk-road-unit-1-middle-high-school
- "The Music of Strangers: Yo-Yo Ma and The Silk Road Ensemble" is a documentary film about the vitality of musical exchange and a vision of global connection through art and culture, in the spirit of the Silk Road. A curriculum based on the film at the high school level is available at silkroadproject.org.

Unit   **8.8**
Topic   **Modern Populations: Case Study of China and India**
Theme   **Global risk: society and health and conflict**
Region   **China and India**
Length   **Six weeks**

Goals and Objectives

1. **Learn** to describe the modern population composition (by ethnicity, race, culture, growth, and migration) in India and China and to describe some policy issues related to population (e.g., policies concerning immigration, workforces, environmental sustainability, population growth, equality, education, and mobility).
2. **Question** the current distribution of people around the world and question current policies with respect to equity.
3. **Act by** creating a project that integrates at least two population issues.

Skills and Knowledge

1. Students will describe the modern population composition (by ethnicity, race, culture, growth, and migration) in India and China and some policy issues related to population (e.g., policies concerning immigration, workforces, environmental sustainability, population growth, equality, education and mobility).
2. Students will evaluate the opportunities and challenges of various population issues (e.g., immigration, population growth or decline, population explosion, integration versus assimilation, and cultural mixing).
3. Students will use information from varied primary and secondary sources to evaluate population policies.

4. Students will synthesize varying viewpoints on population policies and their challenges and opportunities.
5. Students will judge population policies and challenges according to the standards of equity, feasibility, and legitimacy.

Activity 8.8.1
http://nationalgeographic.org/archive/xpeditions/lessons/09/g68/tgmigration.html

Activity 8.8.2
The Population History of India and China
The teacher splits the class into two groups. One will focus on India, and the other will focus on China.

Students will work in groups of four to research the historical migration patterns in India and China. They should produce similar maps and charts as well as narrative explanations of trends in their assigned country.

Students will get into larger groups to present the information they learned about their country to the other groups that researched the same country, to exchange information, and to deepen their understanding of the concepts through discussion.

Students will regroup into mixed groups (i.e., groups of students who studied China and students who studied India) and present to one another the information they learned.

Students will compare the history of population change in China to that of India using a simple chart.

Some key data are available here: www.un.org/esa/population.

Activity 8.8.3
Population Challenges in India and China

The teacher will guide a discussion regarding the many population challenges faced by India and China. These challenges should include poverty, education, urbanization, and health.

Most of the students will choose a challenge of interest to them and work in groups to

1. identify the cause of the challenge and what part population plays in the challenge
2. identify previous attempts to solve the challenge and judge their effectiveness
3. propose a few policy solutions to the challenge.

A small group of students will instead research the broad picture in each country. Rather than focusing on one problem, they will conduct research on the current state of governance and on the overall challenges in each nation. In the mock summit, these students will act as a decision-making body for each nation and choose the most compelling proposal from the groups. This group should research the resources provided by the governments as well as by NGOs and social organizations.

Activity 8.8.4
Mock Summit

Each group will represent its country in a mock summit on the challenges that the countries face. Students will be placed in groups according to the challenge they researched (whether it is in India or China).

They will need to prepare a presentation about their challenge and possible policy solutions.

During the summit, each group will give a brief presentation about its challenge and possible solutions. There will be a question-and-answer session after each presentation.

The few students who make up the decision-making body (see above) present to the group their research on the limits of the resources in the nation. Students get back into small groups to make a case for their policy challenge and solution and for why their challenge should be a priority. Students should prepare to advocate strongly for their policy solution.

Back in the larger summit setting, the students make their cases for why their challenge and policy solution should be prioritized. The decision-making body should meet to discuss the proposals and then make a decision. They should also prepare a rationale for their decision. They will present their decision to the class as a final decision.

To debrief the summit, ask the students for their reflections on this project. Ask them the following questions: What were some of the challenges and opportunities? How did it feel to wait for a decision after making so many preparations? How did it feel to have the decision rest on the shoulders of the decision making body? What did you learn from this experience?

Resources 8.8

- A list of links to sources on US and international demographic data (http://www.ala.org/ala/mgrps/rts/magert/publicationsab/demdata. cfm)

The World Course
Ninth through Twelfth Grade

There are two strands to the World Course in grades nine through twelve: a curricular strand and an individual project. At this level the World Course expects greater self-direction on the part of student in determining what to study, why and how. For this reason, the individual project is the anchor of this activity, with the curricular strand offering the necessary intellectual foundation to support students in developing that project. Ideally the curricular strand will offer many opportunities for personalization, with students helping develop the program of study. For this reason, the semester long courses are presented in less detail than the previous year long courses have been.

The curricular strand is composed of five semester-long in-depth studies of major processes driving globalization, their respective challenges, the past progress made on the challenges, and the current progress being made on the challenges. Each student will choose at least two of these semester-long courses but can take more if he or she wishes. The semester courses are described in the following sections. These courses should be similar to college level courses and we anticipate that as students and their faculty fully flesh them out that they will draw on existing college level courses to identify relevant content. Our hope is that there will be abundant opportunities for personalization at this level, with students pursuing the same topic conceivably accessing different resources and content in ways that is most directly relevant to their interests and to the project students should be working on in high school.

The study of each of the challenges will be rooted in a semester-long course. The case study includes teaching and learning about the following: the skills and knowledge needed to address the challenges associated with that process and various ways to think about the challenge, such as the kinds of questions to ask or the frameworks in which to look at the issues.

The independent (or group) project strand focuses on a multiyear individual (or group) capstone project on an issue that the students will identify by the end of their ninth-grade year, after taking the two semester courses. This project includes independent research, an internship with a mentor and/or an organization working on the issue, the development and implementation of an action plan to help address the issue, and a final senior-year presentation to the rest of the school community on the experience. The students will be placed in advisory groups with peers who are interested in similar issues and will be supervised throughout grades ten through twelve by an assigned advisor and possibly by outside mentors. This project can be executed individually or in groups. The focus is on helping students use their talents and interests to meet global challenges.

- Examples of projects/ issues include the following:
  - o In working on emerging technologies, students will identify (at the end of the semester course) one emerging technology that they believe could address a relevant global challenge. (This is the final activity of the semester course.) They will then identify firms, universities, or other organizations working on the issues; find and do an internship; and write a final paper summarizing their contribution to the issue in their engagement with the firm or university.
  - o In working on the issue of countries in conflict/geopolitical challenge, students will identify organizations working on the issue of interfaith understanding in NYC; map what they do; locate gaps, particularly for high school students; form a student club at their school with other students to develop interfaith

understanding; and leverage resources from other organizations to educate other students on the topic.

o   In working on the issue of health challenges, students will find organizations working on the issue of AIDS in South Africa, do an internship, and develop an art project/book that they will then sell to raise money for an organization identified as doing effective work.

As students work on their independent projects, they will serve as peer coaches for students in the five semester courses. This will serve the dual purpose of tapping into the expertise of more advanced students to teach the courses and keeping the more advanced students engaged in a structured course that will give them the opportunity to deepen their study of the subject they're pursuing in their independent project. Because these projects are likely to be interdisciplinary, a student working on his or her independent project might serve as a resource in multiple semester courses rather than just in the specific semester course in which the project originated. In this way students will maximize their opportunity to explore the interdisciplinary dimensions of their project. For example, a student might initiate a project to study the drivers of youth unemployment in the conflict semester course. This project might evolve into using information technologies to match jobs to candidates or to help candidates develop skills through open-source education. Thus, this student could present his or her project to students in the emerging technology course as well as in the conflict course. The same project might develop some components that would be of interest in the economic-development course. Eventually, the problem that the student is working on will drive the study and integration of the knowledge from various disciplines relevant to the problem.

The World Course
High School Semester Course
The Environment

In this semester-long course, students study the world as it is, as it might be, and as it should be. They use mapping skills to represent the natural and man-made world as it is today in an effort to understand the challenges that humans already face and will face as a result of the destruction of the environment. Students will read one book of fiction (*Oryx and Crake*, by Margaret Attwood) and one book of nonfiction (*Silent Spring*, by Rachel Carson). They will employ systems thinking to understand and predict scenarios for the future if environmental degradation continues unchecked. Finally, they will work together to devise a plan to avoid the disastrous future they predicted.

Overview of the Units

1) The World as It Is
2) The World as It Could Be: Scenario Planning, Part 1
3) The World as it Should Be: Scenario Planning, Part 2

Unit	E.1
Topic	The world as It Is
Theme	ICC: intrapersonal (curiosity about global affairs); ethics: commitment to equality and the value human potential; work and mind habits: innovation and creativity; knowledge: economics, trade, and demography (economic development and poverty); culture: geography; politics; global risk: environment and globalization; arts: literature; skills: investigative and analytical skills (evaluate sources of information, the use of evidence, the local-global link, and creative communication); and global problem solving: produce media, critical consuming, and the use of technology
Region	Global
Length	Six weeks

Goals and Objectives

1. **Learn** about the natural and man-made world and about what threatens the natural and man-made world.
2. **Inspire** students to strive to understand what threatens the natural environment and how those threats can be minimized.
3. **Act** as stewards of the environment.

Skills and Knowledge

1. Students will learn in detail about the main threats to the natural world.
2. Students will use math, science, and research skills to generate information about the natural world.
3. Students will practice mapping and graphing skills.
4. Students will gain in-depth knowledge of six environmental topics.

Overview

The purpose of this unit is to use various methods to represent the world as it is today.

Activity E.1.1
Understanding Sustainable Living

Download the lesson plan "Understanding Sustainable Living" and teach the sixty-minute lesson (https://www.tes.com/worldslargestlesson/).

Study Sustainable Development Goals 11–15 (http://www.un.org/sustainabledevelopment/sustainable-development-goals/).

Activity E.1.2
Mapping the World

Students begin this unit by taking a close look at the world today. They complete a series of mapping activities that challenges them to chart and map the following:

1. Freshwater versus salt water
2. Deserts and forests
3. Endangered animals and plants
4. Energy resources
5. Climactic zones
6. Population

The students create maps, tables, and charts that together should give a picture of the world as it is today. They devote one week to each topic, using multiple sources to gather information and multiples methods to share different aspects of each topic.

For example, for topic 1, the students may make a map showing the major bodies of freshwater and the major bodies of salt water, noting which countries have access to each and which have access to neither. The students may also create a graph that shows the ratio of freshwater to salt water on the planet. They may make tables indicating the primary methods that individuals use to access freshwater around the world. The students may do a brief investigation of where their freshwater comes from (e.g., a water table or an aquifer) and of how it gets to them.

Activity E.1.3
Silent Spring

Students read Rachel Carson's book *Silent Spring* outside of class in preparation for the next two units.

Unit	E.2
Topic	**The World as It Could Be: Scenario Planning, Part 1**
Theme	**ICC: intrapersonal (curiosity about global affairs and conflict-resolution skills); ethics: trust in institutions, breakdown in trust in institutions, common values, commitment to equality, the value of human potential, the importance of global compacts, and commitment to supporting human rights; work and mind habits: innovation and creativity; knowledge: economics, trade, and demography (economic development and poverty); culture: geography; politics; global risk: environment and globalization; arts: literature; skills: investigative and analytical skills (evaluate sources of information, the use of evidence, local-global link, and creative communication); and global problem solving: scenario building, future studies, produce media, critical consuming, and the use of technology**
Region	**Global and China**
Length	**Eight weeks**

Goals and Objectives

1. **Learn** how to use systems thinking and scenario planning to envision our environmental future.
2. **Inspire** students to use critical-reasoning skills to think through a scenario to its probable future.
3. **Act** to avert a potentially disastrous future.

Skills and Knowledge

1. Students will use math and science to calculate risks and to make projections about the future.

2. Students will use systems thinking to make connections between human choices, natural phenomena, and the environment.

Overview

The purpose of this unit is to help students think through the future and about where current trends could lead.

Activity E.2.1
Oryx and Crake

Students begin reading (and continue reading throughout this unit) *Oryx and Crake*, by Margaret Attwood. This book about a fictional future will help the students to think creatively about what the future could look like.

Activity E.2.2
What Are the Issues?

Students come to class with articles and ideas about the most pressing and interesting issues in environmentalism. They evaluate the articles in terms of the information they learned in their analysis of the world as it is (activity E.1.1) and during their reading of *Silent Spring* (activity E.1.2). Combining the three knowledge sources, the students identify environmental risks such as freshwater scarcity, desertification and erosion, extreme weather, climate change, energy choices, biodiversity loss, and more. The class discusses these issues and tries to create linkages between them, perhaps by drawing flow-charts that show, for example, how drought, erosion, and biodiversity loss are interrelated.

Activity E.2.3
A Framework for Understanding the Issues:
Developing Systems Thinking

The environment is a delicate system, and when one variable is altered, it sets off a chain of changes to the system. In order to be able to think about tackling an environmental problem, the students must have an understanding of systems and must practice systems thinking.

Students will be introduced to the concept of systems thinking through a study of the food-energy-water nexus: food production requires water and energy, water extraction and distribution requires energy, and energy production requires water. They will demonstrate their understanding of the concept by creating diagrams that show the interconnections between these three processes and by giving an interactive presentation (maybe of something akin to a Rube Goldberg machine) that shows how water, energy, and food interact. The teacher may want to suggest the human body as a microcosmic representation of this global dynamic.

Activity E.2.4
Case Study: China's Three Gorges Dam

The teacher will lead the class through a study of China's Three Gorges Dam. Using one or more sources (suggestions are included below), the teacher will design a case activity that leads the class through the various dilemmas and scenarios related to the decision to build (and the opposition to building) the Three Gorges Dam. For example, the teacher may first present the class with the following scenario: there is regular, deadly flooding in the Chang Jing River Valley, and China's energy needs are growing at a rapid pace.

The teacher then could ask the class about possible solutions. The students may suggest a dam. When they do, the teacher will reveal the Chinese government's reasoning for the construction of a dam, which includes the facts that

1. a dam emits a small amount of greenhouse gases
2. a dam would prevent the chronic, deadly flooding that affects the region
3. a dam would provide electricity to keep pace with China's growing energy needs.

In this way, the class will learn about how some seemingly environmentally friendly solutions generate may environmental problems. They will also practice thinking about how the dam fits into the larger social, political, and environmental system.

Resource

- American University's case studies on Three Gorges Dam
  - http://www1.american.edu/ted/THREEDAM.HTM
  - http://www1.american.edu/ted/3gorges.htm

Activity E.2.5
Scenario Planning, Part 1

The students look at the list of issues they brought to class during the first activity and are asked to think about how the current environmental system will look if the issues continue along the same course (good or bad). The students will write a creative report describing the scenario, using actual scientific projections whenever possible. The students will share their scenarios with the class and discuss the steps that need to be taken to avoid or improve the scenarios they described.

Unit	E.3
Topic	The World as It Should Be: Scenario Planning, Part 2
Theme	ICC: interpersonal (work in intercultural teams); ICC: intrapersonal (curiosity about global affairs and conflict-resolution skills); ethics: trust in institutions, breakdown in trust in institutions, common values, commitment to equality, valuing human potential, importance of global compacts, and commitment to supporting human rights; work and mind habits: innovation and creativity; knowledge: economics, trade, and demography (economic development and poverty); culture: geography; politics; global risk: environment and globalization; skills: investigative and analytical skills (evaluate sources of information, the use of evidence, local-global link, and creative communication); and global problem solving: scenario building, future studies, produce media, critical consuming, and use of technology
Area	Global
Length	Four weeks

Goals and Objectives

1. **Learn** how to use systems thinking and scenario planning to create a future to their liking.
2. **Inspire** students to use critical-reasoning skills to decide how to create the future they want.
3. **Act** by bringing life to the environmental future they desire.

Skills and Knowledge

1. Students will use creative, visionary thinking to design a healthy future for our world.
2. Students will develop their planning skills.

Overview

The purpose of this unit is to help students to use planning skills to makes something happen.

Activity E.3.1
Making a Plan

Using the ideas generated in the class discussion of the student-generated scenarios, students work in teams (can be international teams if the teacher chooses) to design a detailed plan for avoiding or improving on a scenario that they chose from among the group's work. The teacher continuously prompts each group with questions like, "How will you get people to change their behavior?" and, "How will you get governments to adhere to environmental agreements?" For example, steps may include working with international environmental protection agencies to advocate for sanctions against corporate and governmental polluters. The student product from this activity will be a detailed work plan for how to achieve their desired results that includes action items, roles and responsibilities, projected budgets, and more.

Activity E.3.2:
Scenario Planning, Part 2

After the students come up with a plan as a group, they write new scenarios individually based on the new future that they hope to create. The groups then share their visions and discuss how even with the same plan, their ideas of what the future could look like differ (or are the same). They will share these reports with students in other parts of the world.

Resources:

- Brown, L. 1988. "Analyzing the Demographic Trap" in *State of the World*, 1987. eds. L. Brown and others. New York: W. W. Norton. Pages 20–37 of the PDF.

- Diamond, Jared. 2005. *Collapse: How Societies Choose to Fail or Succeed*. New York: Penguin Books. Chapters 1 and 2.
- United Nations Environment Programme (http://www.unep.org/)
- TED Talks:
  - Innovative water solution (http://www.ted.com/talks/rob_harmon_how_the_market_can_keep_streams_flowing.html)
  - Melting icebergs (http://www.ted.com/talks/camille_seaman_haunting_photos_of_ice.html)
  - Being a weekday vegetarian (http://www.ted.com/talks/graham_hill_weekday_vegetarian.html)
  - Hans Rosling on population growth (http://www.ted.com/talks/hans_rosling_on_global_population_growth.html)
  - Plastic pollution (http://www.ted.com/talks/dianna_cohen_tough_truths_about_plastic_pollution.html)
  - Saving the ocean (http://www.ted.com/talks/greg_stone_saving_the_ocean_one_island_at_a_time.html)

THE WORLD COURSE
HIGH SCHOOL SEMESTER COURSE
SOCIETY AND PUBLIC HEALTH COURSE

In the society and public health course, students will begin with their individual needs for personal health. They will then expand to the public nature of health through an investigation of John Snow's cholera map. They will compare public health from 1900 and today. They will consider the advances that have been made in public health as well as explore careers in public health. Students will then expand their understanding of public health to include the linkages between health, education, and economics through multiple explorations. Students also read Kidder's *Mountains beyond Mountains*, a personal story about the field of public health. Students will use country-level and special-topic study to develop an understanding of health advances and challenges on a global scale. Students create, plan, and execute a public-service campaign around one issue of society and health.

Overview of the Units

1) **Personal Health**
2) **Public Health (What's Public about Public Health?)**

3) **Literacy Link: Kidder's** *Mountains Beyond Mountains* **and Context Studies**
4) **The Health and Wealth of Nations**
5) **An Experiential Learning Project**[17]

---

17 Please see the note in the detailed description of this unit for suggestions regarding the timing of this project.

Unit   **SPH.1**
Topic   **Personal Health**
Themes   **ICC: interpersonal (empathy) and ICC: intrapersonal (ethics)**
Region   **Not applicable**
Length   **Three weeks**

Goals and Objectives

1. **Learn** about public health through an exploration of personal health, about what one needs to be generally healthy, and in particular about a single topic that relates to personal health.
2. **Inspire** in students a desire to maintain personal health for a high quality of life and to show compassion for others who face health challenges.
3. **Evaluate** one's own personal health, the extent to which personal health needs are met, and health resources.

Skills and Knowledge

1. Students will understand broadly their own personal health needs (physical and emotional).
2. Students will compile and organize information on personal health from a variety of sources.
3. Students will explain and describe key information regarding one health topic of interest.
4. Students will identify and explore linkages across multiple components of health.

Overview

In this unit, students will begin their exploration of health by starting with personal, individual health. They will interview members of their family as well as their personal physician regarding health issues. They will compile research on one health topic of interest in a fact sheet to share with peers. Students will also begin to explore some of the important linkages between different aspects of health that will be explored in greater depth in later units.

Activity SPH1.1
What Do You Need to Be Healthy?

Students investigate what they need as individuals to be healthy. Students begin by writing a reflection in their journals about what they need to be physically healthy and emotionally healthy. Students then interview their parents or guardians to determine what those individuals believe they need to be healthy. Students use their reflections to write a list of questions regarding their personal health to ask their pediatrician or family physician. They then interview the physician to gain more clinical knowledge of their personal needs.

Activity SPH1.2
Educating Others about Personal Health

Students should use this list and other information to create a one-page information sheet that will educate others on *one topic* of interest that emerged in their exploration of health. The topics that the students choose should vary widely and should range from prenatal care to exercise, nutrition, vaccination, medical screenings, dental health, physical health, emotional health, mental health, and so on. However, the topics should relate to personal health rather than to public health, which will be addressed later. Students should use the library and online resources to find at least five sources of information to use to develop their information sheet. The information should not be personal to the student but rather an exploration of a topic in personal health that is of interest to them (this is important because this information sheet will be shared). Students should gather in groups of four or five to share their information sheets. They should read the sheets and provide feedback to one another. Students should use their drafts and the feedback to refine their sheets and to create a short presentation for the class.

Activity SHP1.3
Health Mapping: How Healthy Are You?

There are a multitude of self-quizzes on the Internet that evaluate personal health. Students should explore them, take two or three of them, and make notes on the questions that are asked. Students then get into groups of four or five to share the questions that are asked (not their responses) to generate a long list of components of health. Students should also discuss what components of health are left out (usually vaccination and maternal/prenatal care and sometimes mental health).

(Note that the students don't report their own personal health. Rather, they report the types of questions that are asked in the questionnaires and what questions are left out, and then they move on to the linkages. Students should not report their own health, particularly if they aren't healthy and wish to keep that information private. That said, this unit builds from personal health to public health, and the students' levels of health may come up. The teacher should be ready to handle potentially sensitive situations.)

Students use mental-mapping software to brainstorm on the *linkages* between multiple components of health, such as access to prenatal care, economic resources, natural resources, vitamins, clean water, sanitation, and hygiene. Students should report on the linkages they mapped, and when the students present, others should add linkages mentioned by their fellow students to their own work.

Unit	SPH.2
Topic	Public Health (What's Public about Public Health?)
Themes	ICC: interpersonal (one's own identity and culture, others' identities and cultures, and empathy); ethics; work and mind habits: cultural exchange; geography; world history; global risk: society and health; and investigative and analytical skills
Region	London
Length	Three weeks

Goals and Objectives

1. **Learn t**o understand historical changes in perspectives on public health as well as on various treatments and health issues, to understand the impact of advances in public health on populations, and to explore the cultural aspects of health issues.
2. **Inspire** in students compassion for public health issues as well as an interest in the development of knowledge and perspectives on public health over time.
3. **Evaluate** the role of information in advances in public health and demonstrate an understanding of it in classroom presentations.

Skills and Knowledge

1. Students will understand the changes in perspectives on public health as well as the changes in understandings of health issues.
2. Students will evaluate the impact of advances in public health understanding.
3. Students will draw connections concerning the availability of information on public health advances.

4. Students will compile, evaluate, and present information on a particular advancement in public health that is of interest to them.
5. Students will examine the cultural norms and expectations around public health issues.

Overview

In this unit, students will begin with a historical exploration of public health. They will examine John Snow's cholera map in order to make the connection between information, access to information, and advances in public health. They will explore historical and modern perspectives on public health issues as well as the cultural aspects of public health issues.

Activity SPH2.1
What Is Public about Public Health?

Show students an image of John Snow's Cholera map (http://www.ph.ucla. edu/epi/snow/snowmap1_1854_lge.htm), making sure that no map keys are visible. Ask the students to guess the purposes of this map. Students should note that there are bar graphs along the city's streets. Once the students realize that the map documents deaths, reveal that it documents cholera deaths. Ask the students to make observations about the concentration of deaths and the areas from which cholera deaths are absent. (The deaths are clustered around a town pump and are absent from the area near the brewery.) Ask students to guess how the map was used to advance the knowledge of the spread of disease.

Students should independently review the activities on the following website, which features interactive maps and images: http://www. makingthemodernworld.org.uk/learning_modules/geography/05. TU.01/?section=2.

Potential Linked Science Activity

The following in-depth lesson plan could be used either in the World Course as an experiential learning unit or in conjunction with the science department: http://www.cdc.gov/excite/ScienceAmbassador/ambassador_pgm/lessonplans_epi.htm.

Activity SPH2.2
Then and Now: Public Health in the 1900s and Today

The following website provides an interesting historical comparison between public health in the 1900s and today. Advances in tools as well as thinking become apparent. This is an excellent introduction to the history of public health: http://www.lessonplanet.com/register/step-1?keywords=Public+Health&media=lesson&title=Then+and+Now%3A+Public+Health+from+1900+to+Today.

Activity SPH2.3
What Are Some of the Advances That Have Improved Public Health?

Students independently research the following advances in public health and then present them to the class. Even though they are just one component of public health, infectious diseases are used here because knowledge about those diseases has changed over the past one hundred years. Students should present both the historical and modern understandings of the infectious disease and explain how the two understandings have affected public health. Subtopics that may emerge include international preparedness, immunization, sanitation, hygiene, awareness raising, disease and war, screening, diagnostics, and treatment.

Activity SPH2.4
What Are Some of the Cultural Components of Public Health?

After their presentations, students should reflect, either as a whole class or in small groups, on the elements of health that are or have become a part of the relevant culture. Some ideas to think about include the cultural nature of personal hygiene, personal space and distance, and food preparation.

Unit	SPH.3
Topic	*Mountains beyond Mountains*
Themes	ICC: interpersonal (one's own identity and culture, others' identities and cultures, and empathy); ethics; geography; economic development; poverty; global risk: society and health; and investigative and analytical skills
Region	Haiti, Russia, and Peru
Length	Six weeks

Goals and Objectives

1. **Learn** to understand issues of public health in an in-depth way through an analysis of literature and through connecting them with a personal commitment to public health issues and to use the contexts presented in *Mountains beyond Mountains* as case studies on the complexities of health issues and how they vary across contexts.

2. **Inspire** in students a desire to promote public health issues and to work to diminish the impact of poverty on health.

3. **Evaluate** public health policies and their impacts on the lives of many different people.

Skills and Knowledge

1. Students will evaluate the personal story of a person committed to poverty and public health issues.

2. Students will explore the connection between poverty and health.

3. Students will compile, organize, and present information on the variety of health contexts in *Mountains Beyond Mountains*.

4. Students will evaluate and explore careers in public health.

Overview

In this unit, students will begin with literature and with an examination of Dr. Farmer, a character in Tracy Kidder's book *Mountains beyond Mountains* who is committed to health and poverty (http://www.amazon.com/Mountains-Beyond-Healing-World-Farmer/dp/0375506160#_). (Note that the book is 336 pages.) Students will then explore and present information regarding the contexts presented in this book, which can be viewed as case studies on the intersection between health, culture, economics, and policy. Students will then explore careers in public health, primarily by connecting and talking with individuals who have made their own careers in public health.

Activity SPH3.1
Mountains beyond Mountains

(Note this can be ongoing with the following two activities or read more quickly as a stand-alone first activity in this unit.)

Students should read Kidder's *Mountains beyond Mountains*. For lesson plans, see the following:

o   http://www.webenglishteacher.com/kidder.html
o   http://www.bookrags.com/Mountains_Beyond_Mountains

The following are some questions for discussion, reflection, or essay writing:

1. What are the meanings of the metaphor of mountains beyond mountains? What is the relationship between this metaphor and health?
2. What relationship between poverty and health is presented in this book? Do you agree or disagree with this position? Why?
3. What did you learn about the character of Dr. Farmer?
4. How did Farmer's ideas about justice evolve over time?

Activity SPH3.2
Understanding the Contexts Presented in the Book

Students should prepare reports regarding the contexts of public health present in the book. Students should work in small groups to prepare these reports. Each group should investigate one of the following contexts for public health: Haiti, prison populations in Russia, and slums in Lima, Peru. The presentations should answer the following questions:

1. What were the health challenges present in these contexts around the time that the book was written? What are some of the modern health challenges?
2. How would you describe the historical background of these health challenges?
3. What was the historical perspective regarding these challenges? What is the modern perspective regarding these challenges?
4. What is the relationship between health and poverty in these contexts?

Activity SPH3.3
Careers in Public Health

Using the following lesson plan as a starting point, students should explore professions in the field of public health: http://www.discoveryeducation.com/teachers/free-lesson-plans/careers-in-health.cfm. Next, each student should choose one career to explore more deeply. The students will then hold a health-professions career day, and on that day, they will present information on their professions to their classmates. The following is important: To prepare, students should interview professionals in their field as well as investigate the education requirements, job opportunities, and other relevant information of the field. The personal connection to individuals working in the field of public health is key to this activity.

Unit	SPH.4
Topic	**The Health and Wealth of Nations**
Themes	**ICC: interpersonal (one's own identity and culture, others' identities and cultures, and empathy); ethics: commitment to equality and commitment to supporting human rights; geography; global risk: society and health; and investigative and analytic skills**
Region	**Uganda and global**
Length	**Three weeks**

Goals and Objectives

1. **Learn** to understand issues of public health, particularly the connection between the health and wealth of nations, at the national level; to understand, evaluate, and use indicators of public health; to evaluate a public health issue through an in-depth case study of an Ebola outbreak in Uganda; and to collect, evaluate, and present information on a topic in public health.
2. **Inspire** in students a commitment to justice as it relates to public health policies on a national level.
3. **Evaluate** the complexities of national health policies and their inextricable ties with wealth through the use of public health indicators and through presenting information on public health challenges.

Skills and Knowledge

1. Students will understand and articulate the connection between wealth and health at the national level.
2. Students will evaluate and apply the use of national public health indicators.
3. Students will evaluate public health challenges on a national level.

4. Students will compile, organize, and present information on a public health topic.

Overview

In this unit, students will examine public health on a national level. First, they will explore the connection between the health and wealth of nations. They will evaluate and use a variety of health indicators and (time permitting) display their own research on these indicators using StatPlanet software. Students will examine public health issues on a national level as well as with a guided case study of an Ebola outbreak in Uganda. Students will apply what they learn in this unit to an exploration of a special topic in public health.

Activity SPH4.1
The Health and Wealth of Nations

Students use Gapminder's software to describe the connection between the economy and health of nations (http://www.gapminder.org/world/#;example=75). Students define the indicators that are used and evaluate their importance. Students should investigate the variety of health indicators available in this software.

Activity SPH4.2
Worldwide Health Challenges

Students review the Sustainable Development Goal for good health and well-being and use the World Health Organization's website to individually investigate the health challenges of different nations on different continents. Note that each student should pick one country from a list of countries (four or five from each of the continents) and that the teacher should making sure that all of the countries are picked. Students then form groups according to their continents and discuss the health challenges and the challenges that are shared. As a whole class, they then compare the challenges around the world.

Examine specific indicators of SDG 3, good health and well-being: http://www.un.org/sustainabledevelopment/sustainable-development-goals/.

As a possible extension of this activity, students can use Stat Planet software to display their findings using interactive maps (http://www.sacmeq.org/statplanet/).

Activity SPH4.3
Responses to Modern Outbreaks: The Case of Ebola in Uganda

Students view the following video to learn more about the Center for Disease Control's response to disease outbreak: http://www.cdc.gov/CDCTV/RespondOutbreaks/.

Students use this as a model to simulate the response to an outbreak within the school.

As a possible extension of this activity, the World Course could link with the science department at the school and use this in-depth lesson plan that simulates using the scientific method to investigate a fictitious disease outbreak at the school: http://www.cdc.gov/excite/ScienceAmbassador/ambassador_pgm/lessonplans/Johns%20Epi%20Lesson%20Plan.pdf.

The following PowerPoint supports the above lesson: http://www.publichealthtools.com/documents-and-resources/doc_download/59-understanding-epidemiology-steps-to-outbreak-investigation.

Activity SPH4.4
Special Topics in Society and Health

Students expand their understanding of society and health through group investigations into the following special topics: aging populations, population increases (developing nations) and declines (developed nations), poverty and hunger, urbanization, urban planning and sanitation, migration, and equity and resource scarcity.

Teacher Resources

- Lesson Planet lessons on public health (http://www.lessonplanet.com/lesson-plans/public-health)

Resources

- Global Health Council (http://www.globalhealth.org/)
- World Health Organization (http://www.who.int/en/)
- Center for Disease Control and Prevention (http://www.cdc.gov/)

Unit	**SPH.5**
Topic	**Awareness-Raising Campaign Project**
Themes	**ICC: interpersonal (one's own identity and culture, others' identities and cultures, and empathy); ethics: commitment to equality and commitment to supporting human rights; global risk: society and health; and investigative and analytical skills**
Region	**Not applicable**
Length	**Three weeks**

(Note that three weeks is an estimate of how long the in-class portion of this assignment should take. However, the teacher should begin this unit earlier in the semester so that students can work on their own issue in public health while learning about it in class. Some components of the project can be assigned as homework as early as the beginning of the semester. However, the semester should end with the completion of this unit.)

Goals and Objectives

1. **Learn** to understand the components of an awareness-raising campaign and to apply this understanding to the development of a campaign project.
2. **Inspire** in students a desire to advocate for awareness around public health issues.
3. **Evaluate** the complexities of public health issues through the development and execution of an awareness-raising campaign on public health.

Skills and Knowledge

1. Students will understand the components of an awareness-raising campaign and apply that understanding to the development of a campaign project.

2. Students will evaluate awareness-raising campaigns for effectiveness and apply that understanding to campaign projects.
3. Students will reflect on personal experiences with raising awareness around a public health issue.

Overview

In this unit, the students will act on their knowledge of a public health issue and create an awareness-raising campaign on public health. The goals of this project are for the students to see themselves as actors and advocates for equity and fairness in public health issues and to engage in a project that allows them to contribute to public health in a meaningful way. In this project, students should grapple with the complexities of their chosen issue and reflect on their challenges and successes both along the way and after the project's completion.

Activity SPH5.1
An Experiential Learning Project

Students create an experiential learning project in which they tackle a global health problem. They should focus on projects that move the needle on the way people behave, on public policy around public health, or on community access to health care and information. Students should be allowed to choose a topic of interest and should form groups in the class around that topic. For example, they could choose increased resistance to medical treatment and antibiotics, food and water contamination, risk behaviors, sedentary lifestyles, access to vaccination or prevention, substance abuse, mental health, access to preventative care or acute care, or access to affordable healthy food. By this point, students are equipped to explore not only the issue itself but also the linkages between the issue and economics, culture, history, access to resources, and equity.

For this campaign, students should

1. create an educational/PSA video;
2. create a two-page "fact sheet" with information, resources, and a references list; and
3. plan, execute, and reflect on a service activity related to the topic.

The World Course
High School Semester Course
Global Conflicts and Resolutions

Overview of the Semester

1. Introduce frameworks for thinking about conflicts, including about how conflicts build and how they may be resolved, and introduce students to other global conflicts and their causes.
   A. Anatomy of a Conflict
   B. Choices in International Conflict, with a Focus on Security Issues in Asia (optional)
   C. Just-War Theory and World War II
   D. *An Agenda for Peace*
   E. Individuals, Civil Society, and Responses to Conflict
2. Case Study of Israel and Palestine: Conflicts and Resolutions in the Middle East
3. Recovering from Conflict: Transitional Justice (optional)

Ongoing Guided Reading Groups

Either as a whole class or in groups of four or five students, the students will read books together and meet regularly to discuss (with guiding questions from the teacher) the sections they have read. One of the objectives of these reading groups is to supplement the content of the course with human-interest stories on how conflict impacts people and how people, including children, react to conflict. The students will be regularly invited to make connections between what they are learning

344

from these books and the discussions they are having about the ongoing content of the course.

If the students do form groups, they might change groups every three to six weeks, which would allow them to interact with as many peers as possible in small groups and would facilitate the opportunity to confront and resolve the differences in opinion likely to emerge (and thereby to practice one of the themes of the semester, conflict resolution).

The teacher can choose books that match the particular region being studied at the moment or that will broaden the scope of the students' knowledge of different parts of the world, and the books should continue to draw out the common themes of conflicts and resolutions. The following are a few recommendations but others, of course, can be added:

1) Leon Uris's *Exodus* (Israel/Palestine)
2) Le Ly Hayslip's *When Heaven and Earth Changed Places* (Vietnam)
3) Tim O'Brien's *The Things They Carried* (Vietnam)
4) Ishmael Beah's *Long Way Gone: Memoirs of a Boy Soldier* (Sierra Leone)
5) Susan Abulhawa's *Mornings in Jenin* (Palestine/ Israel)
   Starred Review. In this richly detailed, beautiful and resonant novel examining the Palestinian and Jewish conflicts from the mid-20th century to 2002, (originally published as *The Scar of David* in 2006, and now republished after a new edit), Abulhawa gives the terrible conflict a human face. The tale opens with Amal staring down the barrel of a soldier's gun—and moves backward to present the history that preceded that moment. In 1941 Palestine, Amal's grandparents are living on an olive farm in the village of Ein Hod. Their oldest son, Hasan, is best friends with a refugee Jewish boy, Ari Perlstein as WWII rages elsewhere. But in May 1948, the Jewish state of Israel is proclaimed, and Ein Hod, founded in 1189 C.E., was cleared of its Palestinian children…and the residents moved to Jenin refugee camp, where Amal is born. Through her eyes we experience the

indignities and sufferings of the Palestinian refugees and also friendship and love. Abulhawa makes a great effort to empathize with all sides and tells an affecting and important story that succeeds as both literature and social commentary. *(Feb.)*

6) Ibtisam Barakat's *Tasting the Sky: A Palestinian Childhood*

Starred Review. This moving memoir of a Palestinian woman's childhood experiences during the Six-Day War and its aftermath is presented in beautifully crafted vignettes. Barakat, now living and working in the United States, frames the story of her life between 1967 and 1970 with a pair of letters from herself as a high school student in 1981. Detained by soldiers during an ordinary bus trip, she was prompted to try to recall her shattered childhood and share her experiences with others around the world. She begins with a description of her three-year-old self, temporarily separated from her family in their first frantic flight from their Ramallah home as the war began. The author's love for the countryside and her culture shines through her bittersweet recollections. Careful choice of episodes and details brings to life a Palestinian world that may be unfamiliar to American readers, but which they will come to know and appreciate. Readers will be charmed by the writer-to-be as she falls in love with chalk, the Arabic alphabet, and the first-grade teacher who recognizes her abilities.

Culminating Activity

The culminating project will be a series of briefing notes prepared by groups of students on various conflicts and will lead to daylong simulations of attempts to bring resolution to the conflicts. The briefing notes will include

1. The history of the conflict, including major incidences of clashes and the various attempts to resolve the conflict;
2. A list of stakeholders and their grievances and demands; and
3. The economic, social, cultural, personal, and other consequences of the conflict and an explanation of whom it affects.

Unit	**GCR.1**
Topic	**Anatomy of a Conflict**
Theme	**ICC: intrapersonal (conflict-resolution skills); ICC: interpersonal (empathy); work and mind habits: innovation and creativity; politics; and global risk: conflict**
Region	**Various**
Length	**One week**

Goals and Objectives

1. **Learn** that conflicts are composed of different elements and components, that conflicts can have positive as well as negative outcomes, and that these outcomes can determine whether a conflict is constructive or destructive.
2. **Inspire** students to understand that people can respond to conflicts in different ways and that those responses can lead to the resolution or escalation of some components of the conflict, to the creation of new conflicts, or to no change in the original conflict
3. **Act by** translating or applying the framework to current conflicts as they are described in a newspaper.

Skills and Knowledge

1. Students will analyze examples of conflicts and recognize the ways in which they are similar and different.
2. Students will recognize that different people can see the same situation differently.
3. Students will recognize that conflict is a common characteristic of human experience.
4. Students will develop definitions of "conflict."

Overview

Based on material from Stanford's Program on Intercultural and Cross-Cultural Education and the International Security and Arms Control Project this unit introduces international conflict.,

Activity GCR.1.1

1. Students talk about why they are interested in taking this class as an elective, and they are asked to write about a conflict that they have experienced or seen, noting the people involved, the causes and consequences of the conflict, and how it affected them and others. This begins a discussion about the nature and the impact of conflict.

2. Students then view clips from films and television shows of different scenes of conflict illustrating the different types of conflict; the clips listed below are based in the United States, but a quick search would yield clips from shows and movies from other countries that follow the same theme:

   i. A clip from the show *Glee* on how one character faces two different goals, beliefs, or actions that are in conflict with one another or a clip from *The King's Speech* or *Hamlet* (intrapersonal)

   ii. A clip from *The Office* on conflict between individuals (interpersonal)

   iii. A clip from *Modern Family* on a conflict within a group such as a family (intragroup)

   iv. A clip from *Lost* on a conflict between two different groups or a film clip that introduces the idea of ethnic identity separating two groups as a lead-in to later discussions about the Palestinian–Israeli conflict and others (intergroup)

   v. A clip from any variety of superhero movies to illustrate a conflict between two or more nations or a clip from *Thirteen Days* (international)

vi. A clip from any variety of superhero movies or documentaries about the environment or other issues (*The Cove?*) to illustrate issues, actions, or values that have conflicting parties that do not belong to discrete nations or groups (global)

3. In discussing the above clips, students talk about how they know that there is a conflict and about the conflict's causes; impacts, including any positive impacts (emphasizing the idea that not all conflicts are negative and that conflicts should not be avoided but instead viewed as part of everyday life); and personal connections.

4. The clips could be supplemented by pictures (an idea from SPICE) of, for example, car accidents, conflicts in sports, wounds of war, fights between siblings, or protests to visually engage the students. The students could be asked to make up their own miniscene/skit with dialogue to explain the causes and the consequences of one of the conflicts shown in the pictures. The students could choose whether to resolve the conflict in their skits.

5. For homework, students are asked to bring to class more examples of conflicts that would fit into the above categories.

6. An alternative or supplemental activity would be to conduct the following simulation produced by the University of Colorado's Conflict Management Initiatives and the Conflict Research Consortium: http://www.colorado.edu/conflict/civil_rights/simulations/racial_conflict/.

Activity GCR.1.2
Conflict Analysis

1. The teacher chooses a conflict based on a current event and brings in a copy of a newspaper article that gives an account of the conflict (such as an article about the debt-ceiling crisis, an article about the conflict in Sudan, an op-ed on a controversial issue, etc.). The students explore the five elements of conflict defined in the SPICE curriculum: (1) participants (and their feelings and reactions); (2)

goals; (3) interruption (visible evidence or other signals that there is a conflict); (4) management/resolution methods; and (5) results. The students then analyze the event to identify the five elements.

2. The students apply the framework to the other examples of conflicts discussed in the previous day's class.

3. Students are then asked to apply this framework to a conflict they've experienced personally and to discuss it. (SPICE's example involves a student who is trying to study for an exam as a younger sibling plays the TV loudly.) The teacher could continually complicate the situation. Using SPICE's example, the teacher could introduce the fact that there is a history of conflict between the siblings involving the volume of the TV, that one of them had a bad day prior to the interaction, that the TV watching is actually for a school assignment, and so on.

4. Throughout the unit, students are encouraged to raise unanswered and unanswerable questions about the conflict (such as questions about unpredicted events, whether goals are always clear, whether participants will even recognize that there is a conflict, the history behind the conflict, etc.) and are encouraged to avoid simplifying complex situations.

Activity GCR1.3
Conflict Resolution, Management, and Results

1. Students begin to learn the difference between the broad categories of conflict management and resolution by brainstorming a list of resolution methods that they already know. (The list from SPICE curriculum includes negotiation; voting; force/ violence; compromise; manipulation; litigation; pressure such as boycotting, protesting, and striking; denying power; threats and intimidation, competition, and withdrawal.) The lists should also include who might use those methods (e.g., governments, individuals, or other

groups). Students should also examine in which situations they are relevant and in which situations they aren't relevant. (Use the examples of conflicts that students brought to class as part of the previous night's homework.)

2. Students discuss whether there are conflicts that can neither be managed nor resolved and why this might be so.

3. Cover the following points from the SPICE curriculum:
   a. Reactive versus proactive methods of conflict resolution
   b. Unilateral versus bilateral or multilateral ways to manage or resolve a conflict
   c. Violent versus nonviolent methods
   d. Methods that can be used simultaneously or in stages
   e. Methods that encourage common ground, that encourage social change, that operate through institutions, and so on
   f. Other categories (invite students to think of them)

4. Excerpts from the following books would be good supplements to the activity and would encourage the students to talk about the differences between win-win, win-lose, and lose-lose outcomes:
   a. *Getting to Yes: Negotiating Agreement without Giving In*, by Fisher and Ury
   b. *Difficult Conversations: How to Discuss What Matters Most* by Stone, Patton, and Heen

5. Ask students to use some of the conflicts that they've been working on or acting out or some of the conflicts that they brought in as examples on previous days to create several skits that show how the conflicts can be resolved (or not) using the various possible resolution methods discussed above. In all of the following cases, students should be encouraged to talk about the feelings involved for the stakeholders (e.g., the desire for a quick resolution, the fear of escalation, anxiety about uncertainty, hunger for power, etc.) as well as about the values (e.g., national pride, nonviolence, the desire to uphold tradition, etc.) that could influence and determine their choices and decisions.

a. An additional whole-class activity would be for the class to read the following scenario from Thucydides's "The Melian Dialogue" and then role-play as the Athenians and the Melians to try to negotiate a different ending to the conflict (idea borrowed from IAF training): http://www.wellesley.edu/ClassicalStudies/CLCV102/Thucydides--MelianDialogue.html. Half of the students would take part in the role-play activity, and the other half would watch and reflect on it. Then the halves would switch roles, with the second group attempting another resolution and the first group watching and then discussing their observations. Or the class could be divided into two Melian groups and two Athenian groups and then paired up and asked to act out their positions and negotiations, one after another. The whole class would then debrief the scene together, discussing the pros and cons (and similarities and differences) of the two scenes that developed.

b. Or, using SPICE curriculum background notes (http://spice.stanford.edu/catalog/10027/), students examine the following conflict between

> Russia and Japan, with a specific focus on the "Northern Territories" dispute. In this lesson, students will be given the historical background on the "Northern Territories" and on how the islands that make up the "Northern Territories" came to be a barrier to Russo-Japanese relations. Students will be asked to characterize four major perspectives on the issue: Japanese, Russian, US, and Ainu (the indigenous people). They then apply their knowledge of the issue in a simulated international tribunal.

The students then apply to the conflict the frameworks they've learned thus far (identifying the elements) and generate possible resolutions or management techniques.

Resource

- http://spice.stanford.edu/catalog/10096/
- http://spice.fsi.stanford.edu/catalog
- http://hrlibrary.umn.edu/education/4thR-sm94/conflict-sm94.htm

Unit	GCR.2 (Optional)
Topic	**Choices in International Conflict: Security Issues in Asia**
Theme	**ICC: intrapersonal (conflict-resolution skills); ICC: interpersonal (empathy); work and mind habits: innovation and creativity; culture: world history; politics; and global risk: conflict**
Region	**Asia**
Length	**Two weeks**

(Note that www.cfr.org provides academic modules on issues of conflict in other parts of the world that can be used should the teacher choose to focus on other regions besides Asia.)

Goals and Objectives

1. **Learn about** various cases of conflict in Asia and the various types of international conflict resolution and management.
2. **Inspire** students to ask why and when one method is chosen by a conflict's participants over other methods.
3. **Act** by working effectively in small and large groups and managing conflicts.

Skills and Knowledge

1. Students will gain experience in identifying, analyzing, and understanding conflicts.
2. Students will analyze the positive and negative results of particular conflict-resolution and conflict-management methods.

3. Students will learn to interpret and use data to reach conclusions about complex conflicts.
4. Students will recognize that it is necessary to understand the geographic and historical contexts of a conflict in order to understand the current situation.
5. Students will learn skills to enhance awareness and communication.

Overview

Based in part on a SPICE curriculum publication, this unit examines various case studies of international conflict with a focus on security issues in Asia, including the following: (1) US military bases in Okinawa (2) the Korean Peninsula (3) Cambodia, and (4) the effects of long-term conflict

Activity GCR.2.1

"This activity consists of four parts. The focus of parts 1–3 is to provide students with a conceptual framework for dealing with international security issues. Students develop a definition of security and conflict and learn several conflict management and conflict resolution methods. Students also discover how international conflict affects their personal lives and why the maintenance of international security is important."

Activity GCR.2.2

"This activity examines US military bases in Okinawa. Students examine conflicts over the US military bases in Okinawa from varying perspectives. Students incorporate these perspectives into role plays for presentations in front of the class. Following the role plays, the class considers options for resolving or managing the conflicts surrounding the US military bases in Okinawa."

Activity GCR.2.3

"This activity introduces students to security issues related to the Korean Peninsula. Students representing the countries of China, South Korea, North Korea, Japan, Russia, and the United States engage in the development of newspapers that present perspectives from these countries."

Activity GCR.2.4

This activity examines Cambodia and the problem of resolving violent conflicts with long histories. Students learn about multilateral mediation and aid as a means of influencing domestic security and examine the United Nations' multidimensional peacekeeping mission to Cambodia in 1992.

Resource

- http://spice.stanford.edu/catalog/10027/

Unit	GCR.3
Topic	**Just-War Theory and World War II**
Theme	**ICC: intrapersonal (conflict-resolution skills); ICC: interpersonal (empathy); work and mind habits: innovation and creativity; culture: world history and philosophical traditions; politics; and global risk: conflict**
Region	**Japan and the United States**
Length	**Three weeks**

Goals and Objectives

1. **Learn** the principles of just-war theory.
2. **Inspire** students to understand the complexities of making ethical evaluations and of determining whether an act of war or war itself is "just."
3. **Act** by participating in a mock trial of the United States' bombing of Hiroshima to determine whether the act was just.

Skills and Knowledge

1. Students will understand the basis of international agreements, such as the Geneva Conventions, that regulate the conduct of nations in wartime.
2. Students will learn the six principles of a just war ("jus ad bellum").

Overview

Students focus on World War II and discuss the components of just-war theory and its application to conflicts.

Activity GCR.3.1

In this lesson students will read Roosevelt's Joint Address to Congress Leading to a Declaration of War Against Japan (the "day that will live in infamy" speech) in order to assess whether Roosevelt spelled out the case for a just war (http://www.pbs.org/thewar/downloads/just_war.pdf).

Optional Activity

Use the following lesson plan on just wars, which includes a role-playing activity concerning the decision to go into the Korean War and also an evaluation of the My Lai massacre during the Vietnam War: http://www.yale.edu/ynhti/curriculum/units/2002/3/02.03.01.x.html.

Activity GCR.3.2

Students are divided into various roles and take part in a mock trial of the United States' bombing of Hiroshima. Applying discussions and concepts introduced in the unit, they debate whether the bombing of Hiroshima to end World War II was justified.

Possible roles include attorneys for both the defense and the prosecution, a judge, a bailiff, and witnesses.

Optional Activity GCR.3.3

Students take a more contemporary speech made by a president on an act of war (e.g., President Bush's speech after September 11 or President Obama's speech on escalating the troop presence in Afghanistan) and compare it to Roosevelt's speech.

They also evaluate a more contemporary war on the basis of just-war theory and discuss/ debate the terms by which such decisions are made.

Resource

- http://www.pbs.org/thewar/downloads/just_war.pdf

Unit	GCR.4
Topic	**An Agenda for Peace: The Role of the United Nations and the Human Rights Movement**
Theme	**ICC: intrapersonal (curiosity about global affairs); ethics: trust in institutions, breakdown in trust in institutions, common values, the importance of global compacts, and commitment to supporting human rights; work and mind habits: innovation and creativity; culture: world history; politics; and global risk: conflict**
Region	**Various**
Length	**One week**

Goals and Objectives

1. **Learn** the role of an international organization such as the United Nations in resolving and/or managing conflicts.
2. **Inspire students** to determine whether and how international organizations can be effective in conflict resolution.
3. **Act** by participating in a mock summit

Skills and Knowledge

1. Students will gain a better understanding of the concepts of conflict and peace.
2. Students will explore the early history of the United Nations.
3. Students will understand key events and actors in the human rights movement.

Overview

Students analyze the concepts of peace and conflict through the activities of the United Nations. They study how the international organization has attempted to fulfill its goals of maintaining and securing peace.

Activity GCR.4.1

1. Students are asked to apply the UDHR to some of the conflicts introduced in previous units. They should answer the following questions: Which rights are violated in these situations? How could one ensure that human rights are upheld in these kinds of situations? Who, if anyone, is responsible for upholding these rights?
2. Students are reminded (if they are students who have completed the kindergarten through eighth grade curricula) of the conditions in which the UN was founded to set the historical context for the unit.
3. Students are reminded of the history of the human rights movement.
4. Excerpts from books such as Lynn Hunt's *Inventing Human Rights: A History* would be a good supplement to this unit.

Activity GCR.4.2

Students will define "conflict" and "peace" as a way to frame this unit.

Activity GCR.4.3

Students study the three focus areas of the UN—peacekeeping, development and relief, and the environment—within the framework of peace and conflict.

Activity GCR.4.4

Using primary sources from the SPICE curriculum, students analyze the impact of UN peacekeeping missions. They can debate the effectiveness of the UN after reading a variety of articles and op-eds on the UN's role in situations of conflict. Consider having them read the following articles and documents:

- o   http://www.cfr.org/un/effectiveness-un-security-council/p11520
- o   http://www.npr.org/templates/story/story.php?storyId=6138745
- o   The US General Accounting Office's 1997 account of "UN Peacekeeping: Issues Related to Effectiveness, Cost, and Reform" (http://www.fas.org/man/gao/nsiad97139.htm)

They can then reenact the UN Charter Conference in San Francisco and, based on what they discussed during their debate on the effectiveness of the UN, propose amendments and other changes.

Resources

- •   http://spice.stanford.edu/catalog/10009/
- •   http://www.amnesty.org/en/armed-conflict
- •   http://www.hrw.org/category/topic/international-justice
- •   http://www.un.org/en/rights/

Unit   GCR.5
Topic   **Individuals, Civil Society, and Responses to Conflict**
Theme   **ICC: interpersonal (empathy and etiquette); work and mind habits: innovation and creativity; culture: world history; politics; global risk: conflict; and ethics: commitment to human rights**
Region   **Various**
Length   **Two weeks**

Goals and Objectives

1. **Learn** how various individuals and civil societies have responded to conflicts.
2. **Inspire** students to find individuals with whom and organizations with which they feel an affinity in terms of issues and methods of conflict resolution.
3. **Act by** writing letters (via e-mail) to some of the various individuals and/or organizations discussed in this unit.

Skills and Knowledge

1. Students will review and learn new research skills.
2. Students will review and continue to hone their skills concerning group work.
3. Students will review and grow their presentation skills.

Overview

Students will study organizations working toward peace and conflict resolution in groups and will report on them to the rest of the class. They will also individually study the biography of a peacemaker, contact him or her (or his or her living relatives), and then report back to the class.

Activity GCR.5.1

In groups, students will study the following organizations and report back to the class, identifying the following: the history of the organization, its goals, its effectiveness (examples and assessment), the opportunities and challenges that the organization faces, its budget and source of income, its major donors, its list of clients, and other information. Students will be encouraged to contact the organization directly for additional information and possibly to arrange for interviews (using technology) with representatives from the organizations.

Questions for the representatives of the organizations can include the following:

1. In your opinion, what are the differences between peace building, peacekeeping, and peacemaking, and how do you see yourself working in those areas?
2. Do you have a framework for understanding how conflicts build and are managed and resolved? If so, can you share it with the class?
3. What are concrete ways for high school students to get involved in this issue?
4. How did you personally come to care about and work on this issue?
5. What are the skills that one needs in order to be effective in this area?
6. Have you also worked in other organizations on this issue? If so, what were they? How would you compare them (e.g., governmental versus nongovernmental or international organizations, for example)?

The following is a list of some possible organizations (there are many):

1. Global Partnership for the Prevention of Armed Conflict
2. (http://www.gppac.net/)

3. Crisis Management Initiative: Every Peace Matters, which was founded by a Nobel Prize winner (http://www.cmi.fi/)
4. Citizens for Global Action (http://globalsolutions.org/blog/2011/02/diplomacy-action-us-unesco-civil-society)
5. "Learning to Give" lesson plan with a list of organizations working on global issues (http://learningtogive.org/lessons/unit68/lesson1.html)

Also, speakers who work on these issues in various relevant organizations in New York can be invited into the classroom.

Activity GCR.5.2

Individually, students will research one winner of the Nobel Peace Prize (see the suggested priority list).

They will give a presentation on the following information about the Nobel Peace Prize winner:

1. His or her major accomplishments
2. The country and context for his or her work
3. Childhood (where he or she grew up, his or her family and background, etc.)
4. Major factors that motivate him or her to do what he or she does (role models, faith, values, experiences, dreams, etc.)
5. Major personal, political, and other challenges and how he or she overcame them
6. Interesting factoids

Depending on the teacher and students, the presentation can take many forms—it doesn't need to just be a short speech. Consider the following examples:

1. Four or five students can form a moderated panel, pose as the winners, and answer questions.
2. Students can hold interviews in the style of a talk show.
3. Students can hold mock award show where the accomplishments are read aloud and the "winners" give a short speech.
4. Students can throw a "cocktail party" for peacemaking celebrities where they come as the people they researched and are tasked with a list of questions that they then must answer about three or four other people they interact with at the "party."
5. Students can be asked to use as many visuals as they can (e.g., a series of pictures from websites, magazines, or books that illustrate the main points of their presentation) to "narrate" the life of their subject.
6. Students can work individually or in groups to produce video "biopics" of their people.
7. If biographical films of the people they studied are available, students can be encouraged to weave them into their presentations.

The following is a suggested priority list of Nobel Peace Prize winners:

1. Liu Xiaobo (2010)
2. Muhammad Yunus (2006)
3. Wangari Muta Maathai (2004)
4. Shirin Ebadi (2003)
5. Jimmy Carter (2002)
6. Kim Dae-Jung (2000)
7. Médecins Sans Frontières (1999)
8. International Campaign to Ban Landmines (ICBL) and Jody Williams (1997)
9. Yasser Arafat, Shimon Peres, and Yitzhak Rabin (1994)
10. Nelson Mandela and Frederik Willem de Klerk (1993)
11. Rigoberta Menchú Tum (1992)
12. 11)Aung San Suu Kyi (1991)

13. The fourteenth Dalai Lama, Tenzin Gyatso (1989)
14. Desmond Mpilo Tutu (1984)
15. Lech Walesa (1983)
16. Office of the United Nations High Commissioner for Refugees (UNHCR) (1981)
17. Amnesty International (1977)

Study of Nobel Peace Prize winners' biographies

Resources

- http://nobelprize.org/nobel_prizes/peace/laureates/
- http://www.nobelpeacelaureates.org/teach_peace.html
- http://www.amazon.com/Peacemakers-Winners-Nobel-Oxford-Profiles/dp/0195103165

Unit	GCR.6
Topic	**Conflicts and Resolutions in The Middle East**
Theme	**ICC: interpersonal (diverse cultural perspectives and empathy); ICC: intrapersonal (conflict-resolution skills); ethics: religious diversity; work and mind habits: innovation and creativity and variation within cultural groups; culture: world history and philosophical traditions; politics; and global risk: conflict**
Region	**The Middle East**
Length	**Eight weeks**

Goals and Objectives

1. Learn a broad overview of the historical factors that led to the situations of conflict in the Middle East.
2. Learn how conflict affects people, including children.
3. Determine and rank the factors that contribute to the current schism between the two Muslims groups in Iraq.
4. Learn that there is diversity among groups of people regardless of whether those groups are defined by geography, religion, or other categories.

Learn historical, cultural, geographic, and other facts about the Middle East

Inspire students to think of ways to resolve or manage conflicts.

Act by participating in a mock summit on various regional conflicts around the world.

Skills and Knowledge

1. Students will learn diverse perspectives on the same conflict.
2. Students will be able to list concerns that the Sunnis and Shiᵡas will have to address before they heal their rift.

Overview

Students first learn "how the Middle East got that way" by viewing and discussing a documentary and reading and discussing an article. They learn about Muslim diversity as well as diversity within the state of Israel and study the region through geography, demography, and the importance of water as a resource. They delve into the historical background of the Israel–Palestine conflict and examine how the conflict affects families and individuals. They review various responses to the conflict and then participate in a mock summit for conflicts in various parts of the world.

Activity GCR.6.1
How the Middle East Got That Way

Students watch the film *Promises* and discuss the questions and issues that are raised in the film (http://www.pbs.org/pov/promises/).

The film's trailer can be found on the following page: http://www.youtube.com/watch?v=ySJaH7OXzOA.

The following is the website of the film: http://www.promisesproject.org/film.html.

The following is a summary of the film from its website:

> *PROMISES* follows the journey of one of the filmmakers, Israeli-American B. Z. Goldberg. B. Z. travels to a Palestinian refugee camp and to an Israeli settlement in the West Bank, and to the more familiar neighborhoods of Jerusalem where he meets seven Palestinian and Israeli children.

> Though the children live only 20 minutes apart, they exist in completely separate worlds; the physical, historical and emotional obstacles between them run deep.

PROMISES explores the nature of these boundaries and tells the story of a few children who dared to cross the lines to meet their neighbors. Rather than focusing on political events, the seven children featured in *PROMISES* offer a refreshing, human and sometimes humorous portrait of the Palestinian–Israeli conflict.

PROMISES, a film by Justine Shapiro, B.Z. Goldberg and co-director and editor Carlos Bolado, was shot between 1995–2000.

Running time, 106 minutes.
Arabic, Hebrew and English dialogue with English subtitles.

The Children

The 7 children featured in *PROMISES* were filmed over 4 years when they were 9-12 years old:

Yarko & Daniel. Secular Israeli twin boys living in Jerusalem.

Faraj. A Palestinian refugee boy living in the Deheishe Refugee Camp in the West Bank.

Sanabel. A Palestinian refugee girl in the Deheishe Refugee Camp in the West Bank.

Shlomo. An ultra-orthodox Jewish boy in the Jewish Quarter of the Old City of Jerusalem.

Mahmoud. A Palestinian boy living in East Jerusalem.

Moishe & sister Raheli live in the Beit El Settlement in the West Bank.

Students will read a short article as an introduction to an overview of the history of the Middle East after World War II.

They will then make a time line of the key events and raise questions about what they read in the article. In groups, they will investigate the answers to these questions using the Internet and other sources.

Activity GCR.6.2
Muslim Diversity

Refer to the following lesson plan, which introduces the Sunnis–Shi`as conflict: http://www.morningsidecenter.org/teachable-moment/lessons/sunni-shiite-conflict.

Using a lesson plan from the Foreign Policy Association's Great Decisions program, students will learn about broader Muslim Diversity.

Activity GCR.6.3
Israel: Diversity and Identity

Present the various cultural, religious, and ethnic identities of the population of Israel, including Ashkenazim, Mizrahim, Israeli Arabs, and Druze. Discuss the history of Zionism, the creation of Israel, and the ongoing political struggle between religious and secular Jews.

Activity GCR.6.4
Understanding the Middle East through Geography and Demography

Use the following resources:

- o   http://ncmideast.org/outreach/teaching/
- o   http://teachmideast.org/teaching_tools/digital-resources-for-teachers/

Activity GCR.6.5
Water in the Middle East

National Geographic produced this lesson plan on water and oil in the Middle East:

http://www.nationalgeographic.com/xpeditions/lessons/01/g68/iraqoil.html.

Resource

- http://www.al-bab.com/arab/env/water.htm

Activity GCR.6.6
Portraits from the Israeli–Palestinian Conflict

Look at the conflict through the eyes of two families who experienced personal tragedy and loss: http://www.cfr.org/israel/crisis-guide-israeli-palestinian-conflict/p13850.

Culminating Activity (One Week for a Series of Four Simulations)

1. The culminating project will be a series of briefing notes prepared by groups of students on various conflicts, which will then lead to daylong simulations of attempts to bring resolution to the conflicts. Students will be encouraged to think about governmental and non-governmental methods to manage and/or resolve the conflicts.
2. The briefing notes will include the following:
   a. An analysis of the conflict using the frameworks introduced earlier in the semester, including a history of the conflict, the major incidences of clashes, and the various attempts to resolve the conflict
   b. A list of stakeholders and their grievances and demands

    c.   The economic, social, cultural, personal, and other consequences of the conflict and whom they affect

3. Consider the following four possible topics for simulations:
   a. Libya
   b. Israel/Palestine
   c. North Korea
   d. Sudan

4. The fifth day of the week can be devoted to a discussion about the opportunities for personal action, such as the following: http://www.facinghistory.org/resources/units/darfur-now.

Optional

Facing History and Ourselves also has units and a framework on transitional justice (reconstruction, repair, and reconciliation) and South Africa, Rwanda, and Northern Ireland that may be relevant to this semester.

Other Resources

- American Friends Service Committee (http://afsc.org/resource/faces-hope-learn-about-palestinian-israeli-conflict)
- Joseph Nye's book (http://www.alibris.com/search/books/qwork/11896747/used/Understanding%20Global%20Conflict%20and%20Cooperation%3A%20An%20Introduction%20to%20Theory%20and%20History)
- More information on international conflicts (http://www.lessonplanet.com/search?keywords=international+conflicts&media=lesson)
- Envision's resources for teachers on globalization (http://www.globalenvision.org/teachers)
- Optional reading (http://en.wikipedia.org/wiki/The_Man_in_the_High_Castle)

The World Course
High School Semester Course
Development Economics: Growth and
Development in Latin America

In this semester-long course, students learn about global economic dependencies through international trade, investment, and exchange rates. Students question their role in growth and development and seek to find new holistic approaches to development. Students also address conundrums about whether human development and democracy are precedents to growth or follow growth later. Using personal stories, core economic concepts, and data sources, the unit aims to provide students with an opportunity to connect the larger with the personal. Each unit has a data-based activity and a culminating project-based activity. This semester-long unit is derived from introduction to development economics courses at the college level and draws extensively from the advanced-placement economics curriculum. The unit does not aim to supplant the AP economics curriculum but rather to serve as a primer that will pique students' interest in learning more about some of the more challenging economic concepts that the AP economics curriculum addresses.

The unit is divided into three parts, each of which lasts six weeks:

1. International Trade
2. Exchange Rates, FDI, and the Argentinian Crisis
3. Going beyond Economic Growth and the Role of Institutions in Growth

Unit	DE. 1
Topic	International Trade
Themes	ICC: interpersonal (empathy and working in intercultural teams); ICC: intrapersonal (curiosity about global affairs); ethics: trust in institutions, breakdown of trust in institutions, and the importance of global compacts; economic development; and poverty
Region	World Latin America
Length	Six weeks

Goals and Objectives

1. **Learn** about international trade and the concepts of free trade and fair trade.
2. **Inspire** students to learn about the workings of international trade and about how it can be a powerful and efficient tool that can build bridges and create inequalities simultaneously.
3. **Act** as informed agents who can defend their stance when they hear misconceptions about trade (e.g., trade results in unemployment).

Skills and Knowledge

1. Students will draw a personal connection between poverty at the global/regional level and that at the individual level.
2. Students will learn about different indexes of poverty and inequality (e.g., the Gini coefficient and the Lorenz curve).
3. Students will use statistics and data sets on international trade to substantiate and confirm their own intuitive hypotheses.
4. Students will examine protectionist trade policies in Latin America and the use of free trade agreements.

5. Students will analyze the winners and losers in the globalization debate through statistics, personal stories, and core economics–based concepts.

Overview

The unit begins with an introduction to the concepts of sustained, inclusive, and sustainable growth; poverty; and inequality in Latin America, and students read various current articles and reports about these topics. The unit focuses on international trade, why nations trade, the concepts of comparative and absolute advantage, and whether trade is indeed an important ingredient of growth for countries in the region.

Activity DE.1.1
Sustainable Growth

Study SDG 8, sustained, inclusive, and sustainable economic growth; full and productive employment; and decent work for all: http://www.un.org/sustainabledevelopment/sustainable-development-goals/.

Activity DE.1.2
Poverty and Inequality

Students begin by watching snippets of the documentary *The End of Poverty* (http://topdocumentaryfilms.com/end-of-poverty/).

After viewing the film, the students discuss what they found alarming in the film and some of the common characteristics of poverty in the different parts of the world that the film focuses on. Students specifically discuss the differences in poverty in the different countries in Latin America shown in the documentary.

The teacher then introduces the concept of poverty to the students, and they discuss the following questions:

1. How is "poverty" defined? How is it measured?
2. What are the one- and two-dollar-a-day benchmarks for poverty?
3. What does "absolute poverty" mean?

Using portions of the following lesson plan from the Council for Economic Education, students learn about Lorenz curves and about how Gini coefficients are calculated: http://www.econedlink.org/lessons/index.php?lid=885&type=educator.

Advanced students and the teacher may read the following for background information: http://web.worldbank.org/WBSITE/EXTERNAL/TOPICS/EXTPOVERTY/EXTPA/0,, contentMDK:20238991~menuPK:492138~pagePK:148956~piPK:216618~theSitePK:430367,00.html.

Students then collect data on poverty rates and inequality in Latin America, and, based on their analyses, they write an op-ed on the decline of poverty and inequality in the region. Students may choose to pick a country or a group of countries within the region. In particular, students should focus on the differences in the averages of the trends.

Alternatively, time permitting, students may also examine some of the demographic household surveys (DHS) used in Latin American countries to examine how poverty is measured using various different indicators.

Resource

- http://siteresources.worldbank.org/INTLACREGTOPPOVANA/Resources/840442-1291127079993/Inequality_Reduction.pdf

Activity DE.1.3
Latin America's New Promise

As an introduction to the semester and to its focus on economic development within Latin America, students are asked to read the following articles and reports regarding the rise of Latin America and the growth prospects for the region between 2008 and 2011:

- ○ an article in the *Economist* about Latin America's economic renaissance in the past decade and the potential impediments to growth (http://www.economist.com/node/16990967)
- ○ a brief summary of a report by Brookings about how demographics, China's slowing growth, and the global-savings level pave the way for opportunities for growth in Latin America (http://www.brookings.edu/opinions/2011/0711_latin_americas_decade_cardenas.aspx)

(Note that the teacher should be aware that these pieces may throw up more questions regarding, for example, the Latin American debt crisis and some issues around exchange-rate fluctuations. Students should be informed that they will get answers to some of their questions as they proceed through the curriculum and answers to others in more advanced economics classes.)

Students will be asked to review these pieces and to divide into groups. Each group will then pick a few Latin American countries, collect the following data on the countries, and analyze the relevant historical trends from 1970 to the present day in those countries:

1. GDP of the countries
2. Growth rates of the economies
3. Percentage of GDP attributed to the primary sectors (agriculture and natural resources), to the secondary sector (manufacturing), and to the tertiary sector (services) over time

4. Level of exports and imports over time
5. Trading partners
6. Unemployment rates and inflation

Based on their analyses, the students will present to the class their observations on time periods when there were peaks, troughs, and anomalies in the data. They will also examine whether the nature of trade has changed over time, whether it has remained the same, and whether there appear to be any trends in the types of goods that are exported and imported in the region.

Students will also collect similar data on the East Asian "tiger economies" (Hong Kong, Singapore, Taiwan, and South Korea) and draw comparisons between the trends observed in the Latin American countries and those observed in the East Asian "tigers."

The following is a list of data sources and other useful sources for information about the economy of Latin America:

- o   Data and statistics on Latin America by the World Bank (http://web.worldbank.org/WBSITE/EXTERNAL/COUNTRIES/LACEXT/0,, menuPK:258575~pagePK:146732~piPK:146813~theSitePK:258554,00.html)
- o   The tables on page 73 of this academic paper about the historical growth rates and predicted growth rates based on several socioeconomic-political factors http://www.bcentral.cl/eng/studies/working-papers/pdf/dtbc265.pdf)
- o   OECD Latin America desk (http://www.oecd.org/about/0,3347, en_2649_33973_1_1_1_1_1,00.html)

Note that the second listed source may be used as background information for the teacher to draw from.

Activity DE.1.4
Understanding Free Trade and Comparative Advantage

Using the example of Bob and Ann, who are stranded on an island and working toward surviving and trading items with each other, students are introduced to the concepts of absolute advantage and comparative advantage.

The following sample lesson plans introduce the concept of comparative advantage:

- http://www.econlib.org/library/Enc/ComparativeAdvantage.html
- http://www.flatworldknowledge.com/pub/international-trade-theory-and/199668#web-199668
- http://www.imf.org/external/np/exr/center/students/hs/think/lesson4.pdf

After they have developed an understanding of comparative advantage, the students will further extend the concept of comparative advantage to the concept of free trade among nations and will undertake a detailed analysis of the data they collected in activity 1.

In this analysis, students will learn about correlations (this learning will be teacher led) and draw out correlations and associations between growth rates, increases in GDP, unemployment rates, and the levels of trade in Latin America. The goal is for them to understand whether standards of living have indeed increased because of trade in the region as a whole or in particular countries with higher levels of trade.

Finally, using the case of Latin America, students will write a position paper on how international trade might result in greater benefits for all. Students can refer to the following article as an example of what might be expected: http://www.econedlink.org/lessons/docs_lessons/575_international_trade1.pdf.

Teacher Resources

- http://www.crawfordsworld.com/rob/ape/APEBrueNotes/APEBrue18.html
- The "Why Nations Trade" lesson plan (http://www.globalization101.org/teacher/trade) (See the "Why Nations Trade" lesson plan)

Activity DE.1.5
Is Free Trade a Win-Win Situation for All?

Students will revisit some of the numerical problems that they faced when they were introduced to the concept of free trade and will now look at cases of restricted trade and protectionism numerically. In particular, students will closely examine the different ways in which trade between nations may be restricted through quotas, tariffs, embargoes, and voluntary export restraints.

The following is a list of sample lesson plans and readings around a conceptual understanding of protectionism:

- Background reading for teachers (http://www.councilforeconed.org/resources/lessons/Focus_International_Econ_Sample_Lesson.pdf)
- A resource for students that draws from the US embargo on trade with Cuba and examines why some US farmers are advocating for the Cuban embargo to be eliminated (http://www.econedlink.org/lessons/index.php?lid=529&type=educator)
- http://www.globalization101.org/index.php?file=issue&pass1=subs&id=14
- A resource on saving jobs as a rationale for protectionism (http://www.econlib.org/library/Enc/FreeTrade.html)

Students will divide into groups and pick countries in the Latin American region that have had experience with protectionist policies (e.g., Brazil's ban on the export of rice in 2008 to protect its domestic consumers and the 2009 tariff imposed by Mexico on US imports as a response to protectionist US policy). They will then present country profiles to the class, answering the following questions:

1. What is import-substitution industrialization?
2. What is export-oriented industrialization? How does it relate to trade? What caused the shift to this strategy?
3. What is the history of protectionism in that particular country?
4. Who benefits from protectionism in that country?
5. Who loses from protectionism, and who is harmed?
6. Are there noneconomic reasons (e.g., political reasons like HR violations or nuclear proliferation) that might be driving a protectionist policy?
7. Can different interests be balanced, or is it an either-or choice?
8. What are current political opinions about protectionism in that country?
9. Which side of the argument do you find more convincing? Why?

Students could watch a selection of the following films:

1. *The Seattle Syndrome*, a documentary film about the protests at the WTO summit in Seattle and whether protests are the best way to bring a fair agenda to the table (http://www.bullfrogfilms.com/catalog/lsss.html)
2. *Life: The Story So far*, a documentary film about how the globalized economy affects local people (http://www.bullfrogfilms.com/catalog/ls1.html)
3. *The Economics of Happiness*, a documentary about the economics of localization (http://www.theeconomicsofhappiness.org/helena-on-tedx)

As a final culminating activity, students undertake background research on various free trade agreements such as the NAFTA (North American Free Trade Agreement), the CAFTA (Central America Free Trade Agreement), and the Mercosur (economic and political agreement between Argentina, Brazil, Paraguay, and Uruguay to promote free trade and the fluid movement of goods, people, and currency).

Use the following link (click on the tab that says "Lesson Plan on Trade Agreements") for a lesson plan around the NAFTA and its pros and cons: http://www.globalization101.org/index.php?file=issue&pass1=subs& id=19.

At a mock policy summit, students will represent different countries, defend their interests, and balance different perspectives to negotiate a fair trading arrangement and to debate whether trade is indeed an impetus for growth.

Unit	DE. 2
Topic	**Exchange Rates and FDI**
Themes	**ICC: interpersonal (empathy and working in intercultural teams); ICC: intrapersonal (curiosity about global affairs); ethics: trust in institutions; and economic development**
Region	**Latin America, with a focus on Argentina**
Length	**Six weeks**

Goals and Objectives

1. **Learn** how exchange-rate fluctuations influence economic growth through FDI.
2. **Inspire** students examine in depth the international financial market and its intricacies.
3. **Act** as aware students who understand that globalization has its pros and cons and what the breakdown of trust in institutions looks like.

Skills and Knowledge

1. Students will learn about core economic concepts concerning free and floating exchange rates, the various kinds of investment and their determinants, purchasing power parity, and the Big Mac Index.
2. Students will become interested in examining how fluctuations in the international financial market might influence growth and development.
3. Students will become aware of and informed about the Washington Consensus and its role in the Argentinian crisis.
4. Students will learn about the breakdown of trust in institutions in the case of the Argentinian Crisis through studying personal stories.

Overview

Through this unit, students learn about core economic concepts associated with the international exchange market and about how fluctuations are dynamic and affect trade, investment, and overall growth in countries.

Activity DE.2.1
Exchange Rates

Using auctions and simulations as outlined in lesson plans by the IMF, students learn about the demand and supply of foreign currency and how exchange rates are determined. Use the following lesson plans:

- ○ http://www.imf.org/external/np/exr/center/students/hs/think/lesson7.pdf
- ○ http://www.imf.org/external/np/exr/center/students/hs/think/lesson7.pdf

Through these lesson plans, students also get a conceptual understanding of fixed and flexible exchange rates and the various factors that cause changes in flexible exchange rates.

(Note that based on the simulations, the teacher can build in circumstances that force the students to think further about the factors that cause changes in flexible exchange rates.)

Students visit www.xe.com, which has a record of exchange rates between various countries since 1995, and examine some of the trends in the exchange rates of countries in Latin America.

Teacher Resource

- Lesson plan from the Council for Economic Education on exchange rates (http://www.econedlink.org/lessons/index. php?lid=342&type=educator)

Activity DE.2.2
Trade, Exchange Rates, and Purchasing Power Parity (the Big Mac Index)

Using the following lesson plan from the Council for Economic Education, students learn about how exchange rates affect trade levels: http://www. econedlink.org/lessons/index.php?lid=342&type=educator.

Students also learn about concepts of appreciation and depreciation using the lesson plan. Through the following lesson plan from the Council for Economic Education, students learn about the Big Mac Index and the concept of purchasing power parity: http://www.econedlink.org/lessons/index. php?lid=156&type=student.

Each student picks a country from the region and collects information on the currency exchange rate within that country as compared to that of the United States. Using data on the value of the currency, the student estimates whether the currency has appreciated or depreciated and predicts the effect of those changes on the imports and exports within the country.

The students subsequently refer back to the initial data they collected and closely examine how the import and export baskets of their countries might have changed owing to the fluctuations in currency.

Alternatively, students may examine data from the *Economist*'s Big Mac Index and examine whether the currency of the country they picked is overvalued or undervalued and how close it really is to the purchasing power parity.

Activity DE.2.3
Foreign Investments in Latin America

The lesson plan from Globalization101 on foreign investments in Latin America is highly recommended.

Students begin by browsing through some of the content on this website. The following is a list of the questions they should answer and links to the pages where they can find those answers:

1. What are the different kinds of foreign investment (http://www.globalization101.org/issue_sub/investment/investmentintroduction/kinds_of_foreign_investment)?
2. What are the differences between FDI and portfolio investments (http://www.globalization101.org/issue_sub/investment/investmentintroduction/portfolio_and_direct_investments)?
3. How are globalization and the rise of financial investment related? (http://www.globalization101.org/issue_sub/investment/investmentintroduction/portfolio_and_direct_investments)

Optional Activity

http://www.globalization101.org/teacher/investment

1. This activity shows an American apparel-manufacturing company that makes different types of clothing. The company is considering

investing in a foreign country specifically in Central America because it knows that those countries have recently negotiated a free trade agreement with the United States. The students should analyze the information related to every Central American country and recommend a decision about which country should be selected for the investment venture. The company has just enough capital to invest in a single country. Finally, some optional ways to analyze the decision in different circumstances are shown. The scenario is described in handout 4.

2. Read the scenario in handout 4 to the class or provide a copy of handout 4 to each student. Act as the manager of the company, and ask the students firstly about the possible benefits and costs associated with an investment in a Central American country. Then ask the students to list the main criteria or the economic, political, legal, and technological variables related to each country that will need to be analyzed before a decision about where to invest can be made. In order to avoid an overly extensive and complex exercise, you can ask the students to select just the five or six most important variables. Students may answer orally in class as a group or individually in a written in-class or homework assignment.

3. You may have the students to do extra research on the Central American countries that have signed the free trade agreement (Guatemala, Honduras, El Salvador, Nicaragua, and Costa Rica) using the following links:
   - the IMF's website (http://www.imf.org/external/country/index.htm)
   - the IADB's website (http://www.iadb.org)
   - the links page on Auladeeconomia.com (http://www.auladeeconomia.com/links2.htm)
   - the links section on Globalization101.org and also other international organizations' websites or media websites

4. Once the students have selected the variables that they're going to review for each country and compiled information on each one, you can ask them to make a comparison using the following table:

Variables	Country				
	Guatemala	Honduras	El Salvador	Nicaragua	Costa Rica

1. Then ask the students to make a decision. Ask them to study the possible risks associated with their decision.
2. Ask them how their decision change would change if investing in China were an option.
3. Also ask the students to consider how their decision would change if the company wanted to install a client-assistance center in the United States instead of manufacturing clothes.
4. Finally, make a series of conclusions regarding benefits, costs, and risks for companies when they invest abroad, and decide which of those factors determine their decisions regarding investments in other nations.

Activity 4
The Washington Consensus and the Argentinian Crisis (1999–2002)

Students form a reading group and are asked to read portions of the following books and to then discuss and present their views on the texts:

- *The Wind of the Hundred Days: How Washington Mismanaged Globalization*, by Jagdish Bhagwati
- *Globalization and Its Discontents*, by Joseph Stiglitz
- *The End of Poverty: Economic Possibilities for Our Time*, by Jeffrey Sachs
- *The Elusive Quest for Growth: Economists Adventures and Misadventures in the Tropics*, by William Easterly

After reading selected chapters in these books, students are asked to present in class a case study of a country that was impacted by the Washington Consensus reforms (positively and negatively). Students should answer the following questions:

1. What was the Washington Consensus?
2. What were the policy recommendations made by the consensus for the country?
3. Why were some of the recommendations unsuccessful or successful in that country?
4. How was Latin America as a region specifically affected by the consensus?

Students are then asked to view archives of different newspapers and journals that reported on the Argentinian crisis. Use the following sources:

o   http://www.time.com/time/world/article/0,8599,189393,00.html
o   http://www.econedlink.org/lessons/index.php?lid=776&type=educator
    http://www.guardian.co.uk/world/2001/dec/20/argentina1

Students subsequently may watch the following documentary film:

o   *The Take*, a story about how the economic collapse in Argentina affected the middle class and resulted in high unemployment (http://thetake.org/index.cfm?page_name=synopsis)

Culminating Activity

Students divide into two groups and use these sources as well as their understanding of exchange-rate markets and concepts around capital flight to complete a culminating activity.

One group creates a video report on the Argentinian crisis, the situation in the country during the nine days when the banks were closed, and the people's loss of confidence in the currency of the country.

The second group creates a video report on the Argentinian government's response to the crisis.

Unit	DE. 3
Topic	**Poverty and Inequality in Latin America and the Political Economy of Growth**
Themes	**ICC: interpersonal (working in intercultural teams and empathy); ICC: intrapersonal (curiosity about global affairs); ethics: trust in institutions; economic development; poverty; and politics: government)**
Region	**Latin America and Asia (Bhutan)**
Length	**Six weeks**

Goals and Objectives

1. **Learn** about various alternate approaches to growth and development and the role of politics in growth and development.
2. **Inspire** students to further question and examine their own interpretations and understandings of growth within cultural contexts.
3. **Act** as informed agents who understand that growth doesn't occur in isolation and that several intertwining factors determine how countries grow and how disparities converge or diverge.

Skills and Knowledge

1. Students will examine the importance of human-capital development in economic growth and development and its role in the Latin American experience through data.
2. Students will learn about social safety nets and the use of conditional cash-transfer programs in addressing poverty alleviation.
3. Students will reflect upon new approaches to development and their practical uses.
4. Students will address the relationship between politics and economics and the importance of strong governance in promoting growth.

Overview

In this unit, students go beyond traditional measures of economic growth and seek to address what inclusive and holistic development might look like. Students also examine the interrelationship between economics and politics and seek to understand the role of democracy in the Latin American growth experience.

Activity DE.3.1
Study SDG Goal 10: Reduce Inequality within and among Countries

Use the following link: http://www.un.org/sustainabledevelopment/ sustainable-development-goals/.

Activity DE.3.2
Investing in Human Capital in the Region

In this activity, students are asked to pick a country and to collect the following information on it: the country's progress on the education and health SDGs, the historic rates of access to education and health care in the country, and how that access has changed over time with globalization. (Use the data that the students have collected through the year on growth rates and development.)

Resources

- *Unequal Schools, Unequal Chances: The Challenges to Equal Opportunity in the Americas*, by Fernando Reimers
- Chapter 5 "Inequality of Opportunity in Educational Achievement in Five Latin American Countries." Published in a 2008 World Bank Report: *Inequality of Opportunities in Latin America and the Caribbean*

- *Quantity without Quality: A report Card on Education in Latin America*

Based on their analyses, students should aim to address the question of whether higher growth enables greater human capital or higher rates of human-capital development enable higher growth rates.

The teacher introduces the students to the concepts of subsidies and conditional cash transfers. Students undertake background research and present to the class on the use of social safety nets as a poverty-reduction strategy and the use of CCTs within the countries of their choice. Students should aim to answer some of the following questions:

1. When were CCTs introduced? Why?
2. What are the strings attached to the CCT? What does it seek to do?
3. What have experiences with the CCT been thus far? Is the program considered successful?

The students can use the following resources from the World Bank:

- http://web.worldbank.org/WBSITE/EXTERNAL/COUNTRIES/ LACEXT/EXTLACREGTOPLABSOCPRO/0,, contentMDK:21246 201~pagePK:34004173~piPK:34003707~theSitePK:503655,00.html
- http://www.economist.com/node/4408187

Students read the following article about PROGRESA: http://www.economist.com/node/181376.

Activity DE.3.3
Is Growth All That Matters for Development?

Students then read the first and concluding chapters of Amartya Sen's *Development as Freedom* as an introduction to the concept of capabilities and freedom as defining concepts of development.

Students also examine some alternate ways that countries and agencies are working to go beyond just economic growth. Students may be divided into different groups and present in groups on the different approaches being used to examine development. Some topics may include the following:

1. Bhutan and its experience with "Gross National Happiness," including whether this idea is extendable and what "subjective well-being" entails as a marker of development
2. A comparison of the *World Development Report* and the *Human Development Report*
3. Stability and peace as indicators of development
4. Acemoglu, Johnson, and Robinson on the role of geography and institutions in development (2001)

Students may question whether the main thesis of their topic is strong, relevant, and practical in current contexts and whether these new approaches to development can be further expanded. Do they believe there are gaps? If so, what might those gaps be, and how can holistic and inclusive development be defined and measured?

Activity DE.3.4
The Political Economy of Growth and Development in Latin America

Students begin by reading the following pieces:

o a piece on the political economy of Latin America and its role in the growth and development of the region (http://www.economist.com/node/16964114)
o a piece on democracy and growth in Latin America (http://foreign.senate.gov/imo/media/doc/Reid_Testimony.pdf)
o a piece on the need for Panama (Latin America's fastest-growing economy) to address issues of governance (http://www.economist.com/node/18959000)

Students then use those pieces to answer some of the following questions:

1. Is democracy a precedent of growth?
2. What might be the influence of regimes on growth?
3. What have the historical experiences of different countries within the region been?
4. How do crime rates and government debt influence investor confidence and FDI flow?
5. What is the role of corruption and informal economies in growth?
6. How have countries with regimes other than democracies experienced growth and development?

Option 1

Students may use a data set of FDI flows and overlay it with important political developments in a country of their choice to examine the changes over time and the associations between politics and economics. Students may also map growth rates with political-regime characteristics, as done by the Polity IV Project (http://www.systemicpeace.org/polity/polity4.htm).

Option 2

Students may interview the chief investment officer of a Multi National Corporation that has operations in Latin America or different parts of the world about some of the factors that he or she considered while deciding where to invest. Simultaneously, the chief of economic affairs of a consulate from one of the BRIC countries could be invited to give a presentation on some of the reforms and incentives being undertaken by the government to attract investors and to continue restoring investors' confidence.

This one-semester course examines the relationship between technological and social developments and how the acceleration of technological innovation causes social change and can address some of the most critical global challenges. Students will examine various emerging technologies and discuss their social implications and possible uses and the consequences of these developments for globalization.

Unit	TIG.1
Topic	The Marvel of Innovation and the World of Inventors
Themes	ICC: intrapersonal (curiosity about global affairs); ethics: common values; work and mind habits: innovation and creativity; knowledge: politics ; investigative and analytical skills; assessing global affairs: evaluate sources, the use of evidence, and creative communication; and global problem solving: future studies, scenario building, and the use of technology
Region	Not applicable
Length	Three weeks

Goals and Objectives

1. **Learn** to appreciate invention as an ongoing process that underlies improvements to quality of life and to analyze invention

as the product of individuals' work in contexts that support innovation.

2. **Inspire** students to be curious about emerging technologies and to anticipate their likely social impact.

3. **Evaluate** the main technological innovations of the twentieth century and demonstrate an understanding of how the process of technological innovation improves well-being.

Skills and Knowledge

1. Students will identify the major emerging technological innovations in the twenty-first century.

2. Students will explain and describe the likely social consequences of at least one major emerging technological innovation, what technologies it replaced, the costs and benefits associated with it, and how it might be used to address one of the global challenges identified in the SDGs.

This unit introduces the topic of invention and examines how it addresses social challenges. Using episodes from Planet Green TV's *Dean of Invention*, in which inventor Dean Kamen discusses emerging technologies, students examine some of the current technological innovations and discuss their applications. They then examine the contributions of Kamen himself as an inventor.

Activity TIG.1.1.

In small groups students select one of the episodes featured in "Dean of Invention" (http://planetgreen.discovery.com/tv/dean-of-invention/dean-of-invention-episode-guides.html) and study one invention of their choosing. Students might focus on microbots, bionic bodies, wired brains, robots, energy, motion, or flight, for example.

For each innovation, students will prepare a report that answers the following questions:

1. What are the benefits of this technological innovation?
2. What previous technologies does it replace, improve, or build upon?
3. What are the costs of this innovation?
4. How do these costs compare to the benefits?
5. In what way can this innovation address some of the global challenges identified in the Millennium Development Goals?
6. What roles did the government and the private sector play in supporting this innovation?
7. What obstacles is this innovation likely to face as it goes to scale?

Activity TIG.1.2.

Students will then present and discuss their reports in class. In this discussion, they will examine the similarities and differences in the ways in which each invention disrupts an existing approach to addressing a problem. They will examine how emerging technologies have supported the invention and the institutions that have supported it.

Activity TIG.1.3.
The World of Inventors and the Life of Dean Kamen

Students will read the *book Reinventing the Wheel: A Story of Genius, Innovation, and Grand Ambition* (http://www.amazon.com/Reinventing-Wheel-Genius-Innovation-Ambition/dp/0060761385).

They will then write a reflections paper summarizing the main argument of the book and analyzing the contributions of Dean Kamen to society. They will examine in what ways Kamen benefited from social factors (e.g., regulations, access to capital, or other innovations) that supported his work.

The teacher might supplement this activity with the following videos of interviews and speeches by Kamen:

- ○ http://www.youtube.com/watch?v=uHwCPHcKAqY
- ○ http://www.youtube.com/watch?v=rNgqQNovWTc
- ○ http://www.youtube.com/watch?v=bjV11FZXq7E
- ○ http://www.youtube.com/watch?v=AoY1cItRiHA

The Innovators by Walter Isaacson

Unit	TIG.2
Topic	**Technological Developments and Society**
Themes	**ICC: intrapersonal (curiosity about global affairs); ethics: common values; work and mind habits: innovation and creativity; knowledge: politics (global risks); investigative and analytical skills; assessing global affairs: evaluate sources, the use of evidence, and creative communication; and global problem solving: future studies, scenario building, and the use of technology**
Region	**Not applicable**
Length	**Three weeks**

Goals and Objectives

1. **Learn** to recognize invention as a force that shapes life and human history, to understand the relationship between scientific and technological development and innovation, and to understand innovation as a global process that often builds on previous inventions and flawed attempts at invention.
2. **Inspire** student to contribute to the evolution of existing technologies and to the application of those technologies to social problems that are meaningful to them.
3. **Act:** by demonstrating understanding of the historical evolution of one of the major technologies of the twentieth century.

Skills and Knowledge

1. Students will recognize the major technological developments of the twentieth century.
2. Students will identify the ways in which those developments built on previous innovations.

3. Students will explain the major social contributions advanced by at least one of those innovations.

Overview

In this unit, students examine the historical development of several technologies, beginning with a teacher-led lesson on the history of computing. They then complete an independent research project on the history of some of the major technologies of the twentieth century.

Activity TIG.2.1
The History of the Computer

In this activity the teacher will lead the class in a discussion of the history of the computer, starting with the first design in 1884 by English mathematician Charles Babbage of the mechanical "analytical engine." The teacher will present a time line showing the history of computers, and the discussion will examine how the development of electronics, the miniaturization of processors, reductions in costs, and increases in processing power and memory have shaped the development of new applications. The class will then discuss the many uses of computers in modern life and how various activities changed as a result of the introduction of computers. This examination of changes might focus on the effect of computers on hospitals, banks, schools, town administrations, animation, and music compositions and performances.

Activity TIG.2.2.
The Evolution of Computers

In small groups of two or three, students will discuss how computers have evolved over the last thirty years and consider the way these changes have affected their uses. Students will research predictions made about computers thirty years ago and compare them with actual developments. They might, for example, look at newspapers that discussed computers in past years. They will also speculate on likely changes that computers might undergo in the future. Each team will then present a report to the class.

Resources:

- *The History of Computers*, by Les Freed
- A chronology of personal computers (http://pctimeline.info/)
- http://en.wikipedia.org/wiki/History_of_computer_hardware

Activity TIG.2.3.
How Does Technology Evolve?

Students will discuss the following talk about how technology evolves: http://www.ted.com/talks/kevin_kelly_on_how_technology_evolves.html.

Activity TIG.2.4.
History of the Major Inventions of the Twentieth Century (Independent Research Project)

Individually or in pairs, students will study the history of the most important technological developments of the twentieth century, as established by the US National Academy of Engineering:

1. Electrification
2. Automobiles
3. Airplanes
4. Water supply and distribution
5. Electronics
6. Radios and televisions
7. Mechanized agriculture
8. Computers

9. Telephones
10. Air Conditioning and refrigeration
11. Highways
12. Spacecraft
13. The Internet
14. Imaging
15. Household appliances
16. Health technologies
17. Petroleum and petrochemical technologies
18. Lasers and fiber optics
19. Nuclear technologies
20. Materials science

For their project they will identify the contributions of the development, the economic and social applications of the development, the factors that contributed to the development, the roles played by the government and by the private sector in creating the development, how the development built on previous inventions, how the development has continued to evolve, and the possible ways in which this development might evolve in the future.

Students will prepare a PowerPoint presentation summarizing the results of their research, present it in an exhibition to their class, and post it in an online platform.

Resources

- The Franklin Institute's "History of Science and Technology" (http://www.fi.edu/learn/sci-tech/)
- Time lines showing the history of inventions (http://inventors.about.com/od/timelines/Timelines_of_Invention_and_Technology.htm)

Unit	TIG.3
Topic	**Emerging Technologies and Globalization**
Themes	**ICC: intrapersonal (curiosity about global affairs); ethics: common values; work and mind habits: innovation and creativity; knowledge: politics (global risks); investigative and analytical skills; assessing global affairs: evaluate sources, the use of evidence, and creative communication; and global problem solving: future studies, scenario building, and using technology)**
Region	**Not applicable**
Length	**Twelve weeks**

Goals and Objectives

1. **Learn** the roles that emerging technologies play as drivers of globalization and how they can be used to address some of the most significant global challenges.
2. **Inspire** students to address global challenges through the creation of social institutions—for example, businesses, social enterprises, and others—that capitalize on emerging technologies.
3. **Evaluate** the major emerging technologies, their benefits, and their likely uses in addressing significant global challenges.

Skills and Knowledge

1. Students will recognize the major contributions to human health and well being advanced by biotechnology, bioinformatics, brain-computer interfaces and neurotechnology, energy and environmental systems, computing and networks, nanotechnology, and robotics and artificial intelligence.
2. Students will identify the current uses of these emerging technologies.

3. Students will explain and describe the core benefits and potential uses of emerging technologies in addressing global challenges and the barriers to universalizing access to them.

Overview

In this unit, students examine the role of information technology, biotechnology, bioinformatics, brain-computer interfaces and neurotechnology, energy and environmental systems, nanotechnology and robotics, and artificial intelligence in supporting the process of globalization and in addressing current global challenges. For each of these emerging technologies, students will examine the core ideas and concepts, the contributions to human well being enabled by the technology, the likely economic applications of the technology, and the challenges to extending these benefits universally.

Activity TIG.3.1.
The Internet, Computing, Networks, and Communications

Students will discuss the uses of the Internet for communications, businesses, and governments.

Students will read the following page about networked computing and the cloud: http://computer.howstuffworks.com/cloud-computing.htm.

Students will then watch the video "United Breaks Guitars" (http://www.youtube.com/watch?v=5YGc4zOqozo) and discuss the implications of the endless information on the Internet for leadership.

Activity TIG.3.2
Open Sources and Copyrights

The teacher will discuss how the Internet has enabled worldwide collaboration and how that collaboration is typified by open-source software. They will learn about Linus Benedict Torvalds, who initiated the creation of Linux, an open-source operating system that is being developed by a global collaborative of volunteers.

Students will learn about "copyleft," or releasing certain rights, public domain, Creative Commons licenses, and open-source licenses, and about copyright, also known as "closed-source software." They will watch a PowerPoint presentation by Larry Lessig that is based on his book *Free Culture* (http://w2.eff.org/IP/freeculture/free.html).

(See the following reference: http://www.amazon.com/Free-Culture-Nature-Future-Creativity/dp/0143034650/ref=sr_1_1?ie=UTF8&qid=1311818 067&sr=8-1.)

The students will critically examine the case for open sources and the case for intellectual property and copyrights as engines of innovation and creativity in business (http://www.wipo.int/freepublications/en/intproperty/909/wipo_pub_909.pdf).

Activity TIG.3.3
Information Technology and Globalization: Economic and Social Implications

In this class session, the teacher's lecture examines the impact of information technology on industrial structures, jobs, the workforce, and financial markets.

Discussing how technology can address humanity's biggest problems

Students will discuss the following TED Talk about humanity's biggest problems and consider how technology can help address them: http://www.ted.com/talks/nick_bostrom_on_our_biggest_problems.html.

Resources

- http://www.globalization101.org/issue_main/technology
- Castells, Manuel. 1999. "Information, Technology, and Social Development." United Nations.

Activity TIG.3.4
Introduction to Biotechnology, Bioinformatics, and Health Care

The teacher will provide an introductory overview to biotechnology, offering a definition of the field and covering molecular biology, DNA, the recombination of DNA, genetic engineering and stem cells, cloning, and gene therapy.

Students then watch Daniel Reda's "An Introduction to Biotechnology" from Singularity University (http://www.evolution-radar.tv/daniel-reda/an-introduction-to-biotechnology-and-bioinformatics-video_81fbc90a0.html).

The teacher then shows clips from a video that illustrates some contemporary applications of biotechnology. The teacher could show clips on genetically modified food (http://planetgreen.discovery.com/food-health/5-of-the-newest-and-craziest-genetically-modified-foods-3-are-animals.html), regenerating our bodies through medical technology (http://www.ted.com/talks/alan_russell_on_regenerating_our_bodies.html, or folding DNA (https://www.ted.com/talks/paul_rothemund_details_dna_folding?language=en).

Students discuss the video and review likely future applications of these technologies.

Resource

- A curriculum guide for a one-semester introductory course on biotechnology at the high school level (http://www.amazon.com/Biotechnology-Comprehensive-Curriculum-Semester-Community/dp/1419683004)

Activity TIG.3.5
Advancing Global Health through Biotechnology

In this student-led activity, students will select one health application emerging from biotechnology and discuss the present ways in which this application contributes to global health and the likely future ways in which it will contribute to global health. Students will examine the barriers that need to be addressed in order to make the benefits of this development available to all. The following resources provide a range of examples of biotechnology's applications to global health.

Resources

- http://www.technologyreview.com/video/?vid=689 http://planetgreen.discovery.com/videos/deanofinvention/
- https://www.ted.com/talks/juan_enriquez_shares_mindboggling_new_science?language=en
- https://www.ted.com/talks/juan_enriquez_on_genomics_and_our_future?language=en
- Evolving Ourselves, by Juan Enriquez and Steve Gullans

Activity TIG.3.6
Introduction to Brain-Computer Interfaces, Neurotechnology, and Medicine

The teacher will explain how brain-computer interfaces work (http://computer.howstuffworks.com/brain-computer-interface.htm). Then he or she will show and discuss with students the following video from CBS: http://www.cbsnews.com/stories/2008/10/31/60minutes/main4560940.shtml.

From the basic science, the teacher will move on to the contemporary applications of brain-computer interfaces. The students can watch a video on DEKA research and robotic arms (http://www.youtube.com/watch?v=R0_mLumx-6Y).

Resources

- http://www.youtube.com/watch?v=NIG47YgndP8&search=brain
- http://www.technologyreview.com/video/?vid=689

To conclude this activity, each student will individually write a short essay summarizing brain-computer interfaces and neurotechnology. Students will write a short essay summarizing the history and the current state of brain-computer interfaces and discussing their current applications. They will identify contemporary population groups in the world that would benefit from the applications of this technology and discuss current barriers to extending the benefits of this technology universally.

Activity TIG.3.7.
Discussing Energy and Environmental Systems

Students will watch and discuss Al Gore's TED Talk (https://www.ted.com/talks/al_gore_warns_on_latest_climate_trends?language=en).

This video provides background knowledge on the energy crisis and global warming. Students will then analyze the merits and drawbacks of the various technological solutions that have been developed to address these challenges, such as wind power, MIT's initiative to harvest power from walking (http://www.media.mit.edu/resenv/power.html), nuclear energy (study the Three Mile Island and Chernobyl incidents), geothermal energy, hydroelectric energy, and fossil fuels.

Activity TIG.3.8.
Turning Waste into Energy

Students will watch the video "Gonzo for Guano" and individually write a short essay that discusses the benefits and drawbacks of this technology and the likely economic and social consequences of adopting technologies of this sort on a large scale.

Resources

- "Gonzo for Guano" (http://planetgreen.discovery.com/tv/dean-of-invention/dean-of-invention-episodes/gonzo-for-guano.html)
- http://www.technologyreview.com/video/?vid=689

Activity TIG.3.9.
Introduction to Nanotechnology

The teacher introduces the field of nanotechnology and some contemporary applications of it.

Resources

- http://www.understandingnano.com/nanotech-applications.html
- http://www.technologyreview.com/video/?vid=689

Activity TIG.3.10
Introduction to Robotics and Artificial Intelligence

Students will examine the evolution of Kismet, Artificial Intelligence, Machine Learning and Robots.

In small groups students will spend time researching the work of MITs artificial-intelligence group on Kismet, which is documented in numerous videos here: http://www.ai.mit.edu/projects/sociable/videos.html.

The teacher will then lead a discussion on robotics and artificial intelligence.

Students can also watch the following videos, which can serve as introductions to the field of robotics:

- o   http://www.youtube.com/watch?v=Iqf5hHdphX4
- o   http://www.youtube.com/watch?v=QKyDrUonp98

Watson. IBM's supercomputer.

Students will watch the following short video from CBS on Watson and on the ongoing efforts to use it in health care: http://www.youtube.com/watch?v=950fbQfdoj8&feature=fvst.

The teacher will then lead a discussion on the likely positive and negative outcomes of using computers to reduce errors in diagnosis, and students will speculate on the likelihood that machine-based diagnosis can extend these services universally.

Resource

- •   http://www.technologyreview.com/video/?vid=689

Unit	TIG.4
Topic	The Acceleration of Technological Change and the Future
Themes	Work and mind habits: innovation and creativity; knowledge: politics (global risks); investigative and analytical skills; assessing global affairs: evaluate sources, the use of evidence, and creative communication; and global problem solving: future studies, scenario building, and the use of technology
Region	Not applicable
Length	Four weeks

Goals and Objectives

1. **Learn** to understand the exponential rate of technological development, the implications of this acceleration for our ability to address social challenges, and the concept of singularity proposed by Ray Kurzweil.
2. **Inspire** students to engage in the utilization of technology to address social purposes that are meaningful to them.
3. **Evaluate** a development that addresses a global challenge and is based on an emerging technology.

Skills and Knowledge

1. Students will recognize the exponential nature of technological development and the ability of smaller groups of people to design innovative solutions to global challenges through approaches such as the XPRIZE.
2. Students will identify the concept of singularity.
3. Students will explain and describe the ways in which a current global challenge can be ameliorated or solved through the use of an emerging technology.

Overview

In this unit, students examine the changes in the rate of technological development, discuss the concept of singularity, examine alternative approaches to stimulating technological innovation, and develop an idea for a way to address a global challenge using an emerging technology.

Activity TIG.4.1
Film Discussion: *Transcendent Man*

This film introduces the ideas and contributions of Ray Kurzeil and is based on his book *The Singularity is Near* (http://transcendentman.com/).

Students will watch and discuss the film, focusing in particular on the concept of exponential growth in information technology and on the notion that it will lead to the merging of humans with machines. The film examines advances in genetics and the possibility that genetics will allow us to reprogram biology, eliminate diseases, and extend life. Students will also engage in a discussion on the concerns raised by critics of the film.

Teacher Resource

- Kurzweil, Ray. 2005. *The Singularity is Near: When Humans Transcend Biology.* New York: Viking.

Activity TIG.4.2
Global Challenges and Technological Innovation

This is an in-class research activity. First students watch a TED talk on the biggest challenges facing humanity: (http://www.ted.com/talks/nick_bostrom_on_our_biggest_problems.html).

The teacher presents the world economic framework for the assessment of global risks (https://www.weforum.org/reports/the-global-risks-report-2016/) and introduces each of the risks:

ECONOMIC RISKS

1. Food-price volatility
2. Oil price spikes
3. Major fall in the US dollar
4. Slowing Chinese economy (by more than 6 percent)
5. Fiscal crises
6. Asset price collapse
7. Retrenchment from globalization (developed)
8. Retrenchment from globalization (emerging)
9. Burden of regulation
10. Underinvestment in Infrastructure

GEOPOLITICAL RISKS

11. International terrorism
12. Nuclear proliferation
13. Iran
14. North Korea
15. Instability in Afghanistan
16. Transnational crime and corruption
17. Israel and Palestine
18. Iraq
19. Global governance gaps

ENVIRONMENTAL RISKS

20. Extreme weather
21. Drought and desertification
22. Water scarcity

23. National catastrophes (cyclone)
24. National catastrophes (earthquakes)
25. National catastrophes (island flooding)
26. National catastrophes (coastal flooding)
27. Air pollution
28. Biodiversity loss

Societal Risks

29. Pandemics
30. Infectious diseases
31. Chronic diseases
32. Liability Regimes
33. Migration

Technological Risks

34. Critical information–infrastructure breakdown
35. Nanoparticle toxicity
36. Data fraud/loss

Students examine in a whole-group discussion how each of these global risks relates to an emerging technology and the extent to which the risk can be managed and how.

Students review Design for Change (https://www.tes.com/worldslargestlesson/taking-action/) and Design Thinking and discuss the following TED Talk by Tim Brow: https://www.ted.com/talks/tim_brown_urges_designers_to_think_big?language=en.

Then, individually or in small groups, students select one of the Sustainable Development Goals and analyze how the problem area that the goal addresses (e.g., poverty, hunger, health, education, etc.) has been addressed in the past by technological developments. The students then discuss how emerging technologies might help address the challenge. Students make an oral presentation to the rest of the class.

Activity TIG.4.3
Technology and Innovation for All: The XPRIZE

The teacher will lead the class in a discussion of the XPRIZE, a process to stimulate innovation that capitalizes on the ability of relatively small groups of individuals to address significant social challenges using knowledge and technology. The teacher will present the XPRIZE Foundation and the XCHALLENGE, its origins, and its applications to finding innovative solutions to space travel and oil cleanup.

Students will answer the following questions:

1. What is the value of competition as a process to stimulate innovation?
2. Why can small groups of people produce new designs that until recently could only feasibly be produced by large corporations and governments?
3. What are the downsides of providing economic rewards only to the winners of the competitions?
4. What challenges are more likely to be solved using approaches such as the XCHALLENGE, and what challenges are less likely to be solved by similar approaches? Why?
5. What XPRIZE Foundation competitions are currently open? Could the students imagine participating in one of those competitions? What would they need to do in order to produce a competitive design?

Activity TIG.4.4.
Thinking through a Process to Address One Global Challenge through Emerging Technologies

In small groups students will select one global challenge (e.g., one of the challenges identified in the Sustainable Development Goals). Students will then design a concept to support the development of solutions to the challenge using some of the emerging technologies. The concept could involve a business, a social enterprise, a nonprofit organization, or another social institution that would develop and implement an intervention to affect this social challenge using some of the emerging technologies covered in the course.

These designs will then be presented in an "innovation fest," a celebration of innovation open to parents and members of the community. This will be an opportunity to invite inventors from the local community to connect with the students.

Conclusion and Beginnings

G lobal Citizenship is an ongoing process of development of our capacity to make sense of ourselves and those around us in a deeply and increasingly interdependent world. Global citizenship education is therefore a journey more than a destination as we are always in the process of becoming global citizens. We hope the World Course we have offered in this book will offer a beginning in at least two ways.

To students, the World Course provides a foundation to get started in the journey of becoming caring and engaged global citizens, people to whom 'Nothing human will be alien', to use Terentius' words. The world course offers foundational knowledge, skills and dispositions to be curious about the world in which we live and about our own place in it. We hope it provides also the confidence that each of us has a choice, many choices in fact, as to how to face the change and complexity of the growing global interdependence which will affect our lives. We have designed this course with enthusiasm that the global citizenship it will engender will be one of embracing possibilities to work with others in improving the world.

To teachers, the World Course is an invitation to join others in a process of reinventing education to make it more relevant and meaningful to address the serious global challenges we share, to create learning and developmental opportunities for our students to be able to invent the future, a future that is better than the present we are passing on to them. Such process of reimagining education is one that needs serious and concerted efforts of many. It needs to involve students, parents and community members, and many teachers and those who support their work. The framework we have offered in this book is intended to support such process of reimagining and collaboration. We have used a Creative Commons license to disseminate this work to facilitate the deepest possible forms of collaboration among teachers as professionals in building upon our work. In order to succeed globally in educating all students to be empowered global citizens, we will need to see unprecedented collaboration leading to collective intelligence about how to do this. This book is only a small step in that ambitious and necessary global effort to align education with the aspirations reflected in the Universal Declaration of Human Rights and in the Sustainable Development Goals.

We conclude this book with deep hope that from those beginnings will emerge a world in which we can all live in Peace, with one another, and with all forms of life on this earth.

Made in the USA
Middletown, DE
15 March 2019